Corporate Financial Reporting

This book is dedicated
to my mother and is in memory of my father
Ena and Bill Higson

Corporate Financial Reporting

Theory and Practice

Andrew Higson

SAGE Publications
London • Thousand Oaks • New Delhi

SAGE Publications Ltd
6 Bonhill Street
London EC2A 4PU

SAGE Publications Inc
2455 Teller Road
Thousand Oaks, California 91320

SAGE Publications India Pvt Ltd
32, M-Block Market
Greater Kailash – I
New Delhi 110 048

British Library Cataloguing in Publication data

A catalogue record for this book is available
from the British Library

ISBN 0 7619 7140 8
ISBN 0 7619 7141 6 (pbk)

Library of Congress Control Number available

Typeset by Mayhew Typesetting, Rhayader, Powys
Printed and bound in Great Britain by Athenaeum Press,
Gateshead

Contents

Acknowledgements

I would like to acknowledge the influence of the late Professor Tom McRae, who, as my PhD supervisor, allowed me time to read and think about accounting and auditing. I would like to thank Professor John Blake for his encouragement over the years. I would particularly like to thank the person who recommended my name to the publishers of this book. Many thanks go to Kiren Shoman and Keith Von Tersch of Sage Publications. I would like to acknowledge the helpful assistance of the staff at the ICAEW library, who dealt with my many requests in a punctilious way. Many thanks also go to Joyce Tuson, who assisted with the finalization of the text, although I take full responsibility for any errors that may remain.

List of Illustrations

FIGURES

TABLES

Preface

This book is built around the premise that to understand financial reporting, it is necessary to understand the motivations of management, and the work of the external auditors. Conversely, to understand the problems facing the auditors, it is necessary to appreciate the scope and limitations of the financial statements. External reporting and external auditing are inextricably inter-twined (as exemplified by the recent financial scandals), yet these are topics that are often debated and taught in desolate isolation. Bringing these topics together has also enabled the book to adopt a critical review of the nature and scope of financial reporting.

This book is aimed at undergraduate and postgraduate students who already have some knowledge of accounting. Rather than following a techniques-based approach, the book examines the conceptual issues behind financial reporting. Therefore, it is interested in the rationale for, and the limitations of, financial reporting. The book is structured to encourage the reader to reflect on and debate the issues raised.

Special features of the book include:

- a critical examination of accounting 'theory'
- the use of communication theory to help understand why users may misinterpret the financial statements and the audit report
- the suggestion that the external audit needs to be viewed in terms of the audit of management's motivations
- an examination of corporate fraud
- senior practitioners' views on 'a true and fair view'
- an exploration of the financial reporting expectations gap, comprising the much discussed audit expectations gap and the rather less discussed financial statements expectations gap
- a discussion of the nature of 'corporate performance'
- an examination of the implications of 'real-time' reporting by companies.

The book starts with an overview of key issues in financial reporting and auditing – this is to enable the reader to appreciate the breadth of the problems confronting those involved with financial reporting. In order to tackle these problems, it is important to have a firm conceptual base, and so the development of 'accounting theory' is examined. As there is no one generally agreed theory of accounting (probably due to the political nature of theory development), the book then examines the history of accounting and financial reporting in order to see what they were trying to achieve. Consideration is then given to the conceptual framework projects undertaken by the accounting standard-setters. However, as the underlying accounting theory is vague and ill-defined, and given compromises by the standard setters (in order to achieve consensus), the danger is that these conceptual frameworks are not really conceptual. The book then moves on to examine the development of auditing and to see what the auditors are saying about the financial statements. While the standard setters endorse the decision usefulness of the financial statements, there appears to be little support for this from the auditors (and this view was also rejected by the Company Law Review and in case law by the Caparo judgement). The book suggests that there may be a financial reporting expectations gap comprising the much discussed audit expectations gap and a financial statements expectations gap – symptoms of this being the vague specification of the objective of the financial statements and the focus on the myriad of financial statement users. The book goes on to suggest that the focus should be on the reporting entity and its communication of its performance and risks. This then raises the question of how to judge corporate performance and risk.

At the end of each chapter, there are five discussion questions. These aim to be provocative in order to stimulate debate. Too often accounting is thought to be a dry and uninteresting subject – but this should not be the case, and so it is hoped that these questions may go some way to redressing the balance.

This book is based around the following articles and papers which have been developed over a number of years:

- 'An empirical investigation of the external audit process', unpublished PhD thesis, University of Bradford, 1987.
- *Communication Through the Audit Report: What Is the Auditor Trying To Say?*, EIASM Workshop on Auditing Regulation, Copenhagen, Denmark, 18–20 September 1991.
- 'A consideration of the significance and value of the "neutrality" concept in financial accounting' (with J. Blake), Accounting Forum, 1992, September: 5–35.
- 'The true and fair view concept – a formula for international disharmony: some empirical evidence' (with J. Blake), *The International Journal of Accounting*, 1993, 28: 104–15.
- *Corporate Communication: A Conceptual Framework for Financial Reporting (A Potential Outline)*, Financial Accounting and Auditing Research Conference, London Business School, 10–11 July 1995.

- 'Principle matter', *Accountancy Age*, 28 September 1995: 13.
- 'Is stewardship merely a comfort blanket?', *Accountancy*, 1995, November: 104.
- 'Driving force', *Accountancy Age*, 21 March 1996: 16.
- 'In a word, what is research?', *Accountancy*, 1996, December: 81.
- *Bias in the Financial Statements – Implications for the External Auditor: Some UK Empirical Evidence*, Loughborough University Business School Working Paper, December 1996.
- 'Developments in audit approaches – From audit efficiency to audit effectiveness?' in M. Sherer and S. Turley (eds), *Current Issues in Auditing* (3rd edn). London: Paul Chapman Publishing, 1997: 198–215.
- 'Time to bridge the expectations gap', *Accountancy*, September 1997: 93.
- 'Harnessing technology: real-time, real problem?' (with A. Shah), *Accountancy*, October, 1997: 86.
- 'A reconsideration of the nature of stewardship' (with M. Tayles), *The Journal of Applied Accounting Research*, 1998, 4 (2): 61–91.
- *A Reconfiguration of the External Reporting Conceptual Framework Conundrum*, Financial Accounting and Auditing Research Conference, School of Oriental and African Studies, University of London, 13–14 July 1998.
- *Why Is Management Reticent To Report Fraud? An Exploratory Study*, Fraud Advisory Panel Research Paper, London, 1999.
- *Indications of Fraud in SMEs*, Fraud Advisory Panel Research Paper, London, 2002.
- *An Exploration of the Financial Reporting Expectations Gap*, British Accounting Association Annual Conference, Jersey, 3–5 April 2002.
- *Continuous Reporting and Auditing: Conceptual Considerations*, Fourth World Continuous Auditing and Reporting Symposium, Salford University, 18–19 April 2002.

Contact address:

andrew@accounting-research.org.uk

1 Issues in Financial Reporting

The path to knowledge cannot be found without visions and
an overall picture.

– R. Mattessich

T oday's dynamic business environment is heralding a revolution in the
need for, and the way in which, accounting data is utilized. This has
resulted in talk of 'an accounting revolution' (Beaver, 1998) and the
possible 'redefinition of accountancy' (Elliott, 1998: 7). However, it is all too
easy to become caught up in this stampede for change, but how far can
accounting change and for it still to be called accounting?

This chapter seeks to explore the major issues facing contemporary financial
reporting – this will include its interrelationship with external auditing and
the provision of assurance to those outside the reporting entity. After all,
'[e]ffective reporting and accounting, and external scrutiny from auditors, are
essential for effective corporate governance' (Company Law Review Steering
Committee, 2001: para. 8.1). To understand the financial statements, one needs
to appreciate the auditors' work and opinion, and, conversely, to understand
the auditors' work and opinion, it is necessary to appreciate the scope and
limitations of the financial statements. All too often, financial reporting and
external auditing are treated and discussed in isolation despite being
inextricably linked. However, the final figures in the financial statements may
come about as a result of negotiations between management and their
auditors – with the auditors examining the reasonableness of management's
justifications for their representations. Indeed, the modern audit with its
emphasis on high-level business risks could almost be viewed as the 'audit of
motivations' – to understand the figures in the financial statements, it is
important to understand management's motivations. Financial reporting and
auditing are not just technical subjects, but they encompass a multitude of
judgements and assumptions. This may go some way to explain why it is
possible for a company to collapse not long after the publication of a set of
accounts with an unqualified audit opinion. Auditing is not just about vouching the contents of the accounting records – it is just as important to understand accounting data in context. Therefore, this book explicitly recognizes

and seeks to explore the interdependences between financial reporting and auditing.

THE SCOPE OF THE PROBLEMS FACING FINANCIAL REPORTING

The changes taking place in the commercial environment have resulted in the accountancy profession critically reviewing its role and the relevance of its curriculum. A number of these developments in the commercial world are set out by Albrecht and Sack (2000: 5–6):

- technological developments resulting in the inexpensive preparation and dissemination of information, thus decreasing the cost and expertise necessary to produce the financial statements
- the globalization of business arising from 'instantaneous information' in tandem with quick and reliable methods of transportation
- the growth in pension funds and other institutional investors with a resultant increase in their power to influence businesses.

Albrecht and Sack quote a participant in their study as summarizing the situation as follows:

> We are moving into an age of instant gratification – that seems to be true whether it's children, clients, or whatever – they want instant gratification and you have to provide the answers now! We not only have to provide the answers, but the right answers. As companies change, they can't get information fast enough and if they can't get it from us [accountants], they will get it somewhere else. (2000: 6)

This concern may be exacerbated by the view expressed by the US Accounting Principles Board (APB, 1970: para. 40) that '[a]ccounting is a service activity'. It considered that the function of accounting 'is to provide quantitative information primarily financial in nature about economic entities that is intended to be useful in making economic decisions, in making resolved choices among alternative courses of action' (para. 40). This is very different from a definition in 1941 that stated: 'Accounting is an art of recording, classifying and summarizing in a significant manner and in terms of money, transactions and events which are, in part at least, of a financial character, and interpreting the results thereof' (cited by the American Institute of Accountants' Committee on Terminology, 1953: 9). This change in definition shows that the concern about accounting and financial reporting being left behind as the business world develops is not a new phenomenon.

The major driving forces behind the developments in contemporary financial reporting include the following.

Globalization

This has given rise to the push for the international harmonization of accounting standards and the resultant debate about whose standards should be adopted. In the European Union, by 2005 publicly traded EU incorporated companies will have to follow the international financial reporting standards of the International Accounting Standards Board (IASB) – formerly the International Accounting Standards Committee (IASC). Over the final quarter of the twentieth century, there was increasing recognition of the politicization of the standards-setting process (Armstrong, 1977; Solomons, 1978; Zeff, 2002) and the implications of the economic consequences of accounting standards and policies (Zeff, 1978). Therefore, the adoption of international standards needs to be viewed as much in a political context as in an accounting one. However, '[i]nternational accounting standard-setting is currently in crisis' (Horton and Macve, 2000: 26).

The influence of management

This is a critical constituency when it comes to developments in accounting: 'Management is central to any discussion of financial reporting, whether at the statutory or regulatory level, or at the level of official pronouncements of accounting bodies' (Moonitz, 1974: 64). One of the reasons for the failure of the current cost experiment in the early 1980s was the lack of support from financial statement preparers (they were not convinced of the validity of the exercise). Current values are now starting to creep into the financial statements, and '[s]ome corporate executives concerned about the volatility of reported results have claimed that standard-setters have a hidden agenda to undermine the bedrock of historical cost by introducing piecemeal requirements for current value measurement' (Miller and Loftus, 2000: 5). There is a concern that the standard setters may be requiring data for external reporting that management does not find useful for its own internal uses. The debacle regarding current cost accounting in the 1980s should not be forgotten.

Extreme market pressures

The pressures from the capital markets are forcing management to achieve earnings targets:

> These pressures are exacerbated by the unforgiving nature of the equity market as securities valuations are drastically adjusted downward whenever companies fail to meet 'street' expectations. Pressures are further magnified because management's compensation often is based in large part on achieving earnings or other financial goals. (Panel on Audit Effectiveness, 2000: 3)

One consequence of these market pressures is the danger of 'aggressive earnings management' that 'results in stakeholders, and the capital markets generally, being misled to some extent about an entity's performance and profitability' (Auditing Practices Board, 2001: 3). Recent financial scandals may be viewed as coming about as a result of extreme disclosure and earnings management.

The informational perspective of the financial statements

The emphasis is now on the provision of information to enable the users of the financial statements to take decisions and to make assessments of future cash flows of the reporting entity. Since the 1960s, users have been actively involved in dialogue about accounting principles and are represented on some accounting standard-setting bodies. 'An outsider, however, might find it remarkable that accounting knowledge should be articulated not only by professional accountants, but also by accounting information users – much like doctors and patients collaborating on the development of medical knowledge' (Hines, 1989: 80). In 1994, the AICPA issued a report containing the findings of a special committee aimed at improving business reporting. The intention was to 'influence future agendas of standard setters and regulators and the direction of their projects'. Its adoption of 'a customer focus' orientation was explained as follows:

> Just as successful businesses align the features of their products and services with the needs of their customers, so, too, should the providers of business reporting. Recognizing this, the Committee concentrated on the information needs of users to help identify and evaluate ideas for improvement. (AICPA, 1994: 4)

The user-primacy, decision-oriented view has not gone unchallenged, and it may have resulted in unrealistic expectations about what the financial statements are capable of delivering. While analysts may want to predict the future, others may still wish to understand the past – shareholders will want dividends, governments will want taxation and information for their statistics, and employees will be interested in a fair return for their efforts. In Germany, the protection of creditors has been the driving force behind corporate reporting. Bankers are interested in predicting future cash flows, but as they are generally in a privileged position, having access to the company's budgets, they will not have to rely on the financial statements to make their predictions. Increasingly, companies are having private meetings with key stakeholders (Holland, 1997; Marston, 1999).

Scott (1994: 62) considered that there 'is the increasing evidence that investors may not be as rational and security markets may not be as efficient as previously believed. This threatens the foundation upon which most financial accounting research over the last 25 years has been based, and has led to calls for a "return to fundamentals".'

The debate about financial performance

The 'statement of financial performance' (ASB, 2000) combines the statement of total recognized gains and losses and the profit and loss account, one reason for this being that users seemed to be ignoring the 'statement of total recognized gains and losses'. However, there is a question as to what is meant by the word 'performance' and whether just focusing on 'financial performance' will really indicate an enterprise's overall performance. The operating and financial review aims to expand on the contents of the financial statements, but in the management accounting area, the recognition of the limitations of financial performance indicators has resulted in the search for complementary indicators, such as the balanced scorecard (Kaplan and Norton, 1996). These issues are now being recognized in relation to external reporting (Upton, 2001).

Advances in technology

This has resulted in a questioning of the relevance of the financial statements: 'The demand for more timely and broader information comes from decision makers, such as potential investors, creditors, customers and suppliers, who are doing, or may want to do, business with an entity' (CICA, 1999: 2). However, because of the multitude of decisions involved, '[i]t is likely that decision makers' information needs will be met at least in part by real-time access to corporate databases, a possibility that is increasingly feasible given advances in information technology' (CICA, 1999: 2), whereby users would be able to access the data they considered relevant to their decisions.

> Technology-driven information systems are capable of capturing, organizing and disseminating information in 'real time'. Investors can quickly access information and consequently have expanded their demands for both financial and non-financial information. Some of that information is 'traditional' historical financial data, and some of it is new. (Panel on Audit Effectiveness, 2000: 172)

It is even suggested that greater disclosure may result in a lower cost of equity capital for some firms (Botosan, 1997). However, if users are ignoring data in the financial statements, one has to wonder how they would cope with this cornucopia of financial data:

> Accounting is the instrument used to treat a mass of enterprise facts so that the flow of transactions becomes intelligible. . . . It is hard to overestimate the contribution to understanding made by compressing a mass of facts and by setting up the resulting data in ways that permit comparisons to be made. The mind cannot grasp very many separate facts at once, and figures lose most of their significance unless the eyes can see quickly whether they are larger or smaller than they were. (Littleton, 1953: 25)

In the age of the database, the relevance of double-entry bookkeeping has been questioned (Doost, 2000). However, it is likely that some sort of accounting control system will still be required. There is the danger that real-time reporting may be the ultimate in short-termism.

The development of the knowledge economy

This has implications for financial reporting with its current emphasis on tangible assets. There is a concern that the financial statements may not reflect this development:

> *For the past two hundred years, neo-classical economics has recognized only two factors of production: labour and capital. This is changing. Information and knowledge are replacing capital and energy as the primary wealth-creating assets, just as the latter two replaced land and labor 200 years ago. In addition, technological developments in the 20th century have transformed the majority of wealth-creating work from physically-based to 'knowledge-based'. Technology and knowledge are now the key factors of production. . . . We are now an information society in a knowledge economy. (Enterprise Development Website, 2000: 1)*

This is already having an impact and is leading to a questioning of the usefulness of the financial statements:

> *Research by Arthur Andersen into 10,000 public companies showed that by 1998, under 30% of their market capitalization was represented by book value. More than 70% of their value fell outside the public measurement and reporting system. This is a dramatic shift from just 20 years before, when book value provided 95% of market value. (Lindsey, 2001: 117)*

But before the usefulness of the financial statements is criticized, it is important to be clear about what they are trying to show.

The rise of corporate governance

Though accountability has long been seen as one of the reasons for financial reporting,

> *A series of spectacular corporate failures and financial scandals . . . including BCCI, Polly Peck and Maxwell, highlighted concerns about the standard of financial reporting and accountability. These concerns centred around an apparently low level of confidence in both financial reporting and in the ability of the auditors to provide safeguards which the users of company annual reports sought and expected. (Davies et al., 1999: 223)*

Recent years have seen the rise in importance of corporate governance, and this could be seen to culminate in the Company Law Review (2001), which viewed corporate governance as being central to future developments in corporate reporting and accountability. It is important to view the financial statements in the context of corporate governance (and not vice versa), and it should be remembered that corporate governance encompasses much more than just financial reporting (Short et al., 1999). Therefore, it would seem reasonable that issues like corporate social responsibility and environmental accounting should be viewed in terms of corporate governance rather than financial reporting per se. If a problem is greater than accounting, it should not be considered in just an accounting context.

While all these developments have been occurring, the auditors have had to try to respond, as well as react, to criticisms of their own work.

Independence

This can be viewed as the key quality of the external audit; however, auditors have frequently been criticized for their perceived lack of independence: 'How unfair may the financial statements be and yet be deemed fair in accordance with GAAP?' (Briloff, 1986: 27). If auditors are not independent, the relevance of the audit can quite rightly be questioned. In order to help bolster the independence of the external auditors, larger companies have established audit committees.

Globalization

As a consequence of globalization 'today's complex economic world requires a break from the auditing traditions that have evolved from the early balance sheet audit' (Bell et al., 1997: 12) – in particular, the emphasis on the business risk approach to auditing (Lemon et al., 2000).

> *Industrial-age companies ran on tangible assets such as inventory, machinery, buildings and land. Post-industrial, information-age enterprises run on intangible assets, including information, human resources, and R & D. If we are to analyze the risks facing the audited company and understand its operations, we must understand these new ingredients for value creation and destruction. (AICPA chairman-elect, R.K. Elliott, quoted by KPMG [1999: 18])*

Audit developments

As a result of the above factors, there has been a perceived change in audit emphasis – from 'audit efficiency' (aiming to reduce audit costs) to 'audit effectiveness' (with an emphasis on whether the audit is achieving its objective). This has resulted in a re-engineering of the audit process, which will need to continue (Panel on Audit Effectiveness, 2000), and in the drive to add value to the external audit.

Assurance services

The pressure to 'add value' to the external audit has resulted in the consideration of how to extend the audit function. The Elliott Committee (1997a) identified opportunities for assurance services to expand to the new types of information used by decision makers. It defined 'assurance services' as 'independent professional services that improve the quality of information, or its context, for decision makers' (p. 1).

A comprehensive real-time database approach to external reporting

This would have major implications for the external auditors, as '[i]nformation provided on a real-time basis to investors inevitably will raise the question of its reliability' (Panel on Audit Effectiveness, 2000: 172). The perceived need for more timely assurance has given rise to the notion of 'continuous assurance' through a 'continuous audit' (CICA, 1999). Because of the pace of business and the speed of digital communication, it is suggested that the people who were users of the financial statements want continuous assurance about the systems and controls within an organization.

Fraud

'Accounting history is littered with examples of financial information used as a means of deception' (Edwards, 1989: 143).

> *Fraudulent financial statements are of great concern not only to the corporate world, but also to the accounting profession. Every year the public has witnessed spectacular business failures reported by the*

> *media. . . . These catastrophic events have shocked the public, undermined auditors' credibility in their reporting function, and eroded public confidence in the accounting and auditing profession. . . . Events such as unreported revenues, manipulation of losses, inflated sales, fraudulent write-offs of uncollectible accounts, unusual related-party transactions, misappropriation of assets and many other irregularities have spearheaded several court rulings and shaped the auditing standards. (Vanasco, 1998: 60)*

The detection of fraud is an often cited expectation of the external auditors. In Victorian times, the audit did have the detection of fraud as its primary objective (Lee, 1986: 31); however, auditors are now required to plan their work in order to have a reasonable expectation of detecting material misstatements arising from error or fraud (APB, 1995: para. 18).

Given the multiplicity and magnitude of the problems relating to the production and utilization of the financial statements, it is critical that there is a firm conceptual basis underpinning financial reporting in order to have a foundation from which to tackle these issues:

> *Accountants must respond to these challenges. But the response should come after a careful study of the foundations upon which accounting has been constructed. The most dangerous trap that accountants can fall into is to be confused and demoralized by the numerous challenges from the neighboring areas of accounting in business and economics and to justify their theories and practices here and there with a humble apology to these neighbors. Accounting has its own way of thinking about, observing, and organizing business phenomena. What is more important, accounting has its own discipline and philosophy, which have developed over centuries. This does not mean that they should not be changed. It emphasizes that the response to the challenges should be made keeping in mind the effects of this response upon accounting foundations. (Ijiri, 1967: ix)*

One way of tackling the multitude of problems facing financial reporting is to build upon accounting theory. The importance of the interrelationship between theory and practice was set out by Littleton as follows:

> *Because accounting theory and practice are inseparably connected, neither can stand alone. To understand practice fully, we need to*

understand theory as well. And to understand the integrated structure
of accounting theory, we need to know something of the totality that
is accountancy, and something of its related fields. (1953: 1)

The changing nature of accounting does have implications for theory development. What impact would all the developments mentioned have on accounting theory? While it would be expected that practice would change over time, would theory really be expected to change? If it does change, does this mean that it was flawed, or indeed could any proposed changes to the theory be flawed? How far can accounting change for it still to be called accounting?

STRUCTURE OF THE BOOK

Chapter 2 will examine the notion of 'accounting theory', noting that this phrase is usually used in the sense of financial accounting and financial reporting. The main concerns raised in this chapter relate to the ill-defined, broad scope and political nature of 'accounting theory'. It raises the question of whether it is appropriate to think in terms of 'accounting theory'. While decision-usefulness appears to have been the cornerstone of conceptual developments since the 1960s, agency theory and communication theory are explored as alternative conceptual bases from which to view financial reporting.

In order to obtain a feeling for the scope and limitations of financial reporting, Chapter 3 will examine the development of accounting and corporate reporting. It seems that the notion of stewardship predates the earliest forms of accounting by hundreds if not thousands of years. Though early forms of accounting were used for stewardship purposes, the nature of these earliest forms may have been more akin to management accounting than financial accounting; therefore, it may be problematic whether the concept of stewardship can simply be transferred to the external reporting. One of the problems is that most users are so divorced from the running of the business that they may not have the appropriate level of knowledge required to assess the management's stewardship. Early accounting records were forms of internal control – as businesses grew in size, better records were needed for control purposes (hence the development of double-entry bookkeeping). The size of business enterprises continued to increase, leading to the development of permanently invested capital, and thus requiring the life of the business entity to be divided into artificial accounting periods – so that a return could be made to the owners for that period. This led to the development of the periodic calculation of profit (on a prudent basis).

Chapter 3 also emphasizes the importance of viewing financial reporting in the context of corporate governance, and not vice versa.

Chapter 4 will look at more recent developments in financial reporting and the regulation of accounting. In particular, it will examine the development of the belief that the objective of the financial statements is to enable users to take economic decisions and to enable them to make their own predictions of future cash flows. The quest for the development of a conceptual framework will also be examined in this chapter, but given the weakness in 'accounting theory' and the politicization of the standards-setting process, there may be a question as to whether such conceptual frameworks are really conceptual.

In Chapter 5, the development of the company external audit will be examined in order to see how it has changed over time in line with changes in the business environment. The views of senior auditors will be presented on the development of the audit process. In particular, the change in audit emphases – from systems work and vouching to examining the business risks – will be covered. The four 'generations' of audits will be discussed as well as the potential fifth-generation 'continuous audit'. The recognition of 'adding value' to the audit and the extension to assurance services will also be examined.

In Chapter 6, the management–auditor relationship will be explored. External auditors are required to have independence of mind, and there is a concern that this may be compromised by financial and personal considerations. However, auditors can form opinions only on things of which they are aware. The potential for management bias in the preparation and presentation of the financial statements is ever present. This chapter suggests that the external audit may more properly be viewed as the audit of motivations – and this may help to explain some of the problems faced by the auditors. While outsiders may wish the auditors to look specifically for fraud, this is problematic. The word 'fraud' may be a useful umbrella term, but it is very vague – it could encompass anything from a false expense claim to a fictitious overseas subsidiary. Therefore, auditors plan their work with a reasonable expectation of detecting material misstatements. On occasion, it has been known for fraudsters to be unable to identify their own fictitious entries in the accounting records! This does raise implications for the external auditors.

Chapter 7 will examine the message the auditor is trying to communicate at the end of the audit. As communication theory has been identified in Chapter 2 as being applicable to financial reporting, it would also seem to be appropriate to relate it to the audit report. Communication theory may help to explain why readers struggle with the auditor's message. Chapter 7 will report the views of senior auditors on what they consider to be the auditors' message at the end of the audit. Auditors do not seem to view their role as being to eliminate bias or minimize bias, but seem to prefer to view their role as being to examine the reasonableness of management's justifications for its

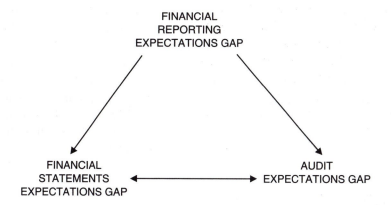

FINANCIAL
REPORTING
EXPECTATIONS GAP

FINANCIAL
STATEMENTS
EXPECTATIONS GAP

AUDIT
EXPECTATIONS GAP

FIGURE 1.1   The financial reporting expectations gap

representations. The development of the phrase 'a true and fair view' will be examined. Interestingly, these auditors were quite critical of the phrase 'a true and fair view'.

Chapter 8 will suggest the possibility of a financial reporting expectations gap, comprising a financial statements expectations gap and an audit expectations gap (Figure 1.1). Much work has been conducted relating to the audit expectations gap, but the notion of a financial statements expectations gap is relatively unexplored. While effort has been put into trying to reduce the audit expectations gap, this may be a futile task if there is a larger expectations gap relating to the financial statements themselves. Chapter 8 goes on to suggest that the imprecise definition of the objective of the financial statements by standard-setters may be contributing to the financial statements expectations gap. It also questions whether the financial statements really reflect 'performance'. After all, the auditors say nothing about economy, efficiency or effectiveness in their audit report. In addition to this, as most readers of the financial statements are very remote from the reporting entity, it is difficult for them to form views on what could have been, or what should have been achieved. Although the financial statements are used as a surrogate performance indicator, it is important that such users are aware of the limitations of such statements.

Having identified the financial reporting expectations gap, Chapter 9 seeks to offer an alternative basis for the construction of a conceptual framework for external corporate reporting, namely, the corporate communication of performance and risk. This would be viewed in terms of corporate governance and would focus on the reporting entity rather than on the myriad of potential users of the financial statements. After the limitations of the financial statements have been recognized, the debate about how to communicate corporate performance and risk can begin. In recognition that traditional accounting information (historically transaction-based financial data) may no longer be considered the language of business (Elliott Committee, 1997b), auditors are being encouraged to expand their assurance services to encompass these other types of information – much of it non-financial. For internal reporting purposes, management has started to supplement the accounting numbers with other performance indicators (including non-financial indicators), but while the objective of the financial statements is so all-embracing the external demand for such data is likely to be stifled.

CONCLUSION

This chapter has tried to explore the diversity of crucial issues currently facing financial reporting. It must be remembered that the second half of the twentieth century saw a number of subtle changes in the way the financial statements are viewed, but their ramifications have been profound. The focus of financial reporting has moved from providing the financial statements to shareholders, to the provision of general-purpose financial statements to enable users to take decisions and make predictions of future cash flows. Users of the financial statements have been keen to expound their requirements, but

> *if the responses of receivers [users] to accounting stimuli is to be taken as evidence that certain kinds of accounting practices are justified, then we must not overlook the possibility that those responses were conditioned. . . . The receivers are likely to have gained the impression that they ought to react, and have noted that others react, and thereby have become conditioned to react. The fact that Pavlov's dog reacted to the sound of a bell does not provide justification for the existence of the bell. (Sterling, 1970: 453)*

The current emphasis appears to be on assisting almost instantaneous decision making and the prediction of the future possibly at the expense of understanding the past. Capital markets are considered to impound information into a share price as soon as it is available, but it must not be forgotten that markets are comprised of a multitude of human judgements. As with any judgement, its validity depends on the experience, the evidence and understanding of the person who has to form the opinion. Just because the users of the financial statements may want something, at what point is it necessary to say that accountants (and indeed anyone else) cannot provide them with it? Awareness of the limitations of the financial statements is a key starting point in the quest for alternative/supplementary disclosures. However, this does not mean that accountants should be embarrassed about the limitations of the financial statements – the financial statements do have their uses, it is just that they may not satisfy the needs of some very vocal users.

The advances in information technology now mean that there has been a proliferation in the number of producers and users of accounting data. This 'mass access' is probably accompanied by half-remembered warnings (or even worse, no knowledge) about the limitations of this data. It is important that advances in technology are matched with advances in common sense; however, the vagueness of 'accounting theory' may mean that this 'common sense' is not so common.

DISCUSSION QUESTIONS

1 Given all the issues discussed in this chapter, do you consider that external financial reporting has lost its focus? Prepare an argument to defend the stance you take.

2 Most financial advertisements that appear in newspapers specifically warn that past performance may not necessarily be a guide to future performance. How do you reconcile this with the standard setters' emphasis on enabling users of the financial statements to predict future cash flows?

3 Real-time reporting would presumably result in profits/losses and gains/losses being calculated on a minute-by-minute basis. How useful/realistic do you think this would be?

4 With the rise of the 'knowledge economy', it is likely that companies will have more and more intangible assets that at present are not recognized in the financial statements. What are the implications of this for accountants, companies and those outside the reporting entity?

5 What is the distinction between aggressive earnings management and fraud?

REFERENCES

Accounting Principles Board (APB) (1970) *Statement No. 4: Basic Concepts and Accounting Principles Underlying Financial Statements of Business Enterprises*. New York: AICPA.

Accounting Standards Board (ASB) (2000) *FRED 22, Revision of FRS 3, 'Reporting Financial Performance'*. London: ASB.

Albrecht, W.S. and Sack, R.J. (2000) *Accounting Education: Charting the Course Through a Perilous Future*, Accounting Education Series, Volume No. 16. Sarasota, FL: American Accounting Association.

American Institute of Accountants, Committee on Terminology (1953) *Accounting Terminology Bulletin No. 1*. New York: AIA.

American Institute of Certified Public Accountants (AICPA) (1994) *Improving Business Reporting – A Customer Focus: Meeting the Information Needs of Investors and Creditors, Comprehensive Report of the Special Committee on Financial Reporting*. New York: AICPA.

Armstrong, M. (1977) 'The politics of establishing accounting standards', *The Journal of Accountancy*, February: 76–9.

Auditing Practices Board (APB) (1995) *SAS 110 – Fraud and Error*. London: APB. January.

Auditing Practices Board (APB) (2001) Aggressive Earnings Management – Consultation Paper. London: APB.

Beaver, W.H. (1998) *Financial Reporting: An Accounting Revolution*. Upper Saddle River, NJ: Prentice Hall.

Bell, T.B., Marrs, F.O., Solomon, I. and Thomas, H. (1997) *Auditing Organizations Through a Strategic-Systems Lens: The KPMG Business Measurement Process*. USA: KPMG Peat Marwick LLP.

Botosan, C. (1997) 'Disclosure level and the cost of equity capital', *The Accounting Review*, 72 (3): 323–49.

Briloff, A.J. (1986) 'Standards without standards/principles without principles/fairness without fairness', *Advances in Accounting*, 3: 25–50.

Canadian Institute of Chartered Accountants (CICA) (1999) *Continuous Auditing*. Toronto: CICA.

Company Law Review Steering Committee (2001) *Modern Company Law for a Competitive Economy: Final Report*. London: DTI.

Davies, M., Paterson, R. and Wilson, A. (1999) *UK GAAP* (6th edn). London: Butterworths Tolley.

Doost, R.K. (2000) 'Has Pacioli's rule ended?', *Managerial Auditing Journal*, 15 (7): 326–30.

Edwards, J.R. (1989) *A History of Financial Accounting*. London: Routledge.

Elliott Committee (1997) AICPA Special Committee on Assurance Services: *Report of the Special Committee on Assurance Services*. New York: AICPA. To be found on websites:
(a) http://www.aicpa.org/assurance/about/opportun.htm (viewed on 11/09/01),
(b) http://www.aicpa.org/assurance/about/environ.htm (viewed on 11/09/01).

Elliott, R.K. (1998) 'Assurance services and the audit heritage', *Auditing: A Journal of Practice and Theory*, 17 (Supplement): 1–8.

Enterprise Development Website (2000) 'Knowledge economy', http://www.enterweb.org/know.htm, updated: 6/09/00.

Hines, R.D. (1989) 'Financial accounting knowledge, conceptual framework projects and the social construction of the accounting profession', *Accounting, Auditing and Accountability Journal*, 2 (2): 72–92.

Holland, J. (1997) *Corporate Communications with Institutional Shareholders: Private Disclosures and Financial Reporting*. Edinburgh: Institute of Chartered Accountants of Scotland.

Horton, J. and Macve, R. (2000) '"Fair value" for financial instruments: how erasing theory is leading to unworkable global accounting standards for performance reporting', *Australian Accounting Review*, 11 (2): 26–39.

Ijiri, Y. (1967) *The Foundations of Accounting Measurement: A Mathematical, Economic, and Behavioural Inquiry*. Englewood Cliffs, NJ: Prentice Hall.

Kaplan, R.S. and Norton, D.P. (1996) *The Balanced Scorecard: Translating Strategy into Action*. Boston, MA: Harvard Business School.

KPMG (1999) *The Financial Statement Audit: Why a New Age Requires an Evolving Methodology*. New York: KPMG LLP.

Lee, T. (1986) *Company Auditing* (3rd edn). London: Van Nostrand Reinhold.

Lemon, W.M., Tatum, K.W. and Turley, W.S. (2000) *Developments in the Audit Methodologies of Large Accounting Firms*. London: ABG Professional Information.

Lindsey, R. (2001) 'New economy, new accounting, new assurance', *Accountancy*, February: 116–17.

Littleton, A.C. (1953) *Structure of Accounting Theory*, American Accounting Association Monograph No. 5. Sarasota, FL: American Accounting Association.

Marston, C. (1999) *Investor Relations Meetings: Views of Companies, Institutional Investors and Analysts*. Glasgow: Institute of Chartered Accountants of Scotland.

Mattessich, R. (1995) *Critique of Accounting: Examination of the Foundations and Normative Structure of an Applied Discipline*. Westport, CT: Quorum Books.

Miller, M.C. and Loftus, J.A. (2000) 'Measurement entering the 21st century: a clear or blocked road ahead?', *Australian Accounting Review*, 11 (2): 4–18.

Moonitz, M. (1974) *Obtaining Agreement on Standards*, Studies in Accounting Research No. 8. Sarasota, FL: AAA.

Panel on Audit Effectiveness (2000) *Report and Recommendations*. Stamford, CT: Public Oversight Board.

Scott, W.R. (1994) 'Research about accounting and research on how to account', in Ernst & Young Foundation (eds), *Measurement Research in Financial Accounting: Workshop Proceedings*. Waterloo, Ont.: Ernst & Young Foundation and Waterloo University, School of Accountancy. pp. 62–7.

Short, H., Keasey, K., Wright, M. and Hull, A. (1999) 'Corporate governance: from accountability to enterprise', *Accounting and Business Research*, 29 (4): 337–52.

Solomons, D. (1978) 'Politicization of accounting', *The Journal of Accountancy*, November: 65–72.

Sterling, R.R. (1970) 'On theory construction and verification', *The Accounting Review*, July: 444–57.

Upton, Jr., W.S. (2001) *Business and Financial Reporting, Challenges from the New Economy, Special Report*. Norwalk, CT: FASB.

Vanasco, R.R. (1998) 'Fraud auditing', *Managerial Auditing Journal*, 13 (1): 4–71.

Zeff, S.A. (1978) 'The rise of "economic consequences"', *The Journal of Accountancy*, December: 56–63.

Zeff, S.A. (2002) '"Political" lobbying on proposed standards: a challenge to the IASB', *Accounting Horizons*, 16 (1): 43–54.

2   An Exploration of the Nature of Accounting 'Theory'

Some may deliberately muddy the water to make it appear deep.

– Nietzsche

T heory is something that usually underpins the development of a discipline. One of the major problems encountered in the accounting area is that 'a single universal accepted basic accounting theory does not exist at this time', the result being that a 'multiplicity of theories has been – and continues to be – proposed' (AAA, 1977: 1). Sterling (1970: 44) considered that this was because '[o]ne of the difficulties encountered in accounting theory construction and verification is that different accounting theories are often theories about different subject matters'. However, '[w]e assume, as an article of faith, that an accounting theory is possible' (Riahi-Belkaoui, 2000: 65). This chapter aims to explore the reason for the myriad of theories facing accounting scholars.

There are numerous discussions of the classifications, descriptions and examples of the major approaches adopted in relation to accounting theory construction (e.g., AAA, 1977; Mattessich, 1995; Riahi-Belkaoui, 2000; Whittington, 1986); therefore, it is not the intention of this chapter to repeat them. The objective of this chapter is to try to understand why agreement on the nature and content of accounting theory has been so elusive. Before it is possible to discuss meaningfully the term 'accounting theory' it is important to try to be clear about what is meant by the individual words 'accounting' and 'theory'. The chapter commences by exploring the interpretations of these words. It then goes on to examine some of the approaches that have been used in the context of 'accounting theory' construction. In order to have an appreciation of the problems encountered in theory development, the impact of vested interests is also explored. The concern of this chapter is that 'accounting theory' is ill-defined, vague in scope and highly political in nature – however, this may go some way to appreciating the reasons for the often vehement disagreements about developments in financial reporting.

AN EXAMINATION OF THE PHRASE 'ACCOUNTING THEORY'

In the setting of 'accounting theory', the discussion of 'accounting' usually revolves around financial accounting (that is, establishing the content and format of the financial statements for external reporting purposes) and financial reporting (the communication of accounting data about an enterprise to a user or group of users). Therefore, the essential distinction that could be made between 'financial accounting' and 'financial reporting' is that the former relates to the generation of accounting data, while the latter is the communication of this data to interested parties outside the reporting entity. Therefore, financial accounting theory can be said to relate to what is contained in the financial statements, whereas financial reporting theory should place more emphasis on the problems of the communication process. The routine double-entry bookkeeping system could be said to end where financial accounting begins.

In terms of understanding the problems relating to the generation of accounting data (financial accounting theory) and the communication process (financial reporting theory), it would seem pertinent to mention the impact of the external auditor. Most discussions of 'accounting theory' pay very little attention to the implications of the external audit. However, other than the directors and company accountants, the external auditors are the people nearest to the compilation of the financial statements, and, as will be seen in Chapter 6, it is the negotiations between the auditors and management that result in the final figures in the financial statements.

'The way accounting theorists and researchers shape and understand the world of organization and management is influenced by the images which they bring to their subject of investigation' (Davis et al., 1982: 307). Davis et al. (1982: 309–13) identified four different images of accounting – firstly as a *historical record,* secondly as a descriptor of *current economic reality,* thirdly as an *information system,* and fourthly as a *commodity.* It is probable that different images of accounting will contribute to the development of different theories.

The word 'theory' is defined (by *Webster's Third New International Dictionary,* 1961: 2371) as a 'coherent set of hypothetical, conceptual, and pragmatic principles forming the general frame of reference for a field of inquiry'. This was essentially the definition employed in *A Statement of Basic Accounting Theory* (ASOBAT) (AAA, 1966: 1). The importance of theories is that:

> Theories . . . enable us to understand in general terms how the world works, to move around, mentally, among the objects and relationships to which they relate, and to act in ways that, as far as we can tell, will not defeat our reasonable expectations. A theory will not save us from unreasonable expectations nor from the vagaries of chance in any

form. A theory will not tell us what to do; but it will tell us what it is possible to do and what it is not possible to do. In that way it removes countless things from consideration when we are confronted with the necessity of choosing or acting. (Chambers, 1996: 125)

In accounting it is valid to question which should come first – theory or practice. Does practice follow theory, or should practice dictate theory? Indeed, in accounting, it has been questioned whether there is a relationship between theory and practice:

Most writers are concerned with what the contents of published financial statements should be; that is, how firms should account. Yet, it is generally concluded that financial accounting theory has had little substantive, direct impact on accounting practice or policy formu-lation. (Watts and Zimmerman, 1979: 22)

A possible explanation of this could be the view of accounting as an ideology (Burchell et al., 1980): 'Ideologies are world views which, despite their partial and possible crucial insights, prevent us from understanding the society in which we live and the possibility of changing it' (Shaw, 1972: 33).

The social allegiances and biases of accounting are rarely apparent, usually they are 'masked' by pretensions of objectivity and inde-pendence. Academics have contributed some of the more sophisticated 'masks' in the form of accounting theories (theories in accounting) and epistemological theories (theories about theorizing in accounting) such as Positivism, Empiricism and Realism. Whatever their specific form, we argue . . . that these theoretical masks act to mystify the socially partisan role of accounting and elevate instead its technical, factual and seemingly objective aspects. (Tinker et al., 1982: 167)

The AAA's *Statement on Accounting Theory and Theory Acceptance* (1977: 6) considered that '[i]n the first decades of the [twentieth] century, most accounting writers dealt with the particulars of accounting practice rather than with conceptual underpinnings'; consequently, '[a]ccounting theory, especially in the majority of textbooks, consisted of special pleadings, without an evident trail of logic, for or against specific accounting practices'. Cushing (1989: 23) considered that '[r]egulation created a demand for accounting theories justifying alternative accounting methods; accounting scholars responded to this demand by creating "accounting theory"'.

One problem that has been encountered in theory development relates to the specification of the purpose of accounting theory. Demski (1973: 718) considered that 'A primary goal of accounting theory is to explain which accounting alternative should be used (in some particular circumstances).' Watts and Zimmerman (1986: 2) held that '[t]he objective of accounting theory is to explain and predict accounting practice', and Schroeder and Clark (1995: 1) that 'accounting theory should be able to explain why business organizations elect certain accounting methods over other alternatives and predict the attributes of firms that elect various accounting methods'. Sterling (1990: 97, emphasis in original) stated 'the fundamental question of accounting' as 'What ought accounting practices to be? More fully, which objects and events, and which attribute(s) of them, should be represented in accounts and on financial statements?' He contended that 'one function of a theory of a discipline is to provide guidelines to the practitioners of that discipline' (Sterling, 1990: 116). However, Littleton (1953: 30) held that

> The central purpose of accounting is to make possible the periodic matching of costs (efforts) and revenues (accomplishments). This concept is the nucleus of accounting theory, and a benchmark that affords a fixed point of reference for accounting discussion.

There is also a debate about whether the theories produced are 'of accounting', 'about accounting', or 'about accountants'. 'Probably the most ancient and pervasive method of accounting theory construction is to observe accountants' actions and then rationalize those actions by subsuming them under generalized principles' (Sterling, 1970: 449). However, Sterling considered that '[t]he result is not a theory about accounting or a theory about the things to be accounted for; instead it is a theory about accountants'. As such, it was an 'anthropological interpretation' of accounting. Christenson (1983) also considered that Watts and Zimmerman (1978; 1979) had confused theories about accounting with theories about the behaviour of people who develop and use accounting information. Thus, even the specification of the basis for the construction of an 'accounting theory' is elusive.

Given the lack of consensus in specifying what accounting theory is trying to achieve, Hendriksen (1977: 2) suggested a classification based on three levels of accounting theory related to 'prediction levels':

1 the explanation of current accounting practices and prediction of how accountants would react in various circumstances – '[t]hese theories relate to the structure of the data collection process and financial reporting'

2   interpretational theories based on relationships between a phenomenon and its representation
3   behavioural theories based on the behavioural or decision-oriented impacts of the financial statements.

It can be seen that that there is a wide range of views about the purpose of 'accounting theory'; in fact,

> There are nearly as many definitions of accounting theory as there are accountants. Sometimes we find theory confused with methods and procedures or rules. Correctly viewed, accounting theory consists of the reasoning and logic used to justify, or arrive at, a method, procedure, or rule. It is quite important to understand that rules themselves are not theory; rather, they are, or should be, the result of applied theory. (Hylton, 1962: 22)

Buckley et al. (1968: 282) considered that '[a]greement on the scope of accounting theories would be a major step toward developing models and theories leading to a logical set of rules and procedures'. They concluded: 'If a general methodology in accounting could be agreed upon, theories developed within this framework would stand a better chance of gaining widespread approval. As it is now, both the ends and the means are constantly in dispute' (1968: 274). Schroeder and Clark (1995: 1) suggested that '[i]n its simplest form theory may be just a belief, but in order for a theory to be useful it must have wide acceptance', however, just because a belief is widely accepted, this alone would not make it valid – it could still be misguided.

It should come as no surprise that if there is very little agreement on the nature and function of 'accounting theory', this may help to explain why its impact on practice appears to have been so marginal. The lack of consensus probably encapsulates the crux of the problem relating to the development and operationalization of 'accounting theory'. This does not mean that the quest for understanding or theory development should be abandoned – indeed, understanding the real nature of a problem is a major step in trying to solve it. The next section tries to understand how such a diversity of approaches to 'accounting theory' could come about.

APPROACHES TO THEORY DEVELOPMENT

A number of informal and formal approaches have been used in the formulation of accounting theories (e.g., Hendriksen, 1977; Story, 1963). Riahi-Belkaoui has set out more recent variations: events and behavioural approaches (2000: 297–329) and predictive and positive approaches (2000: 331–83). Generally, theory development can be either formal or informal. Some of the major approaches will now be explored.

Non-theoretical (informal) – practical (or pragmatic) approaches

These approaches 'involve the development of ideas that are in agreement with the real world and find usefulness in realistic situations' (Hendriksen, 1977: 23).

> *The practical approach is an important part of theory in accounting because it enables the theory to have operational utility, based on an understanding of relations between business phenomena, of constraints on the measurement system, and of the needs of users of accounting information. Practitioners are the most knowledgeable and experienced in these matters. (Buckley et al., 1968: 277)*

Hendriksen (1977: 23) considered that '[o]ne of the advantages of the pragmatic approach is that accounting serves a function only if it is useful', but '[t]he most serious criticism is probably that there are no basic criteria for determining what is meant by "useful"'. Moonitz (1961: 4) had already raised the question of useful to whom, and for what purpose. Hendriksen considered that '[a] clear statement of the objectives of financial accounting must precede an analysis of how specific procedures can help accounting fulfill its functions' (1977: 23).

Non-theoretical (informal) – authoritarian approaches

These can be viewed as attempts by professional bodies to regulate accounting practices and to provide solutions to practical problems. As such, the authoritarian approach could be viewed as a variation of the pragmatic approach. Storey (1963: 64) considered that the authoritarian approach to the formulation of accounting principles 'has created almost as many problems as it has helped to solve'.

Thus, it can be seen that the non-theoretical approaches have been criticized mostly because of the vagueness of the specification of the objective of the financial statements. It has been questioned whether an approach without theoretical underpinnings could in itself be successful.

There are a number of approaches to formal theory building.

Theoretical (formal) – inductive reasoning

This approach attempts to draw generalized conclusions from detailed obser-vations and measurements: 'Applied to accounting, the inductive approach begins with observations about the financial information of business enter-prizes and proceeds to construct generalizations and principles of accounting from these observations on the basis of recurring relationships' (Riahi-Belkaoui, 2000: 70).

> The advantage of the inductive approach is that it is not necessarily constrained by a preconceived model or structure. The researcher is free to make any observations he may deem relevant. But once generalizations or principles are formulated, they should be confirmed by the logical process of the deductive approach. However, the main disadvantage of the inductive process is that the observer is likely to be influenced by subconscious ideas of what the relevant relationships are and what data should be observed. (Hendriksen, 1977: 10)

In view of the sun's apparent movement in the sky, it is easy to see how people concluded that it was revolving around the earth. Therefore, obser-vation alone may not necessarily ensure a sound theoretical basis.

Theoretical (formal) – deductive reasoning

Hendriksen (1977: 7) defined the deductive approach to theory construction as 'the process of starting with objectives and postulates and, from these, deriving logical principles that provide the bases for concrete or practical applications'. He set out a structure for the deductive process; namely: 1. specify the objectives; 2. set out postulates/hypotheses; 3. set out the constraints; 4. structure; 5. definitions; 6. generalized statements of policy; 7. specific applications. Hendriksen considered (1977: 7) that: 'In the deduc-tive process, the formulation of the objectives is most important because different objectives might require entirely different structures and result in different principles.' However, '[o]ne of the main disadvantages of the deductive method is that if any of the postulates and premises are false, the conclusions may also be false' (p. 9).

Both deductive and inductive approaches to theory development may be normative or positive in nature (as may the other approaches that are dis-cussed later). Normative theories aim to set out what should be done (that is, they are prescriptive). Most institutional and personal conceptual frameworks for financial reporting (which will be discussed in Chapter 4) could be labelled as normative in nature. Given the emphasis on decision making as being the objective of the financial statements (Chambers, 1955; Staubus, 1954, 1961), such approaches tend to make judgements about what the users of the financial statements need in order to be able to do this. However, for example, the FASB's hierarchy of accounting qualities 'all flow from the overriding objective of providing accounting information useful for decisions. They therefore suffer from our lack of understanding of the models used for decision making' (Bromwich, 1992: 287):

> We have no generally accepted theory which tells us which elements of investor decision models will be affected by any signals provided by accounting systems. Any messages obtained by investors from accounting information may be expected to lack precision. This is because the theoretical roles of investor decision models of many accounting concepts, such as the accrual concept and realization principles, are still unknown. The complexity of these concepts may mean that any signals generated by accounting systems are indirect and imprecise. (Bromwich, 1992: 202)

Therefore, while decision-making theory might seem to be relevant to determining what should be reported, this lack of appreciation of decision models would appear to be a hindrance. Another problem is that accounting data would only be part of the overall decision process, and therefore its relative impact is problematic. Accounting can have feedback value; that is, investors and analysts can compare their estimates of corporate results with the actual results and then base their decisions on how close they were to the published figures. However, this again does not really give any guidance on the content of the financial statements. Watts and Zimmerman were concerned about the impact of the development of accounting regulation:

> Accounting theorists became more concerned with policy recommendations; they became more normative – concerned with what should be done. Very little concern was exhibited for the empirical validity of the hypotheses on which the normative prescriptions rested. These theorists thought that the nature of accounting, its role, the effects of different procedures on stock prices, and so on were self-evident, so deriving prescriptions was only a matter of assuming an objective for accounting and applying logic. (Watts and Zimmerman, 1986: 4–5)

In contrast to normative statements, positive (also labelled descriptive or empirical) propositions are concerned with describing how the world works (positive accounting theory [PAT], as advocated by Watts and Zimmerman [1986], is an example of a positive approach to theory development). Watts (1995) described the development of positive accounting theory. Jensen (1976: 11) considered that 'research in accounting has been (with one or two notable exceptions) unscientific . . . [b]ecause the focus of this research has been overwhelmingly normative and definitional'. Therefore, '[t]he major thrust of the positive approach to accounting is to explain and predict management's choice of standards by analysing the costs and benefits of particular financial disclosures in relation to various individuals and to the allocation of resources within the economy' (Riahi-Belkaoui, 2000: 369).

Even without external regulation, managers of companies might be expected to have an interest in providing credible accounts to users. Jensen and Meckling (1976: 306) argue that agency theory explains 'why accounting reports would be provided voluntarily to creditors and stockholders, and why independent auditors would be engaged by management to testify to the accuracy and correctness of such reports'. It appears that managers have been willing to incur costs to improve the credibility of accounting reports long before they were required to do so by law, and in many cases voluntarily submitted to audit. Watts and Zimmerman (1983) trace the provision of audited reports back to late sixteenth-century England, and suggest that the historical development of both financial reporting and auditing would appear to support the agency theory argument. Watts and Zimmerman (1986: 197) considered that: 'The hypothesis that accounting reports are demanded to monitor that [manager/shareholder] relationship is called the stewardship concept and was popular in the literature in the late nineteenth and early twentieth centuries.' They further point out that '[t]he hypothesis that accounting and auditing arose as a monitoring device for a firm's contracts contrasts with the common hypothesis that investors demand accounting reports as a source of information for investment and valuation decisions'. Although they considered that these two hypotheses were not mutually exclusive, they advocated concentration on the contracting hypothesis (p. 198).

Agency theory (Ross, 1973; Spence and Zeckhauser, 1971) has been used to explain management's choice of a particular accounting approach. Jensen and Meckling (1976: 308) define an agency relationship as a 'contract under which one or more persons (the principal[s]) engage another person (the agent) to perform some service on their behalf which involves delegating some decision-making authority to the agent'. It is postulated that individuals act in their own best self-interest. The problems of information asymmetry (the owners have incomplete information and are unable to view all the actions of the managers) and moral hazard (the actions of management may differ from owners' preferred options) may result in owners calling on the auditors or providing incentives so as to align management's preferences with their own: 'Minimizing agency monitoring costs is an economic incentive for managers to report accounting results reliably to the ownership' (Wolk and Tearney, 1997: 90). It is assumed that managers and owners will contract in order to restrict opportunistic behaviour, and, as such, the external audit is viewed as a monitoring activity.

> *Agency theory may help to explain the lack of existence of a comprehensive accounting theory. It implies that a framework of accounting theory cannot be developed because of the diverse interests involved in financial reporting. However, there is an even more basic reason why agency theory will have limited direct impact on financial accounting. Agency theory is a descriptive theory in that it helps to explain why a diversity of accounting practices exists. Therefore, even if subsequent testing supports this theory, it will not identify the correct accounting procedures to be used in various circumstances, and thus accounting practice will not be changed.* (Schroeder and Clark, 1995: 67)

There have been major debates about the relative merits of the normative and positive approaches. For example, Demski (1973: 721) 'interpreted accounting theory as providing a complete and transitive ranking of accounting alternatives at the individual level'. He considered that 'generally speaking, we cannot rely on standards to provide a normative theory of accounting'. Departing from individual preferences 'creates an insurmountable difficulty', and 'no normative theory of accounting can be constructed using any such set of standards [such as relevance, usefulness, objectivity, fairness and verifiability]; the standards are bound incompletely and/or incorrectly to rank the accounting alternatives – thus leading to an incorrect or undefined accounting specification' (Demski, 1973: 718). In the following year, Demski concluded that the selection of financial reporting alternatives 'ultimately must entail trading off one person's gain for another's' (1974: 232). Given the debate about the purpose of 'accounting theory', Demski's interpretation of the phrase may be open to question, as it is problematic whether standards could be produced that would maximize the expected utility of the different user groups. This raises the question of whether it would be an appropriate basis for the construction of an accounting theory.

Demski's stance was criticized by Chambers (1976), and in turn positive accounting theory, in particular, PAT, has been heavily criticized (Christenson, 1983; Sterling, 1990). 'One widespread criticism of PAT is that it does not provide prescription and therefore does not provide a means of improving accounting practice' (Deegan, 2000: 235). The strength of feeling generated by it is such that it has been likened to a cult – Chambers (1993), in challenging it, considered:

> *Inventing names, attaching labels, classifying and pigeonholing are all useful devices in their place. But too often they are made to stand in place of careful analysis and disciplined thought. The disputatious and the merely captious resort to them to advance or dismiss, to promote or put down, to set up or demolish argument, rather than to distinguish with care between what they consider meritorious and what objectionable. (Chambers, 1993: 8–9)*

However, the idea of a dichotomy between normative and positive approaches is probably more descriptive than practical. Tinker et al. (1982: 167) pointed out 'that "positive" or "empirical" theories are also normative and value-laden'. Christenson (1983: 6) argued that 'the development of good "positive" theory at the primary level requires sound "normative" theory – methodology – at the metalevel', and Watts and Zimmerman (1986: 9) themselves acknowledged that 'positive theory does not make normative propositions unimportant'. One wonders how great the difference would be between a realistic normative framework and a reasonable positive one (realistic in the sense that the component parts are achievable; reasonable in the sense that the preparers and the users fully appreciate the limitations of the accounting data) – if the starting point for theory construction and the function of the financial statements could be agreed.

The dichotomy between inductive and deductive may also be artificial. 'Far from being either/or competitive approaches, deduction and induction are complementary in nature and are often used together' (Wolk and Tearney, 1997: 35). Therefore, it may be more appropriate to view them as iterative; 'it is not possible to divorce the inductive from the deductive approach because the latter provides a guide to the selection of the data to be studied' (Hendriksen, 1977: 9):

> *Obviously the two processes of generalizing from experience and inferring from premises work hand in hand. Convictions derived inductively from the particulars of experience may form the premises from which to derive, deductively, additional convictions; and conclusions reasonably inferred from acceptable truths may become the expression of accepted standards of practice. (Littleton, 1938: 17)*

Therefore, while there may be debates about normative or positive/inductive or deductive approaches to theory development, this may be more rhetoric than real – the key thing would appear to be the clarification and agreement on the function of theory and the objective of the financial statements.

Communication theory

Hendriksen (1977: 20) considered that 'little has been done in applying communication theory to accounting'; however, the discussion of communication theory in an accounting context is not a new phenomenon (Barnett, 1989; Bedford and Baladouni, 1962; Bedford and Dopuch, 1961; Parker, 1986; Sullivan, 1983). While decision making has been used to underpin the construction of a conceptual framework for financial reporting, communication theory has not.

Bedford and Baladouni (1962: 658), in describing a communication theory approach to accounting, quote Hylton (1962: 27) as stating that the problem of accounting theory was 'not in the existing differences of opinion but in the lack of any sense of direction in which we should be moving to make accounting what it should be'. As a consequence, Bedford and Baladouni contended 'that the communication theory approach to accountancy is one way of providing the desired "sense of direction"'. Chambers (1966, Chapter 8) recognized the importance of the communication process in relation to financial accounting. Parker's (1986: 1) study was 'founded upon the argument that corporate annual reports represent a process of mass communication as advocated by Gerbner (1969)'. Parker (1986: 29) quotes a practitioner, Goch (1979: 305), as stating that '[m]ost accountants have probably never thought of themselves as being in the communication business'. A concern expressed by Parker was that there may have been 'a lack of official recognition of the importance of communicating through accounting reports by academic journal editors and their review boards' (1986: 8).

Communication theory (Lasswell, 1948; Shannon and Weaver, 1949) splits the communication process into the message, the means of communication and whether the recipient receives the message that was sent. In terms of applying this to financial reporting, it would mean identifying the message(s) that the directors were trying to communicate. The financial statements, the chairman's statement, etc., could be viewed as the means of communicating this message. The users' understanding of the reporting process, their interpretation of the financial statements and any related documents, would determine whether they received the message the directors were trying to send. Therefore, in utilizing communication theory, the critical starting point would be the identification of the directors' message(s).

The users may read the financial statements, but problems can arise in the transfer of the directors' message due to what has been termed 'noise' and 'distortion' (Figure 2.1). In relation to the financial statements, 'noise' could

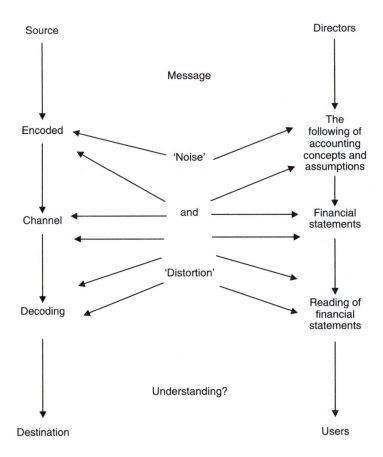

FIGURE 2.1   Communication through the financial statements

relate to the technical accounting terms, whilst 'distortion' would refer to the users' interpretations of the financial statements. Where the processes of thought and understanding are involved, it follows that a given set of data can have different meanings to different users (Haried, 1973; Oliver, 1974). A key aspect of communication theory relates to the word 'information'. It holds that 'information' is conveyed only if the message sent is the message received. The financial statements contain data, and only if this is correctly interpreted can 'information' be said to flow.

Rogers and Kincaid's (1981) criticisms of the preceding communication models include: 1. their treatment of communication as a linear one-way act, rather than a cyclical two-way process; 2. the possible occurrence of bias in the message as a result of the receiver's being dependent on the sender for information; and 3. the fact that their foci tended to be on the object of communication and the message rather than on interactions/silence/timings. Ironically, these criticisms of the usual communication process would appear to mirror what happens in financial reporting (although the feedback loop could be closed by including share price reactions, press comment regarding the financial statements, and corporate meetings with analysts and institutional investors).

Just like agency theory, communication theory will not help in the determination of financial accounting standards, but, in terms of financial reporting, communication theory may help in understanding why the financial statements can be misinterpreted. The key to this is the clear identification of the message that the financial statements are trying to communicate.

Other theoretical (formal) approaches

Two other approaches to developing accounting theory are the ethical and the sociological approaches. Riahi-Belkaoui (2000: 73) differentiates between these as follows: the ethical approach focuses on a concept of 'fairness' while the sociological approach focuses on 'social welfare'. Therefore, 'concepts such as justice, truth and fairness would be discussed and extended to accounting' (Moonitz, 1961: 3). The 'truth' and 'fairness' envisaged here are much broader concepts than are encompassed by the phrase 'a true and fair view'. With the sociological approach:

> One of the objectives of accounting is, therefore, the reporting of the effects of business operations on all related groups in society whether or not they are direct users of accounting information. While accountants are not and should not be called upon to make judgements regarding welfare, it is occasionally suggested that accounting reports should provide the information necessary for broad welfare judgements. The main difficulty with this approach is that adequate principles and procedures cannot be established unless accountants have a basis for determining what welfare judgements are important and what information will aid in making these judgements. (Hendriksen, 1977: 21)

Indeed, it could be argued that decisions regarding social welfare are really beyond the remit of the 'accountant'. Such decisions are political – if the problem is greater than accounting, the accountant alone cannot solve it.

THEORY DEVELOPMENT AND RESISTANCE

Sterling reported that '[t]here are many disputes over the way in which theories are constructed' (1970: 444). Kuhn (1970) has suggested that the finding of 'anomalies' in existing theories results in insecurity and crisis, while there are debates over their implications. When these 'anomalies' can no longer be ignored, theoretical developments are said to occur.

An important aspect of theory development is that of creativity: 'Creativity is defined as the ability to formulate new combinations from two or more concepts already in mind' (Haefele, 1962: 5). A key starting point is the clear identification of the topic or problem: 'In technical work, as well as in business, to "define the problem" has become a practical cliché and a sacred cow. But it is also good advice' (Haefele, 1962: 6). However, there also needs to be an initiating drive – for without it nothing will happen. Haefele (1962) set out the emotional factors relating to creativity:

• The problem should be significant or important.
• The researcher needs confidence – 'confidence feeds upon the expressed faith by others' (Haefele, 1962: 20), as in a commission to undertake a project or write a report.
• There should be competition to solve the problem.
• Finally, there is the joy of solving the problem, thus gaining freedom from the frustration of struggling and thinking about it.

But should one strive to be creative? Despite the rhetoric of research aiming to make a contribution to knowledge, one may often be forgiven for thinking that the last thing that people want is a contribution to their knowledge!

> The belief in the sanctity of the human body for twelve centuries (from Galen to Vesalius) stood in the way of advances in the study of human anatomy. The belief in a geocentric universe persisted a similar interval, from Ptolemy to Copernicus. Sentiment, habit, fear, and jealousy stood in the way of the acceptance of the views of Harvey on the circulation of the blood, of Jenner on inoculation against smallpox, of Semmelweiss on the prevention of puerperal fever. (Chambers, 1966: 348)

In the seventeenth century, Galileo was imprisoned for challenging the doctrine that the earth was the centre of the universe. '[E]minent scientists such as Kelvin, Mach and Rutherford held firmly to beliefs that were discarded, because disproved, within a generation of their utterance' (Chambers, 1980: 167). Koestler (1970: 59) explained that '[w]hen reality becomes unbearable, the mind must withdraw from it and create a world of artificial perfection'.

This raises questions about the implications for the development of accounting theory. Watts and Zimmerman (1979: 24) considered that it was the 'diversity of interests which prevents general agreement on accounting theory'. 'Too often, accounting theory is invoked more as a tactic to buttress one's preconceived notions, rather than as a genuine arbiter of contending views' (Zeff, 1974: 177). 'My hypothesis is that the setting of accounting standards is as much a product of political action as of flawless logic or empirical findings' (Horngren, 1973: 61). Therefore, one must question how theoretical are accounting theories and consequently how conceptual are the conceptual framework projects undertaken by the accounting standard-setters. An example of conceptual confusion follows:

> The apotheosis of hotchpot accounting at the hands of the U.K. Sandilands Committee (1975) is the crowning consequence of the chaos of indeterminacy. Faced with conflicting submissions and argu-ments, the Committee seems to have tried to appease all. Some asset amounts (and the consequential charges or credits in income or reserve accounts) were to be based on independent current valuations, some on index-based replacement costs, some on net realizable values, some on discovered money amounts or money equivalents, some on discounted present values, some at original cost and some at the lower of replacement cost and net realizable value. The result of such an aggregation and the income amount it yields are beyond description and mortal understanding. (Chambers, 1980: 177)

Current cost accounting was introduced in the USA in 1979 and in the UK in 1980; '[b]y 1985 it was clear that the UK standard had failed and it ceased to be mandatory; a year later the Financial Accounting Standards Board (FASB) withdrew its standard' (Miller and Loftus, 2000: 4). 'Standard-setters around the world were badly burnt by the current cost fiasco' (Miller and Loftus, 2000: 5). One cannot help but wonder whether this was because of a lack of a firm theoretical base, the political nature of the debate and a lack of conviction by the preparers and users of the financial statements about the validity of such adjustments.

MEASUREMENT IN ACCOUNTING

One of the first topics usually covered in a book on accounting theory relates to accounting measurement and the ongoing debate regarding the appro-priateness of historical costs, current values, fair values, etc. So far there has been little mention of 'measurement' issues relating to accounting – this has been deliberate. This emphasis on measurement does raise two problems – firstly as to whether an accounting system per se is a measurement system, and secondly, if it is, what is it measuring? 'Measurement presupposes something to be measured, and, unless we know what that something is, no measurement can have any significance' (Caws, 1959: 3). A committee of the American Accounting Association (AAA, 1971: 46) considered that: 'Accounting measurement is the core of accounting, both in theory and in practice, since accounting without measurement is inconceivable.' Ijiri (1975: 29) also thought that *accounting measurement* . . . is the central function of accounting systems' and 'in order to understand accounting measurement in current accounting practice, accounting measurement must be analyzed from the point of view of *performance measurement*' (p. 34, emphasis in original). However, Churchman (1971: 57) questioned whether accounting was a system of measurement; 'accounting is a systematic method of gathering data. . . . But to be systematic in gathering data does not mean to measure.' Indeed, Larson (1969) advocated the separation of measurement from the discussion of accounting theory. Therefore, the distinction between measurement and calculation is an important one (Sterling, 1989). It may be questionable whether historical cost is a measurement process – it is certainly a calculation because the preparation of the financial statements comes about because of the nature of the double-entry system. Indeed, 'measurement' (if this is the right term) should become an issue only once the objective of the financial statements has been settled. An interesting question is, if the focus of accounting were to move to discounted future cash flows, how would one 'measure' the future?

In terms of the discussion of performance, the word 'measurement' is often deliberately avoided because of the implication of precision (ICAEW, 1995); instead, the term 'performance indicator' is preferred. This should raise the question of whether it is appropriate to talk about accounting measurement, or whether this in itself could lead to the danger of artificial precision being associated with accounting.

CONCLUSION

What is clear from this examination of 'accounting theory' is that its nature, scope and purpose are vague. The term 'accounting theory' generally encompasses financial accounting and financial reporting. Different theories may have come about because of the different views of accounting. Different theorists may have different starting points and have ended up going in different directions. It has been seen that the purpose of 'accounting theory' may be to:

- facilitate the matching of costs and revenues
- explain and predict accounting practice
- explain which accounting alternative should be used
- provide guidelines for practitioners

- justify accounting practice (in the early days of theory development)
- explain the impact of accounting data on users.

Whether 'accounting theory' can provide all this is problematic. What needs to be clarified is the appropriate starting point for the theory's development. The specification of the problem is crucial. However, the political nature of theory development may mean that vested interests try to obstruct such developments.

While there has been much discussion about how the financial statements are used and the impact that accounting data has on various stakeholder groups, many of the approaches to 'accounting theory' development do not help identify the content of the financial statements. Financial reporting has developed over time, and Bedford and Dopuch (1961: 355) were concerned about 'the suggestion, and its implications, that the structure of accounting theory be developed from a base of shifting goals and standards'. Whittington (1987: 335) considered that 'all approaches to accounting theory are, at the present time, in a fairly rudimentary stage of evolution and desperately need further constructive development'. Disturbingly, Vasarhelyi et al. (1988) report a decreasing trend in published articles over the period 1963–84 dealing with accounting theory as a school of thought – and it is likely that this trend has continued. The discussion of the redefinition of accountancy presumably would also require the redefinition of 'accounting theory'; however, once one starts to alter theory, the implication is that the previous theory was defective or the new theory could be misconceived. Indeed, there may even be a question as to whether it is appropriate to talk about 'accounting theory'.

DISCUSSION QUESTIONS

1   Explain whether or not you believe that it is appropriate to attempt to construct a theory of accounting.

2   In the context of accounting theory construction, consider whether the normative/positive dichotomy is appropriate. Construct a case to justify your stance.

3   Does the multitude of approaches to accounting theory represent a rich diversity of intellectual paradigms or merely confusion about the scope and limitations of accounting?

4   Explain the dysfunctional behaviour that may occur in the course of theory development.

5   In the context of financial reporting, it has been suggested that measurement issues are of secondary importance, and the primary concern should be clarity about what is to be reported. Support or refute this line of reasoning.

REFERENCES

American Accounting Association (AAA) (1966) Committee to Prepare a Statement of Basic Accounting Theory, *A Statement of Basic Accounting Theory*. Sarasota, FL: AAA.

American Accounting Association (AAA) (1971) 'Report of the Committee on Foundations of Accounting Measurement', *Accounting Review*, Supplement: 1–48.

American Accounting Association (AAA) (1977) Committee on Concepts and Standards for External Financial Reports, *Statement on Accounting Theory and Theory Acceptance*. Sarasota, FL: AAA.

Barnett, G.A. (1989) 'Communication of accounting information', in G. Siegal and H. Ramananskas-Marconi (eds), *Behavioral Accounting*. Cincinnati, OH: South-Western Publishing Co.

Bedford, N.M. and Baladouni, V. (1962) 'A communications theory approach to accountancy', *The Accounting Review*, 37 (4): 650–9.

Bedford, N.M. and Dopuch, N. (1961) 'Research methodology and accounting theory – another perspective', *The Accounting Review*, July: 351–61.

Bromwich, M. (1992) *Financial Reporting, Information and Capital Markets*. London: Pitman Publishing.

Buckley, J.W., Kircher, P. and Mathews, R.L. (1968) 'Methodology in accounting theory', *The Accounting Review*, April: 274–83.

Burchell, S., Clubb, C., Hopwood, A., Hughes, J. and Napier, J. (1980) 'The roles of accounting in organizations and society', *Accounting, Organizations and Society*, June: 5–28.

Caws, P. (1959) 'Definition and measurement in physics', in C.W. Churchman and P. Ratoosh (eds), *Measurement, Definitions, and Theories*. London: Wiley.

Chambers, R.J. (1955) 'Blueprint for a theory of accounting', *Accounting Research*, January: 17–25.

Chambers, R.J. (1966) *Accounting, Evaluation and Economic Behavior* (reprinted 1974). Houston, TX: Scholars Book Co.

Chambers, R.J. (1976) Correspondence: 'The possibility of a normative accounting standard', *Accounting Review*, 51 (3): 646–52.

Chambers, R.J. (1980) 'The myths and science of accounting', *Accounting Organizations and Society*, June: 167–80.

Chambers, R.J. (1993) 'Positive accounting theory and the PA cult', *Abacus*, 29 (1): 1–26.

Chambers, R.J. (1996) 'Ends, ways, means and conceptual frameworks', *Abacus*, 32 (2): 119.

Christenson, C. (1983) 'The methodology of positive accounting', *The Accounting Review*, January: 1–22.

Churchman, C.W. (1971) 'The systems approach to measurement in business firms', in R.R. Sterling and W.F. Bentz (eds), *Accounting in Perspective*. Cincinnati: South-Western Publishing Co. pp. 51–7.

Cushing, B.E. (1989) 'A Kuhnian interpretation of the historical evolution of accounting', *Accounting Historians' Journal*, 16 (2): 1–41.

Davis, S.W., Menton, K. and Morgan, G. (1982) 'The images that have shaped accounting theory', *Accounting Organizations and Society*, December: 307–18.

Deegan, C. (2000) *Financial Accounting Theory*. Roseville, NSW: McGraw-Hill Australia.

Demski, J.S. (1973) 'The general impossibility of normative accounting standards', *The Accounting Review*, October: 718–23.

Demski, J.S. (1974) 'Choice among financial reporting alternatives', *The Accounting Review*, April: 221–32.

Gerbner, G. (1969) 'Institutional pressures upon mass communicators', in P. Halmos (ed.), *The Sociology of Mass-Media Communicators*. The Sociological Review Monograph 13. Keele: University of Keele.

Goch, D. (1979) 'Company reporting – the state of the art', *Certified Accountant*, October: 305–7, 309.

Haefele, J.W. (1962) *Creativity and Innovation*. New York: Reinhold.

Haried, A.A. (1973) 'Measurement of meaning in financial reports', *Journal of Accounting Research*, Spring: 117–45.

Hendriksen, E.S. (1977) *Accounting Theory* (3rd edn). Homewood, IL: Richard D. Irwin, Inc.

Horngren, C.T. (1973) 'The marketing of accounting standards', *The Journal of Accountancy*, October: 61–6.

Hylton, D.P. (1962) 'Current trends in accounting theory', *The Accounting Review*, January: 22–7.

Ijiri, Y. (1975) *Theory of Accounting Measurement*, Studies in Accounting Research No. 10. Sarasota, FL: AAA.

Institute of Chartered Accountants in England and Wales (ICAEW) (1995) Faculty of Finance and Management, *Developing Comprehensive Performance Indicators*. London: ICAEW.

Jensen, M.C. (1976) 'Reflections on the state of accounting research and the regulation of accounting', *Stanford Lectures in Accounting 1976*. Stanford, CA: Stanford University, Graduate School of Business.

Jensen, M.C. and Meckling, W.H. (1976) 'Theory of the firm: managerial behavior, agency costs and ownership structure', *Journal of Financial Economics*, 13 (4): 305–60.

Koestler, A. (1970) *The Sleepwalkers*. London: Penguin.

Kuhn, T. (1970) *The Structure of Scientific Revolutions*. Chicago: Chicago University Press.

Larson, K. (1969) 'Implications of measurement theory on accounting concept formulation', *The Accounting Review*, January: 38–47.

Lasswell, H. (1948) 'The structure and function of communications in society', in L. Bryson (ed.), *Communications of Ideas*. New York: Institute for Religious and Social Studies.

Littleton, A.C. (1938) 'Tests for principles', *The Accounting Review*, March: 16–24.

Littleton, A.C. (1953) *Structure of Accounting Theory*, American Accounting Association Monograph No. 5. Sarasota, FL: AAA.

Mattessich, R. (1995) *Critique of Accounting: Examination of the Foundations and Normative Structure of an Applied Discipline*. Westport, CT: Quorum Books.

Miller, M.C. and Loftus, J.A. (2000) 'Measurement entering the 21st century: a clear or blocked road ahead?', *Australian Accounting Review*, 11 (2): 4–18.

Moonitz, M. (1961) *The Basic Postulates of Accounting*, American Accounting Association Research Study No. 1. New York: AICPA.

Oliver, B.L. (1974) 'The semantic differential: a device for measuring the interprofessional communication of selected accounting concepts', *Journal of Accounting Research*, Autumn: 299–316.

Parker, L.D. (1986) *Communicating Financial Information Through the Annual Report*. London: ICAEW.

Riahi-Belkaoui, A. (2000) *Accounting Theory* (4th edn). London: Business Press (Thomson Learning).

Rogers, E.M. and Kincaid, D.L. (1981) *Communication Network: Towards a New Paradigm for Research*. New York: Free Press.

Ross, S.A. (1973) 'The economic theory of agency: the principal's problem', *American Economic Review*, 62, May: 134–9.

Sandilands Committee (1975) *Inflation Accounting*, Report of the Inflation Accounting Committee. London: HMSO.

Schroeder, R.G. and Clark, M. (1995) *Accounting Theory: Text and Readings* (5th edn). New York: Wiley.

Shannon, C. and Weaver, W. (1949) *The Mathematical Theory of Communication*. Urbana, IL: University of Illinois Press.

Shaw, M. (1972) 'The coming crisis of radical sociology', in R. Blackburn (ed.), *Ideology in Social Sciences*. New York: Fontana.

Spence, M. and Zeckhauser, R. (1971) 'Insurance, information and individual action', *American Economic Review*, 61 (2): 380–7.

Staubus, G.J. (1954) 'An accounting concept of revenue', unpublished PhD thesis, School of Business, University of Chicago.

Staubus, G.J. (1961) *A Theory of Accounting to Investors* (reprinted 1971). Houston, TX: Scholars Book Co.

Sterling, R.R. (1970) 'On theory construction and verification', *The Accounting Review*, July: 444–57.

Sterling, R.R. (1989) 'Teaching the correspondence concept', *Issues in Accounting Education*, 4 (1): 82–93.

Sterling, R.R. (1990) 'Positive accounting: an assessment', *Abacus*, 26 (2): 97–135.

Storey, R.K. (1963) *The Search for Accounting Principles*. New York: AICPA.

Sullivan, J.J. (1983) *Handbook of Accounting Communications*. Reading, MA: Addison-Wesley.

Tinker, A., Merino, B. and Neimark, M. (1982) 'The normative origins of positive theories: ideology and accounting thought', *Accounting, Organizations and Society*, 7 (2): 167–200.

Varsarhelyi, M., Boa, D.H. and Berk, J. (1988) 'Trends in the evolution of scholarly accounting thought: a quantitative examination', *Accounting Historians Journal*, Spring: 45–64.

Watts, R.L. (1995) 'Nature and origins of positive research in accounting', in S. Jones, C. Romano and J. Ratnatunga (eds), *Accounting Theory: A Contemporary Review*. Sydney: Harcourt Brace. pp. 295–353.

Watts, R.L. and Zimmerman J.L. (1978) 'Towards a positive theory of the determination of accounting standards', *The Accounting Review*, January: 112–34.

Watts, R.L. and Zimmerman, J.L. (1979) 'The demand for and supply of accounting theories: the market for excuses', *The Accounting Review*, April: 273–304, reprinted in R. Bloom and P.T. Elgers (1987), *Accounting Theory and Policy: A Reader* (2nd edn). Orlando, FL: Harcourt Brace Jovanovich. pp. 22–57.

Watts, R.L. and Zimmerman, J.L. (1983) 'Agency problems, auditing and the theory of the firm: some evidence', *Journal of Law and Economics*, October: 613–34.

Watts, R.L. and Zimmerman, J.L. (1986) *Positive Accounting Theory*. Englewood Cliffs, NJ: Prentice Hall International.

Webster's Third New International Dictionary (1961). Springfield, MA: G. & C. Merriam Co.

Whittington, G. (1986) 'Financial accounting theory: an overview', *The British Accounting Review*, Autumn: 4–41.

Whittington, G. (1987) 'Positive accounting theory: a review article', *Accounting and Business Research*, 17, Autumn: 327–36.

Wolk, H.I. and Tearney, M.G. (1997) *Accounting Theory: A Conceptual and Institutional Approach* (4th edn). Cincinnati, OH: South-Western College Publishing.

Zeff, S.A. (1974) 'Comments on accounting principles – how they are developed', in R.R. Sterling (ed.) (1974), *Institutional Issues in Public Accounting: Paper and Responses from Accounting Colloquium III*. Lawrence, KS: Scholars Book Co.

If you wish to understand something, observe its beginnings
and development.

                                                        – Aristotle

I n view of the lack of a generally accepted accounting 'theory', this
      chapter seeks to examine the development of accounting. Edwards
      (1989: 4) considered that '[t]he study of accounting history helps us to
understand our past and gives us an appreciation of how our current practices and problems came into being'. 'While accounting procedures have not
always been logically conceived, it is relevant to study their development and
change to understand why accounting is what it is today. The historical
perspective also permits a better evaluation of the objectives and postulates of
accounting theory' (Hendriksen, 1977: 27). Studying this should help to clarify
what accounting, or, more precisely, what financial accounting, was intended
to achieve. As was noted in the previous chapter, the identification of objectives is the key starting point for solving any problem.

An examination of the literature on the subject of the history of accounting
shows that it has developed in line with industrial, commercial and social
changes in society. There has been a debate (Sombart, 1902; Tinker, 1985;
Winjum, 1971; Yamey, 1964) as to whether accounting is socially constructed
(developments in accounting arise as a result of social, economic and political
events) or socially constructing (because of its power, accounting actually
influences the development of society). Given all the concern about current
developments and their impacts on accounting, it would seem that at the
moment accounting is very much socially constructed.

In view of the debates about the nature of and lack of agreement on
'accounting theory', this chapter seeks to shed some light on this topic by
examining developments in the use of accounting data. In particular, it should
be noted that:

• The original notion of 'stewardship' appears to predate the production of
  accounts by hundreds if not thousands of years (originally, it was to do
  with honesty and integrity).

- The earliest uses of 'accounting' data were in what we would now call a 'management accounting' setting, and accounting could be classified as an internal control. As early 'accounting' was used for 'stewardship' purposes, it can be seen that in the early days 'stewardship' and 'management accounting' were linked.
- The development of double-entry bookkeeping is another example of accounting being used as an internal control.
- Permanently invested capital required the splitting up of the life of an enterprise into artificial accounting periods, and eventually resulted in the development of the financial accounts and the calculation of 'profit'. The accounting records (which were originally for internal control purposes) were utilized. The separation of ownership and management meant that 'stewardship' evolved into a 'financial accounting' context. Given the recent emphasis on corporate governance, this chapter will examine the implications for financial reporting.

In Chapter 4, conceptual developments in financial reporting will be considered:

- The 1960s saw the emphasis on users' needs, and the development of the objective of the financial statements as being to enable users to take economic decisions.
- This has now been extended to emphasizing the need to enable users to make their own predictions of future cash flows.

While accounting has come a long way over the past ten thousand years, some of the most dramatic changes have occurred in the past forty years. Although it may be argued that recent developments have simply mirrored the increase in complexity in the world of commerce and business, there must be a concern about how much financial accounting has changed in such a short space of time – especially given its problematic theoretical base.

The study of history involves the interpretation and reinterpretation of past events. As Popper (1966: 268) stated, 'there can be no history of "the past as it actually did happen"; there can only be historical interpretations, and none of them final'.

THE ORIGINS OF STEWARDSHIP

Stewardship in one form or another goes back to the most ancient of times. Boyd (1905: 17) quotes from the code of laws issued by Hammurabi (who ruled in ancient Babylon) as an example that a stewardship relationship could be discerned to exist between a merchant and a person acting as his agent (though in the Near East rudimentary business records in the form of tokens for record keeping may have existed six thousand years before this [see Mattessich, 1995: 15–31]). Boyd considered that there was ample evidence that stewardship predated the production of accounts (in the modern sense of the word) by hundreds of years. In the royal treasury of ancient Egypt, a system of checks was used to try to prevent theft and thus reinforce the stewardship function of the officials (Boyd, 1905: 21). The ancient Greeks were also concerned about the accountability of people working for the state. Though the classical Greek period is too early for documentary papyri (de Ste. Croix, 1956: 23), more permanent records do exist, '[t]o ensure publicity the accounts of public officials were engraved on stone and exposed in public' (Boyd, 1905: 25). It was the view of de Ste. Croix (1956: 14–15) that 'Greek and Roman accounting took the form of individual records of debts and of receipts and payments, and miscellaneous inventories, rather than accounts in the modern sense'. He continues (p. 29): 'No doubt some men of business other than bankers would find it necessary to keep detailed accounts of their operations, if only to make sure that they were not cheated by their slaves or their associates.' However, records were not required for taxation purposes, as 'at no time in the ancient world were taxes assessed upon money incomes' (p. 29). An important example of accounting in Ptolemaic Egypt from the mid-third century BC can be found in the 'Zenon archive' (Mickwitz, 1937). This contains the detailed accounts (kept by Zenon) of the private estate of Apollonius (the chief finance minister of Ptolemy II). While these accounts contained greater detail than accounts of earlier periods, the system was essentially the same, as was their purpose:

> Elaborate and minutely detailed as the Zenon accounts are, their purpose was much more limited than that of comparable estate accounts today: it was not to enable Apollonius to draw up at regular intervals complete 'profit and loss accounts' and 'balance sheets' (nothing of this sort appears in antiquity), nor to assist him to obtain the highest possible rate of profit out of his estate, but simply to prevent theft, embezzlement, fraudulent conversion and other avoidable losses due to carelessness and the like. This, indeed, was the one major aim of all ancient accounting. (de Ste. Croix, 1956: 32)

Descriptions can be found (e.g., Mickwitz, 1937; Rathbone, 1991) of accounting on a large estate in Roman Egypt (AD 249–68), where monthly accounts were submitted by *phrontistai* (managers) to the owners of the Appianus estate – a variety of other records was also produced by the *phrontistai* for their own uses: 'Efficient management of production was the job of the phrontistes [manager]; failure on his part would have been evident from small crops and high total figures for expenditure' (Rathbone, 1991: 26). However, 'the whole purpose of ancient accounting was not to measure the rate of profit or loss but to keep accurate records of acquisitions and outgoings, in money and kind, and to expose any losses due to dishonesty or negligence' (de Ste. Croix, 1956: 38).

Following the fall of the Roman Empire, western Europe was thrown into turmoil; '[f]or centuries education was practically eliminated' (Littleton, 1933: 16) and so the next stages in accounting development that are recorded relate to the city-republics of northern Italy (in the wake of the Crusades) and Norman England. Manorial accounts first appeared in the very early thirteenth century. Harvey (1984: 91) described the situation in England as follows:

> If the landlord entrusted his manor to a local official who was answerable to him for all moneys received or spent, all the corn and livestock, there would clearly have to be a regular reckoning to show what resources remained in hand and how much cash was due from the official to the lord or vice versa. It is this regular reckoning that the manorial account records: its aim was to show the state of account between the lord and his official, to show how much was owing to one or the other once every transaction had been allowed for.

The manorial account was always a charge-and-discharge account (Harvey, 1984: 93). A charge-and-discharge statement 'is plainly the report of an agent, not a statement of indebtedness or of ownership' (Littleton, 1933: 126). Littleton continues, 'the steward does not owe the lord of the manor; neither is it a receipt and disbursement statement nor a calculation of loss or gain. It is simply a well organized report upon an agent's responsibilities.' Macve (1985: 64) considered that '[m]edieval estate accounts recorded receipts and issues of cash and produce in essentially the same way as estate accounts, like those of Zenon or Appianus . . . [t]heir primary purpose was to control the accountable officials'. Just as in ancient Egypt, so in Norman England, the development of an early form of audit (during the early part of the twelfth century) supported the stewardship function.

EARLY STEWARDSHIP IN A MANAGEMENT ACCOUNTING CONTEXT

The use of the term 'management accounting' developed after the Second World War, and encompasses the term 'cost accounting' which is much older.

Littleton (1933: 321) considered that '[c]ost accounting . . . is one of the many consequences of the industrial revolution'. There has been much discussion of the development of cost accounting from the end of the eighteenth century (e.g., Johnson, 1981; Johnson and Kaplan, 1987; Kaplan 1984). Solomons (1968) identified a 'costing renaissance' as taking place in the 1880s and 1890s, although he acknowledged that rudimentary cost accounting could be traced as far back as the fourteenth century. Edwards and Newell (1991) show that the use of costings in business was not a product of the eighteenth or nineteenth centuries, but was much older. They considered (p. 411) that Boulton and Watt's Soho works and Josiah Wedgwood's use of costings were unlikely to have been exceptional 'but the scarcity of well-documented examples has, perhaps, conveyed this impression'.

Rathbone (1991) makes a direct comparison of the Appianus estate with Andrew Carnegie's methods of managing his steelworks. Commenting on the work of Johnson and Kaplan (1987), Rathbone expressed the following view (1991: 54–5):

> As the authors of a recent study conclude: 'Carnegie's success depended upon good information about direct operating costs. For that, accounting systems mattered. For the rest, faith and intuition sufficed.' The same might be said about the Appianus estate, which could perhaps be put in the category of 'multiprocess, hierarchical, managed enterprises', with a geographically distinct central office and production units and a need to cost internal transfers, which the same authors assume emerged only in the nineteenth century.

As the earliest forms of accounting were used for stewardship purposes, these were very early forms of what could probably be termed 'management accounting'. In its earliest form, stewardship involved the custodianship of goods on behalf of another person – ensuring the prevention of theft or fraud. The earliest forms of accounting were developed to assist with this. The key aspect of this type of stewardship is an assessment of whether the 'stewards' have done what was required of them; that is, it was necessary for the landowner or master to form a judgement. Although '[t]he purpose of periodic financial statements of a corporation is to furnish information that is necessary for the formulation of dependable judgements' (AAA Committee quoted in AAA, 1957: 52), it must be remembered that, in terms of external reporting, the users are very remote from the reporting entity. However, in terms of early accounting, there would have been a relatively close relationship between the steward and the owner, and a comparatively simple (in relation to modern financial statements) means of assessment.

The much-cited biblical parable of the talents is often used to show that the relationship between accounting and stewardship is thousands of years old. This parable illustrates that proper accountability requires that the person to whom the report is being made is able to make an informed judgement about the outcome. In the parable, the owner was interested in what could have been done. As Collinson et al. (1993: 63) state: 'One fascinating element of that story is the implicit reference to financial opportunity cost, for the owner indicated that he could have made interest on the money assigned to the steward if it had been deposited with a banker!' However, modern financial statements say nothing about what could have been achieved, but this should be an essential piece of information if one is trying to judge management's performance. Rosenfield (1974: 127–8) considered that in judging management's performance: 'The criterion is not how well they did compared with how well others did or how well they previously did, but how well they might have done in the circumstances.' This requires detailed knowledge of the situation. Therefore, in some ways, this parable is more akin to an example of a management accounting situation (where a board of directors would know what to expect of a divisional manager) than a financial accounting situation (where the shareholders tend to be completely divorced from the running of the business).

Two aspects of stewardship can be discerned; firstly, custodianship linked with a responsibility for the prevention of theft or fraud, and, secondly, the evaluation of performance. Noke (1981: 137) considered that: 'One objective of modern financial reporting is traditionally described as "accounting for stewardship", but the analogy with the administration of manorial estates does not strictly hold.' At the same time as the widening of the notion of stewardship, there has been a weakening in the relationship between the managers (stewards) and the people to whom they now report. It can be seen that stewardship involves both the management and accounting disciplines – it refers to the responsibilities assumed by management and also encompasses management's actions to fulfil its obligations. The nature of stewardship has changed over time, and the concept itself is not well defined. The 1990s saw the rise of corporate governance, and therefore it would appear to be appropriate to view financial reporting as part of this process.

CORPORATE GOVERNANCE

The work of Adam Smith (1776) and Berle and Means (1932) show that concern about corporate governance is not a new phenomenon, but it certainly came to prominence in the 1990s. The Cadbury Committee was established by the Financial Reporting Council, the London Stock Exchange and the accountancy profession in order to examine the financial aspects of corporate governance. This was because 'concerns about the working of the corporate system were heightened by some unexpected failures of major companies and by criticisms of the lack of effective board accountability for such matters as directors' pay' (*Cadbury Report*, 1992: 14). Tricker (1984) considered that 'management' is to do with running a business, whereas 'governance' is about ensuring that it is run properly. He viewed the corporate governance process in terms of four principal activities:

1 *Direction*:   formulating the strategic direction for the future of the enterprise in the long term
2 *Executive action*:   involvement in crucial executive decisions
3 *Supervision*:   monitoring and oversight of management performance
4 *Accountability*:   recognizing responsibilities to those making a legitimate demand for accountability. (Tricker, 1984: 7)

The *Cadbury Report* (1992: 15) defined corporate governance as 'the system by which companies are directed and controlled' (1992: 15). It continued:

> *Boards of directors are responsible for the governance of their companies. The shareholder's role in governance is to appoint the directors and the auditors and to satisfy themselves that an appropriate governance structure is in place. The responsibilities of the board include setting the company's strategic aims, providing the leadership to put them into effect, supervising the management of the business and reporting to shareholders on their stewardship. . . .*
>
> *The role of the auditor is to provide the shareholders with an external and objective check on the directors' financial statements which form the basis of that reporting system. (Cadbury Report, 1992: 15)*

The perceived benefits of corporate governance (CIMA, 1999) are seen as reduced risk, improved performance, better access to capital markets, greater marketability of goods and services, improved leadership, and the demonstration of transparency and social accountability. Whittington (1993) discussed four separate themes driving the developments in corporate governance, namely: creative accounting, the business failures and scandals of the late 1980s and early 1990s, concern about the level of directors' pay, and short-termism. The *Cadbury Report* (1992: 32) was concerned that '[a] basic weakness in the current system of financial reporting is the possibility of different accounting treatments being applied to essentially the same facts, with the consequence that different results or financial positions could be reported, each apparently complying with the overriding requirement to show a true and fair view'. It considered that there were advantages 'in financial reporting rules which limit the scope for uncertainty and manipulation'. The report recommended

> *that boards should pay particular attention to their duty to present a balanced and understandable assessment of their company's position. Balance requires that setbacks should be dealt with as well as successes, while the need for the report to be readily understood emphasises that words are as important as figures. (p. 33)*

The boards of directors should 'aim to ensure the integrity and consistency of their reports and they should meet the spirit as well as the letter of reporting standards' (p. 33). Whittington (1993: 314) considered that '[f]inan-cial reporting . . . is a crucial element which is necessary for the corporate governance system to function effectively', but, if users do not use the data or the monitoring cost are too high, the mere 'provision of good financial reporting information is not a sufficient condition for the effectiveness of corporate governance'. Dewing and Russell (2000: 372) were concerned about the effectiveness of corporate governance as 'the process of setting and amending the codes has been, to a large extent at least, *ad hoc*; and . . . the mechanisms for monitoring and enforcing compliance are at least weak and at worst non-existent'.

So, while there are concerns about the effectiveness of corporate governance procedures, it is still important to think of corporate financial reporting within the overall context of corporate governance – as opposed to viewing cor-porate governance in a financial reporting context.

EARLY DEVELOPMENTS IN ACCOUNTING

Until the thirteenth century, accounting records were still no further advanced than account keeping. Harvey's view (1984: 91) was that '[t]here is every indication that until the mid-thirteenth century it was unusual to set down in writing the details of accounts; they would be presented by the local official and examined – audited, that is, heard – by the lord or his rep-resentative entirely by word of mouth, with no other aids than counters for the calculations, tally-sticks as vouchers, and perhaps a few brief notes as memoranda'. Brown (1905: 94) described them as containing 'nothing more than a series of unconnected jottings related to those portions of business on which it would have been unwise to rely on memory alone'. It was the transition of the accounting records from merely being a memorandum containing a number of detached notes, to containing information for the settlement of amounts to be paid and amounts to be received that marks the birth of systematic bookkeeping. The growth in the number of transactions required the development of a systematic method of recording this information. Double entry was first recorded, in 1340, in Genoa. The first trader's books, containing double entry, related to the period 1410 to 1434. The practice of double-entry bookkeeping was described by Luca Pacioli in 1494 in his *Summa de Arithmetica, Geometria, Proportioni et Proportionalita*. However, it was not until the seventeenth century that the practice of periodically balancing the ledger became generally accepted – therefore, it was common for the ledger not to be balanced until it was completed. This also meant that there was no periodic calculation of profit (Littleton, 1933).

At this time, the concept of permanent capital did not exist. Individuals ran their own businesses, or groups of entrepreneurs would come together to finance individual trading expeditions. This could involve buying a ship, hiring a crew and filling it with goods for exchange. If the venture was successful, the exchanged goods would be sold, the wages of the crew and other expenses would be paid, and any remainder would be divided up between the entrepreneurs. Therefore, provided the expedition was a success, each merchant would be repaid his original capital invested in the enterprise plus a share of the profit.

In England, overseas trade was controlled by the Crown, and this privilege was usually conferred by Royal Charter on corporations with monopoly rights in specific parts of the world. Even though the trade was carried out by a corporation, the principle of settling up after each expedition or venture was continued. This was through the issue of terminable stock. As these corporations grew, both in size and scope of operation, the impracticalities of this method of accounting became apparent. One of the first steps in the development of the idea of permanent capital came in 1613 when the East India Company issued capital for a term of four years. This was followed by a new charter which, in effect, established the principle of permanently invested capital. Accounting had been directed previously at periodic settlements for each venture, from which each subscriber was paid a sum representing capital and profit without distinction. Permanent capital changed all this and produced the difficulties of determining profit while retaining capital intact.

A concept of profit was known prior to this, but '[w]hat . . . is less clear is what the thirteenth century mind understood by the concept of profit, and the purposes for which the concept was used' (Noke, 1981: 146). The study of the accounts for Norwich Cathedral Priory (Noke, 1981; Stone, 1962) during the thirteenth and fourteenth centuries indicates a concern with profit and loss accountancy and even the adoption of an opportunity cost approach. This was 'presumably so as to enable the monks to judge not merely the efficiency of arable husbandry but also whether they should be engaged in that rather than some alternative' (Noke, 1981: 148). However, the calculation of profit was relatively uncommon in early forms of business, and this situation persisted until the nineteenth century. Yamey (1962: 38) gave the following reason for this: 'Periodic calculations of a firm's profits and statements of the value of its assets are of little interest to the businessman who is closely and continuously concerned with his own business operations.' As a consequence:

> the problems we associate with the concept of profit and the careful calculation of periodic profit do not appear to have been problems worrying the early practitioners or teachers of double entry accounting in England. Accounting requirements of business men did not call for any serious concern with these matters. (Yamey, 1962: 37)

The seventeenth and eighteenth centuries saw rapid developments in economic life. Berle and Means (1932: 125–6) considered that up to approximately 1835, when shareholders were few, the situation could be described as follows:

> We have the picture of a group of owners, necessarily delegating certain powers of management, protected in their property rights by a series of fixed rules under which management had a relatively limited play. The management of the corporation indeed was thought of as a set of agents running a business for a set of owners . . . they were strictly accountable and were in a position to be governed in all matters of general policy by their owners.

As early as 1776, Adam Smith was concerned about the management of these joint-stock companies:

> The directors of such companies, however, being the managers rather of other people's money than of their own, it cannot well be expected, that they should watch over it with the same anxious vigilance with which the partners in a private copartnery frequently watch over their own. Like the stewards of a rich man, they are apt to consider attention to small matters as not for their master's honour, and very easily give themselves a dispensation from having it. Negligence and profusion, therefore, must always prevail, more or less in the management of the affairs of such a company. (1776: 741)

In the wake of the Industrial Revolution, there was a need to bring together large amounts of capital. In the UK, apart from incorporation by Royal Charter, the only other ways of achieving corporate status, prior to the enactment of the Joint-Stock Companies Act, 1844, were by a special Act of Parliament or letters patent (Edey and Panitpakdi, 1956: 356). These methods were both time-consuming and costly. Moreover, at this time incorporation did not automatically mean that the stockholders were entitled to limited liability status. This was another privilege that had to be obtained separately.

The complexities of incorporation prior to 1844 meant that the most prevalent form of business entity was that of the joint-stock partnership. The increase in business activity and scale of operations created a demand for capital that was beyond the means of the individual entrepreneur. The widespread use of the partnership as a means of combining capital was seen as an answer to this problem. Edey and Panitpakdi (1956) report that in the 1840s there was great concern regarding the large, unregistered, and unregulated joint-stock partnerships. Fraud appears to have been rife. They quote from the British Parliamentary Papers of 1844 as follows: 'Periodic accounts, if honestly made and fairly audited, cannot fail to excite attention to the real state of a concern, and by means of improved remedies, parties to mismanagement may be made more amenable for acts of fraud and illegality' (Edey and Panitpakdi, 1956: 357). It seems that it was the status of these partnerships which brought about the enactment of the Joint-Stock Companies Act, 1844. This act was responsible for two major innovations. It revolutionized the method of company formation. For the first time, it was possible to obtain corporate personality by merely registering with a government official, namely, the Registrar of Joint-Stock Companies. Though a company registered this way had a separate legal personality, it still did not automatically have the right of limited liability for its stockholders. This act also contained the first statutory requirement for an audit of a company's accounts.

During the nineteenth century, as business corporations increased in size, the number of stockholders also increased, and greater powers were delegated to management. It was this concentration of economic power in the hands of management and the dispersion of ownership which resulted in what Berle and Means (1932: 7) called 'the quasi-public corporation'. This, they contended, 'has destroyed the unity that we commonly call property – has divided ownership into nominal ownership and the power formerly joined to it'. They considered that: 'Where ownership is sufficiently subdivided, the management can thus become a self-perpetuating body even though its share in the ownership is negligible'. This form of control was called 'management control' (p. 82).

Berle and Means (1932: 114) were concerned as to whether the interests of management and the owners would be the same: 'If we are to assume that the desire for personal profit is the prime force motivating [those in] control, we must conclude that the interests of control are different from and often radically opposed to those of ownership; that the owners most emphatically will not be served by a profit-seeking controlling group.' Pannell (1978: 37) also had reservations: 'It is not unreasonable to assume that stewardship responsibility is more likely to be fulfilled between parties who know one another personally than between those who are strangers.'

Another problem which emerged related to the calculation of profits. Permanently invested capital had brought about the need to divide the life of a business into artificial accounting periods. While it had previously been unimportant, Yamey (1962: 38) reported that during the nineteenth century, profit calculation dominated the accounting world, and so '[w]hat had often been incidental, became central'. Periodic profit was significant because the profits figure set an upper limit on the amount of dividends that could be distributed to shareholders and, secondly, because the shareholders did not have close contact with the operations of their business – '[t]he periodic profit figure not unnaturally came to be regarded as an indicator of the profitability of operations, a summary of the results of the interaction of numerous business decisions and economic circumstances of which the shareholders had no detailed knowledge' (Yamey, 1962: 39). In addition to this separation of owners and management, the changes brought about by the Industrial Revolution meant that:

> still more significant has been the great investment of fixed capital characteristic of modern production and made possible by the organization of corporations. The use of fixed capital on a large scale increases incalculably the difficulty of determining the profits earned in any given year. (Hatfield, 1924: 251)

It was the increase in complexity and the greater dependence of the shareholders on the financial statements that, by the start of the twentieth century, resulted in the demand for greater information and publicity. Brief (1987: 144), quoting from *The Journal of Accountancy* of October 1906, considered that this 'has proceeded from a public conscience which is shocked by corporate immorality'. Yamey (1962: 42–3) reported the dependence of shareholders as follows:

> The use of secret reserves in company accounting represented the victory of the needs of company management over the developing accent on meticulous accounting calculation (an accent which is seen,

for example, in the careful appointment of prepaid and accrued
expenses). It also reflected an attitude taken by company management
towards the shareholders; it was deemed axiomatic that, provided they
acted in good faith, the management should decide, within limits,
what to tell the shareholders in accounting statements prepared for
their information.

Yamey (1956: 13) considered that 'it may have been pure chance which in the nineteenth century required the final accounts of companies to serve in several possibly incompatible capacities – as accounts of stewardship (in a narrow sense) rendered to absentee owners, as statements of profitability and financial condition for the information of shareholders as well as of potential investors and creditors, and as statements of divisible profits which were inevitably influenced by considerations of financial and general managerial policy'. The problem of dividing 'profits' is probably as applicable today as it was in the nineteenth century and still underpins much of the work done by modern accountants and auditors: 'Nine-tenths of the problems of the accountant are due to this demand to express results in terms of years. The accountant is wrestling with it. That it has not been solved is apparent to anyone who opens a text on the subject or enters into the intricacies of the income tax' (Littleton, 1933: 11). Throughout most of the twentieth century, there was a close relationship between accounting and taxation. In the USA, '[w]hile the Revenue Act of 1913 provided for the calculation of taxable income on the basis of cash receipts and disbursements, the 1918 Act was the first to recognize the role of accounting procedures in the determination of taxable income' and so 'set the stage for the beginning of a harmonization between tax accounting and financial accounting' (Riahi-Belkaoui, 2000: 7).

THE RECOGNITION OF INCOME AND EXPENDITURE

On the basis of the discussion so far, it would appear that the problem facing the financial accountant is that of how to divide the life of the business into artificial accounting periods. This had arisen from the development of permanently invested capital which required periodic returns to be made to the people who had invested in the business. The financial statements were the means by which management rendered their report to their shareholders. In 1970, Sterling considered that:

Arguments about the 'correct' method of calculating income have
persisted for over a century. When an argument persists for that length

of time, one may suspect that there is no possibility of resolution. In the sense that one is free to define 'income' in any way that he likes, the problem is merely a definitional dispute. (p.3)

'The major concern of accounting during the early 1900s was the development of a theory that could cope with corporate abuses that were occurring at the time, and capital maintenance emerged as a concept' (Schroeder and Clark, 1995: 4):

The distinction between capital and income, which every one recognizes and the economist attempts to state with refined accuracy, is fundamental in accounting. Making effective and effectively maintaining as near as may be the distinction between capital and income of a particular enterprise are the ultimate objectives which determine the activities of accountants and the functions of accounting. (Sanders et al., 1938: 1)

The problem would appear to be that '[a]rguments in favor of measuring income could be extended ad infinitum' (Riahi-Belkaoui, 2000: 386). In an economics setting, one of the most respected definitions of income comes from Hicks:

The purpose of income calculations in practical affairs is to give people an indication of the amount which they can consume without impoverishing themselves. Following out this idea, it would seem that we ought to define a man's income as the maximum value which he can consume during a week, and still expect to be as well off at the end of the week as he was at the beginning. Thus, when a person saves, he plans to be better off in the future; when he lives beyond his income, he plans to be worse off. Remembering that the practical purpose of income is to serve as a guide for prudent conduct, I think it is fairly clear that this is what the central meaning must be. (1946: 172)

Alexander (1962: 127) considered: 'A year's income is, fundamentally, the amount of wealth that a person, real or corporate, can dispose of over the course of the year and remain as well off at the end of the year as at the beginning.' Alexander was concerned with the problem of valuation at two points in time. Sterling (1970: 12) stated that 'the definition or concept of income as being "the difference between wealth at two points in time plus consumption" is agreed upon by almost all writers'. Although much has been made of the differences between the economists' and the accountants' concepts of income, Sterling (1970: 11) suggests that the accountants accept the economists' definition, but 'their method of valuation is the variant' and therefore '[t]he quarrel is semantic'. Therefore, the problem comes from the phrase 'as well off', as there are numerous approaches to the 'measurement' of this.

The accounting tradition could be said to be primarily based on cost and past acts. Examining the development of accounting makes it easy to see why historical costs came to be used in the compilation of the financial statements – these were the figures that were already recorded in the accounting records. But '[o]nly in the last 75 years did the historical cost doctrine crystallize and come to dominate the literature and practices of accounting' (Wells, 1976: 473):

> Historical cost is a natural basis for accounting in a double-entry system primarily concerned with recording transactions under conditions of price stability. For such a purpose and in such conditions, it is relevant and reliable, in that it is both representationally faithful and verifiable. (AAA, 1990: 394)

The trial balance was extracted from the accounting records (which were essentially used for internal control purposes), and thus the historical costs formed the bedrock of the financial statements (after the adjustment of the trial balance for the accruals, prepayments and any other adjustments). Given that a prime purpose of the financial statements was to enable the calculation of 'profit' and thus the determination of a return (in the form of a dividend) that could be made to shareholders (and later the calculation of taxation), it is understandable why this would be done on a prudent basis (that is, recognizing only realized gains but anticipating losses). Edwards (1989: 4) explained the accountant's conservative approach in the late nineteenth century as follows:

> Investment in business, at that time, was an even more speculative activity than it is today; liquidations and bankruptcies were everyday features of business life, creditors were the main users of accounting reports and prices were falling. In these circumstances the development of the concept of conservatism was perfectly natural.

In the preconceptual framework era, four fundamental accounting concepts can be discerned – these were the broad basis assumptions which underlie the periodic financial accounts of business enterprises:

- The going concern concept is the presumption that the enterprise will continue in operational existence for the foreseeable future.
- The accruals concept matches revenue and expenditure and tries to ensure that they are charged to the profit and loss account in the period to which they relate (unless the prudence concept requires the immediate recognition of a loss or a write-down).
- The consistency concept relates to treatment of items in a particular accounting period and from one period to another.
- The prudence concept aims to ensure that revenue and profits are not anticipated, but only recognized on realization, whereas provision should be made for all anticipated future losses.

Historical cost has been criticized – particularly by those 'influenced by the neoclassical theory of the firm, in which historical costs are ignored entirely' (AAA, 1977: 6). For example, the normative deductive school of accounting thought 'drew on neoclassical economic theory and on their observations of economic behaviour to propose that accounting, which had been preoccupied with historical record-keeping, should be reconstructed to reflect current costs or values'. This school generally 'concluded that income measured using a single valuation base would ideally meet the needs of all users' (AAA, 1977: 6) – they were described 'as advocates of a "true income" theory' (the notable exception was Alexander (1962), who advocated different incomes for different purposes where the economy was characterized by changing prices and changing expectations of future earning power). The normative deductivists 'borrowed from economics the terms "income" and "wealth" and sought to make them operational in an accounting context' (AAA, 1977: 6–7):

> Particularly by borrowing from economics, accountants have long attempted to find a correspondence between accounting measurements and economic or physical concepts of real-world phenomena. This search has been necessary in order to give some meaning to accounting theory and accounting practice. (Hendriksen, 1977: 4)

Indeed, '[t]he only basis for accounting numbers having any significance whatsoever is that they are approximations of properties that have significance' (Larson, 1969: 40).

The market-value approach emphasizes that '[i]t is probably obvious to most people that the market value is the appropriate measure of well-being associated with each item in a man's possession' (Alexander, 1962: 137). This approach has been criticized for its lack of objectivity and lack of realization. 'Taxation theorists argue that value increments cannot be considered income because they are not in a form that would permit the payment of taxes. Accountants argue similarly that value increments are not income because they are not in a form that would permit the payment of dividends' (Sterling, 1970: 18).

An alternative method based on the Fisher tradition (Sterling, 1970: 13) is whereby the expectations about the future are the basis of measurement of income. 'In the absence of dividend payments and new contributions by stockholders, income is measured at the end of the period by adding up the discounted values of all net receipts which the managers then expect to earn on the firm's existing net assets and subtracting from this subjective value a similar computation made at the beginning of the period' (Edwards and Bell, 1961: 24–5). 'Since future receipts must be predicted and cannot, by definition, be measured, what one is measuring under this tradition is the owner's and/or manager's expectations or feelings about the future' (Sterling, 1970: 13). As one is measuring management's feeling and expectations about the future, this is very subjective and uncertain.

Once the historical cost basis for the construction of the financial statements was under attack, particularly since the 1920s, numerous alternatives have been proposed. This, however, has intensified the debate about the objective of the financial statements, which will be discussed in the next chapter.

CONCLUSION

This chapter has examined the early developments in accounting in order to try to appreciate their implications for accounting today. The earliest forms of accounting (early records and the development of double-entry bookkeeping) were for internal control purposes, and the setting was more akin to a 'management accounting' context than that of a 'financial accounting' one. The development of permanently invested capital gave rise to the need to split the life of a business enterprise into artificial accounting periods so that a return could be made to stockholders (shareholders). This was also the start of the separation of ownership and management. The Joint-Stock Companies Act, 1844, brought about a formalization of financial reporting for companies incorporated under it – this included the drawing up of a balance sheet and the necessity for an annual audit. These financial accounts were used to assess the stewardship management (the notion of stewardship having moved on from 'honesty and integrity' to assessing performance). Given the recent emphasis on corporate governance, it is suggested that financial statement development should be viewed in this context.

Increasingly, accountants have taken terms from economics in order to try to give meaning to the accounting data. The terms 'income' and, in particular, 'wealth' have been adopted. Consequently, one reason that historical costs have been criticized is that they are viewed as being irrelevant in terms of decision making, this focus having gained considerable popularity since the 1960s. The next chapter goes on to examine this development.

DISCUSSION QUESTIONS

1   Why is it important to understand the historical development of a subject?

2   What do you consider the word 'stewardship' to mean?

3   In terms of corporate governance, what is the role of financial reporting?

4   If there is no one right way to calculate profit/income, does it really matter how this is done as long as people understand the procedures that have been followed? Justify your stance.

5   Why is it more difficult to calculate the 'income' of a going concern business than that of an individual (assume similar time periods)?

REFERENCES

Alexander, S.S. (1962) 'Income measurement in a dynamic economy', revised by D. Solomons, in *Studies in Accounting Theory* (2nd edn), W.T. Baxter and S. Davidson (eds). Homewood, IL: Richard D. Irwin Press. pp. 126–200.

American Accounting Association (AAA) (1957) *Accounting and Reporting Standards for Corporate Financial Statements and Preceding Statements and Supplements.* Evanston, IL: AAA.

American Accounting Association (AAA) (1977) Committee on Concepts and Standards for External Financial Reports, *Statement on Accounting Theory and Theory Acceptance.* Sarasota, FL: AAA.

American Accounting Association (AAA) (1990) *Report of the American Accounting Association Committee on Accounting and Auditing Measurement, 1989–1990,* reproduced in, R. Bloom and P.T. Elgers (1995) *Foundations of Accounting Theory and Policy.* Orlando, FL: Dryden Press.

Berle, A.A. and Means, G.C. (1932) *The Modern Corporation and Private Property* (rev. edn, 1967). New York: Harcourt, Brace & World.

Boyd, E. (1905) 'Ancient systems of accounting', in R. Brown (ed.), *A History of Accounting and Accountants.* Edinburgh: T.C. & E.C. Jack.

Brief, R.P. (1987) 'Corporate financial reporting at the turn of the century', *The Journal of Accountancy*, May: 142, 144, 147–9.

Brown, R. (ed.) (1905) *A History of Accounting and Accountants*. Edinburgh: T.C. & E.C. Jack.

Cadbury Report (1992) Report of the Committee on the Financial Aspects of Corporate Governance. London: Gee and Co.

Chartered Institute of Management Accountants (CIMA) (1999) *Corporate Governance: History, Practice and Future*. London: CIMA.

Collinson, D.J., Grinyer, J.R. and Russell, A. (1993) *Management's Economic Decisions and Financial Reporting*. London: ICAEW.

de Ste. Croix, G. (1956) 'Greek and Roman accounting', in A.C. Littleton and B.S. Yamey (eds), *Studies in the History of Accounting*. London: Sweet & Maxwell.

Dewing, I.P. and Russell, P.O. (2000) 'Cadbury and beyond: perceptions on establishing a permanent body for corporate governance regulation', *The British Accounting Review*, 32: 355–74.

Edey, H.C. and Panitpakdi, P. (1956) 'British company accounting and the law 1844–1900', in A.C. Littleton and B.S. Yamey (eds), *Studies in the History of Accounting*. London: Sweet & Maxwell.

Edwards, E.O. and Bell, P.W. (1961) *The Theory and Measurement of Business Income*. Berkeley, CA: University of California Press.

Edwards, J.R. (1989) *A History of Financial Accounting*. London: Routledge.

Edwards, J.R. and Newell, E. (1991) 'The development of industrial cost and management accounting before 1850' (first published in *Business History*) in R.H. Parker and B.S. Yamey (eds), 1994, *Accounting History: Some British Contributions*. Oxford: Clarendon Press.

Harvey, P.D.A. (1984) 'Manorial accounts' (first published as 'Accounts' in *Manorial Records*), in R.H. Parker and B.S. Yamey (eds), 1994, *Accounting History: Some British Contributions*. Oxford: Clarendon Press.

Hatfield, H.R. (1924) 'An historical defense of bookkeeping', *The Journal of Accountancy*, 37 (4): 241–53.

Hendriksen, E.S. (1977) *Accounting Theory* (3rd edn). Homewood, IL: Richard D. Irwin, Inc.

Hicks, J.R. (1946) *Value and Capital* (2nd edn). Oxford: Oxford University Press.

Johnson, H.T. (1981) 'Toward a new understanding of nineteenth-century cost accounting', *The Accounting Review*, 56: 510–18.

Johnson, H.T. and Kaplan, R.S. (1987) *Relevance Lost: The Rise and Fall of Management Accounting*. Boston, MA: Harvard Business School Press.

Kaplan, R.S. (1984) 'The evolution of management accounting', *The Accounting Review*, 59: 390–418.

Larson, K. (1969) 'Implications of measurement theory on accounting concept formulation', *The Accounting Review*, January: 38–47.

Littleton, A.C. (1933) *Accounting Evolution to 1900*. New York: American Institute Publishing Co.

Macve, R.H. (1985) 'Some glosses on "Greek and Roman accounting"' (first published in *History of Political Thought*), in R.H. Parker and B.S. Yamey (eds), 1994, *Accounting History: Some British Contributions*. Oxford: Clarendon Press.

Mattessich, R. (1995) *Critique of Accounting: Examination of the Foundations and Normative Structure of an Applied Discipline*. Westport, CT: Quorum Books.

Mickwitz, G. (1937) 'Economic rationalism and Graeco-Roman agriculture', *English Historical Review*, 52: 577–89.

Noke, C. (1981) 'Accounting for bailiffship in thirteenth century England', *Accounting and Business Research*, 42: 137–51.

Pannell, R.L. (1978) 'An inquiry into the meaning of stewardship in financial accounting', PhD thesis, New York University, Graduate School of Business Administration, reproduced 1988 by University Microfilms International.

Popper, K.R. (1966) *The Open Society and Its Enemies, Volume II, The High Tide of Prophecy: Hegel, Marx, and the Aftermath* (5th edn). London: Routledge & Kegan Paul.

Rathbone, D. (1991), 'Accounting on a large estate in Roman Egypt' (first published in *Economic Rationalism and Rural Society in Third-Century A.D. Egypt: The Heroninos Archive and Appianus Estate*), in R.H. Parker and B.S. Yamey (eds), 1994, *Accounting History: Some British Contributions*. Oxford: Clarendon Press.

Riahi-Belkaoui, A. (2000) *Accounting Theory* (4th edn). London: Business Press Thomson Learning.

Rosenfield, P. (1974) 'Stewardship', in J.J. Cramer, Jr and G.H. Sorter (eds), *Objectives of Financial Statements, Vol. 2 Selected Papers*. New York: AICPA.

Sanders, T.H., Hatfield, H.R. and Moore, U. (1938) *A Statement of Accounting Principles*. USA: American Institute of Accountants.

Schroeder, R.G. and Clark, M. (1995) *Accounting Theory: Text and Readings* (5th edn). New York: Wiley.

Smith, A. (1776) *An Inquiry into the Nature and Causes of the Wealth of Nations, Volume 2* (1976 reprint), R.H. Campbell, A.S. Skinner and W.B. Todd (eds). Oxford: Clarendon Press.

Solomons, D. (1968) 'The historical development of costing', in D. Solomons (ed.), *Studies in Cost Analysis* (2nd edn). London: Sweet & Maxwell.

Sombart, W. (1902) *Der moderne Kapitalismus*. Leipzig: Dunker and Humblot.

Statement of Standard Accounting Practice 2 (SSAP2)

Sterling, R.R. (1970) *Theory of the Measurement of Enterprise Income*. Houston, TX: Scholars Book Co.

Stone, E. (1962) 'Profit-and-loss accountancy at Norwich Cathedral Priory', *Transactions of the Royal Historical Society*, 5th series, 12: 25–48.

Tinker, T. (1985) *Paper Prophets: A Social Critique of Accounting*. London: Holt, Rinehart and Winston.

Tricker, R.I. (1984) *Corporate Governance: Practices, Procedures and Powers in British Companies and Their Boards of Directors*. Aldershot: Gower.

Wells, M.C. (1976) 'A revolution in accounting thought', *The Accounting Review*, 51: 471–82.

Whittington, G. (1993) 'Corporate governance and the regulation of financial reporting', *Accounting and Business Research*, 23 (91A): 311–19.

Winjum, J.O. (1971) 'Accounting and the rise of capitalism: an accountant's view', *Journal of Accounting Research*, 9: 333–50.

Yamey, B.S. (1956) 'Introduction', in A.C. Littleton and B.S. Yamey (eds), *Studies in the History of Accounting*. London: Sweet & Maxwell Ltd.

Yamey, B.S. (1962) 'Some topics in the history of financial accounting in England 1500–1900', in T.W. Baxter and S. Davidson (eds), *Studies in Accounting Theory* (2nd edn). London: Sweet & Maxwell Ltd.

Yamey, B.S. (1964) 'Accounting and the rise of capitalism: further notes on a theme by Sombart', *Journal of Accounting Research*, 2: 117–36.

4 Financial Reporting: Frameworks Without Foundations?

Those are my principles. If you don't like them, I have others.

– Groucho Marx

The use of the financial statements for stewardship purposes may have been central to financial reporting in the first half of the twentieth century, but from the 1960s onwards the focus moved to user needs and the provision of information to enable users take economic decisions. This change of emphasis was reflected in the various attempts by the accounting standard-setters to produce a conceptual framework for financial reporting. A generally accepted conceptual framework has been one of the most elusive goals in financial reporting.

This chapter considers the impact of accounting regulation on the development of financial reporting (see Zeff [1972] for a detailed description of developments up to 1971 in the USA and the UK). Standard setters have been criticized for being reactive in the setting of standards rather than adhering to a consistent theoretical framework as a basis of choice. In this chapter, the struggles of the standard-setters to develop a conceptual framework for financial reporting will be examined. In view of the state of development of 'accounting theory' and the recognition of the politicization of the standard-setting process, the controversies regarding the attempts at producing a conceptual framework should come as no surprise. The problems encountered in defining the 'objective of the financial statements' will be studied. As was appreciated in Chapter 2, the specification of an objective is a key starting point of any project. If there is disagreement about the objective, it is likely that different people will be debating different things. It would be logical that fundamental to the construction of a conceptual framework for financial reporting is the clear specification of the objective of the financial statements. Until the objective has been clearly articulated, the development of any conceptual underpinnings must be problematic.

ACCOUNTING REGULATION

Accounting regulation has been defined as 'the imposition of constraints upon the preparation, content and form of external reports by bodies other than the preparers of the reports, or the organizations and the individuals for which reports are prepared' (Taylor and Turley, 1986: 1). In the nineteenth century, statutory requirements were fairly general about what needed to be disclosed in terms of financial reporting; 'the prevailing attitude was for *laissez-faire* and this implied that financial affairs were a private matter' (Taylor and Turley, 1986: 19). The accountancy profession (which only started to develop in the middle of the nineteenth century) did influence the development of financial reporting, but prior to the development of accounting regulation, '[t]he diffusion of stock ownership gave management complete control over the format and content of accounting disclosures' (Riahi-Belkaoui, 2000: 6). This was obviously not a satisfactory situation – especially if management were judged on its 'stewardship' on the basis of these figures. Therefore, '[c]ritics of accounting theory during the 1920s suggested that accountants abdicated the stewardship role, placed too much emphasis on the needs of management, and permitted too much flexibility in financial reporting' (Schroeder and Clark, 1995: 5). In the USA, in the wake of the stock market crash of 1929 and the Great Depression, efforts were made to examine the problems of the investors, the stock market and the accountants in relation to financial reporting. The Securities and Exchange Commission (SEC) was established by the US Congress in 1934. As part of its remit, the SEC could prescribe the format and content of the balance sheet and the earnings statement. Unless the accounting profession established a standards-setting body, the SEC threatened to develop accounting principles (Riahi-Belkaoui, 2000: 7–8). The AICPA's Committee on Accounting Procedures (CAP) commenced issuing *Accounting Research Bulletins* in 1938. In 1959, the CAP was superseded by the establishment of 'the Accounting Principles Board and the Accounting Research Division with the mission to advance the written expression of what constitutes generally accepted accounting principles' (Riahi-Belkaoui, 2000: 9). Following the recommendations of the Wheat Report (1972), the Financial Accounting Standards Board (FASB) replaced the Accounting Principles Board in 1973.

In the UK, the Cohen Committee was established in 1941 to consider the reform of the Companies Acts. 'The ICAEW [Institute of Chartered Accountants in England and Wales] formed the view that the committee was likely to recommend a significant increase in legal control over financial reporting unless the accountancy profession acted to make improvements' (Taylor and Turley, 1986: 21). This would almost seem to be a repeat of the US situation in the previous decade. In 1942, the ICAEW issued the first of its *Recommendations on Accounting Principles*. Altogether, 29 'recommendations' were issued until 1969 (Zeff, 1972: 10–23), but they were not mandatory. As a result of the flexibility of accounting practice afforded by these 'recommendations' and a number of financial scandals in the 1960s, '[a]ction to increase the standardization of accounting was needed, both to deal with the real problem of too much flexibility in the choice of accounting policies and also to divert criticism that the accounting profession was complacent about the apparent deficiencies in accounting practice' (Taylor and Turley, 1986: 49).

In 1970, the Accounting Standards Steering Committee (ASSC) met for the first time. Initially, the ASSC was a committee of the ICAEW, but it rapidly incorporated members from other accountancy bodies. In 1976, it was reconstituted as the Accounting Standards Committee (ASC) – a joint committee of the Consultative Committee of Accountancy Bodies (CCAB).

> The Accounting Standards Committee (ASC), whose membership consisted entirely of accountants, was criticised as being self-serving. . . . The 1989 Companies Act transferred control of the standard-setting and enforcement process from the professional accountancy bodies to the Financial Reporting Council (FRC), a legally mandated body set up in January 1990. Subsidiary bodies include the Accounting Standards Board (ASB), which deals with standard-setting, the Urgent Issues Task Force (UITF), which deals promptly with emerging issues, and the Financial Reporting Review Panel (FRRP), which has the power to take court proceedings against companies that are seen to depart from generally accepted accounting principles, with a view to enforcing compliance. (Beattie et al., 1999: 70)

Since the 1970s, standard setters all around the world have been attempting to ensure that they have a conceptual basis to underpin the promulgation of their standards. This has resulted in a quest to develop a 'conceptual framework'.

CONCEPTUAL FRAMEWORK DEVELOPMENTS

A conceptual framework could be seen as an attempt to operationalize the accounting theory – this could be done by either individuals or standard-setters. Those who have thought about accounting have probably formed some sort of conceptual framework in their own mind. 'Those who comment on proposed accounting standards do so in terms of their personal conceptual frameworks, and the members of the Financial Accounting Standards Board vote in accordance with their personal conceptual frameworks' (Anthony, 1983: 2). Yet, while there was support for the development of such a framework, no one framework has gained overall acceptance. Worldwide political, legal and cultural differences may all have contributed to this (Davidson et al., 1996). Hines (1991: 313–14) considered that 'the meaning and significance of CF [conceptual framework] projects is not so much functional and technical, but rather social and cultural'. The potentially conflicting driving forces behind the conceptual framework projects will be examined later in this chapter.

Chambers (1996: 124) stated that Storey (1964) first used the term 'conceptual framework' in an accounting context:

> Principles distilled from practice are capable of leading so far and no further. A point is reached at which principles of this type become meaningless unless and until a conceptual framework is developed which gives meaning to the procedures followed, or points out that the procedures followed do not make sense and should be replaced by others which do . . . a conceptual framework . . . [provides] at once both the reasoning underlying procedures and a standard by which procedures are judged. (Storey, 1964: 60–1)

A 'conceptual framework' was succinctly defined by Davies et al. (1999: 53) as follows:

> In general terms, a conceptual framework is a statement of generally accepted theoretical principles which form the frame of reference for a particular field of enquiry. In terms of financial reporting, these theoretical principles provide the basis for both the development of new reporting practices and the evaluation of existing ones.

The FASB (1976a: 2) described a conceptual framework as 'a coherent system of interrelated objectives and fundamentals that can lead to consistent standards and that prescribes the nature, function and limits of financial accounting and financial statements'. The importance of such a framework is such that 'one cannot make a rational choice of accounting procedures without some framework of principle' (Macve, 1981: 9). In fact, it is surprising that accountants have managed for so long without such a framework:

> Every science, methodology, or other body of knowledge is oriented to some conceptual structure – a pattern of ideas brought together to

TABLE 4.1   An outline of conceptual framework developments

Paton (1922) *Accounting Theory.*
Sprague (1923) *Philosophy of Accounts.*
Canning (1929) *The Economics of Accountancy.*
AAA (1936) *A Tentative Statement of Accounting Principles Affecting Corporate Reports.*
Sanders, Hatfield and Moore (1938) *A Statement of Accounting Principles.*
Paton and Littleton (1940) *An Introduction to Corporate Accounting Standards.*
Moonitz (1961) *The Basic Postulates of Accounting.*
Sprouse and Moonitz (1962) *A Tentative Set of Broad Accounting Principles for Business Enterprises.*
Grady (1965) *Inventory of Generally Accepted Accounting Principles for Business Enterprises.*
AAA (1966) *A Statement of Basic Accounting Theory.*
APB (1970) APB Statement No. 4: *Basic Concepts and Principles Underlying Financial Statements of Business Enterprises.*
Trueblood Report (1973) *Objectives of Financial Statements.*
FASB (1974–85) The FASB conceptual framework project.
ASSC (1975) *The Corporate Report.*
Stamp Report (1980) *Corporate Reporting: Its Future Evolution.*
AARF (1987–95) The Australian conceptual framework project.
CICA (1988–90) The Canadian conceptual framework project.
IASC (1988–89) The International Accounting Standards Committee's conceptual framework.
ASB (1991–99) The development of the UK conceptual framework.

> form a consistent whole or a frame of reference to which is related the
> operational content of that field. Without some integrating structure,
> procedures are but senseless rituals without reason or substance;
> progress is but a fortunate combination of circumstances; research is
> but fumbling in the dark; and the dissemination of knowledge is a
> cumbersome process, if indeed there is any 'knowledge' to convey.
> (Vatter, 1947: 1)

The first attempts at constructing conceptual frameworks tended to be by individuals. By the 1970s and 1980s, the standard-setters were the prominent producers of them. There have been a number of reviews of these developments (Gore, 1991, 1992; Mathews and Perera, 1996; Riahi-Belkaoui, 2000; Zeff, 1999). Gore (1994) examined the practical usefulness of conceptual frameworks, while Power (1993) considered the idea of a conceptual framework (Table 4.1).

Paton in 1922 (Zeff, 1999: 89) and Sprague in 1923 (Anthony, 1983: 17) may be considered to have made the earliest attempts at producing 'unofficial' conceptual frameworks. Canning (1929) 'was the first to develop and present a conceptual framework for asset valuation and measurement founded explicitly on future expectations' (Zeff, 1999: 90). After the establishment of the SEC and its concern about accounting principles, the first institutional attempt at a conceptual framework was the 'tentative statement' produced by the American Accounting Association in 1936. In 1938, Sanders et al.

produced a monograph 'which was, in large measure, a defence of accepted practice' (Zeff, 1999: 91). Zeff considered the Paton and Littleton (1940) framework to be the most influential of the early conceptual framework attempts: 'it was an elegant explication and rationalization of the historical cost accounting model that was already widely accepted in the U.S.' (Zeff, 1999: 90).

It was not until the 1960s that major consideration was given to further conceptual framework projects. Zeff (1972: 174–5) reports that there was almost no reaction to Moonitz's study in 1961: 'It was not clear from Moonitz's study whether he favored historical cost accounting or a version of current value accounting: thus many readers found his study to be too abstract and general to engage their interest and critical thought' (Zeff, 1999: 93). However, the following year, there was an adverse reaction to the Sprouse and Moonitz (1962) document (including nine of the twelve members of the project's advisory committee). This report had recommended that 'the use of current values should be expanded' (Zeff, 1999: 94). In 1965, Grady's 'Inventory' attempted to pull together the objectives, concepts and principles contained in the then current professional pronouncements. The following year saw the publication of *A Statement of Basic Accounting Theory* (ASOBAT) by the academic American Accounting Association (AAA). It focused on the needs of the users of the financial statements: 'The committee defines accounting as the process of identifying, measuring, and communicating economic information to permit informed judgments and decisions by the users of the information' (AAA, 1966: 1). External users were identified as 'present and potential investors, creditors, employees, stock exchanges, governmental units, customers, and others' (p. 20):

> *Many persons use accounting information as an aid to some kind of prediction. We accordingly point out some of the more important efforts at prediction for which accounting information is considered particularly relevant. It is important to emphasize that accountants (with good justification) have avoided the role of forecasters in connection with reports to external users. The committee suggests that accounting information for external users should reflect their needs by reporting measurements and formulations thought to be relevant in the making of forecasts without implying that the information supplied is wholly adequate for such prediction . . .*
>
> *Almost all external users of financial information reported by a profit-oriented firm are involved in efforts to predict the earnings of the firm for some future period. Such predictions are most crucial in the case of present and prospective equity investors and their representatives – considered by many to be the most important of user*

groups. *Future earnings are the chief determinant of future dividends and future market prices of shares (given some predetermined price-earnings ratio), which, when taken together, are generally considered to provide the primary basis for establishing a subjective value for shares in the mind of the user. The past earnings of the firm are considered to be the most important single item of information relevant to the prediction of future earnings. It follows from this that past earnings should be measured and disclosed in such a manner as to give a user as much aid as practicable in efforts to make this prediction with the minimum of uncertainty [footnote omitted]. (AAA, 1966: 23–4)*

With such a change in emphasis, a change in the characteristics of accounting data was also required. ASOBAT recommended four basic standards for accounting data:

Relevance *is the primary standard and requires that the information must bear upon or be usefully associated with actions it is designed to facilitate or results desired to be produced. Known or assumed informational needs of potential users are of paramount importance in applying this standard.*

Verifiability *requires that essentially similar measures or conclusions would be reached if two or more qualified persons examined the same data. It is important because accounting information is commonly used by persons who have limited access to the data. The less the proximity to the data, the greater the desirable degree of verifiability becomes. Verifiability is also important because users of accounting information sometimes have opposing interests.*

Freedom from bias *means that facts have been impartially determined and reported. It also means that techniques used in developing data should be free of in-built bias. Bias information may be quite useful and tolerable internally but it is rarely acceptable for external reporting.*

Quantifiability *relates to the assignment of numbers to the information being reported. Money is the most common but not the only quantitative measure used by accountants. When accountants present non-quantitative information in compliance with the other standards they*

should not imply its measurability. Conversely, when quantitative
information is reported without a caveat the accountant must assume
responsibility for its measurement. (AAA, 1966: 7)

The Accounting Principles Board's Statement No. 4 (1970) also endorsed the decision-usefulness view of the financial statements: 'The basic purpose of financial accounting and financial statements is to provide quantitative financial information about a business enterprise that is useful to statement users, particularly owners and creditors, in making economic decisions' (APB, 1970: 32). The APB considered that because financial information was used by a variety of groups and for diverse purposes, '[t]he needs and expectations of users determine the type of information required' (1970: 18). Sterling's (1972: 198) opinion was as follows: 'Almost all the literature on accounting states that accounting reports must be "useful" or that accounting is a "utilitarian art".' The Trueblood Report (AICPA, 1973: 13) supported the decision-usefulness approach:

> *Accounting is not an end in itself. As an information system, the*
> *justification of accounting can be found only in how well accounting*
> *information serves those who use it. Thus, the Study Group agrees with*
> *the conclusion drawn by many others that the basic objective of*
> *financial statements is to provide information useful for making*
> *economic decisions.*

The Trueblood Report also endorsed the focus on future cash flows: 'An objective of financial statements is to provide information useful to investors and creditors for predicting, comparing, and evaluating potential cash flows to them in terms of amount, timing and related uncertainty' (p. 20). Peasnell (1982: 245) reported that 'the public hearing arranged by the FASB showed that there was considerable opposition from industry to the Report's emphasis on user needs and to some of the forms of disclosure mentioned in the Report'.

In 1974, the FASB published its consideration of the Trueblood Report; in 1976, it published the *Tentative Conclusions on Objectives of Financial Statements for Business Enterprises* (1976a) – user needs and decision usefulness were becoming ingrained in the fabric of financial reporting. In 1978, the FASB specified the objective: 'Financial reporting should provide information that is useful to present and potential investors and creditors and other users in making rational investment, credit and similar decisions' (FASB, 1978: para. 34). Dopuch and Sunder (1980: 17) considered than an 'objective' is unclear when applied to an activity. They point out that people have goals and objectives, and activities do not. However, standard setters have continued to use the phrase 'objective of the financial statements'.

The FASB's qualitative characteristics concept statement (1980a) was built on 'understandability', 'relevance' (comprising 'predictive value', 'feedback value' and 'timeliness') and 'reliability' (comprising 'verifiability', 'representational faithfulness' and 'neutrality') of accounting data for decision making. 'Comparability' and 'cost/benefit' were also recognized. Joyce et al. (1982: 670) considered the usefulness of the FASB's qualitative characteristics and found: 'Nine of the 11 qualitative characteristics clearly fail the tests of operationality.' The only two that met the tests were verifiability and cost. They considered that, '[n]ot only is there considerable disagreement among experienced policy makers on what the qualitative characteristics mean in the context of particular accounting policy issues, there is considerable disagreement on their relative importance' (p. 670).

In 1976, the FASB had issued a discussion memorandum relating to *Elements of Financial Statements and Their Measurement* (1976b), which contained a discussion of defining earnings using the 'asset and liability view' as well as the more conventional 'revenue and expense view'. The FASB eventually (1980b) came to favour the 'asset and liability view', whereby 'the definition of earnings depends on the definitions of assets and liabilities, so that a balance sheet test must be invoked to validate the existence of earnings, revenues and expenses' (Zeff, 1999: 104). This was to be the most controversial part of the FASB's conceptual framework project because it was seen as a means of implementing current value accounting (Storey and Storey, 1998). With SFAC 3 (FASB, 1980b), '[t]he asset/liability view focuses on what the entity owns and owes, and income occurs if there are more net assets at the end of a time period than at the beginning, after adjusting for owners' contributions and distributions' (Miller, 1990: 26). 'Assets are probable future economic benefits obtained or controlled by a particular entity as a result of past transactions or events' (FASB, 1980b: para. 19) and '[l]iabilities are probable future sacrifices of economic benefits arising from present obligations of a particular entity to transfer assets or provide services to other entities in the future as a result of past transactions or events' (para. 28). The other elements of the financial statements were defined in terms of being an asset or a liability, and thus the 'FASB set the stage for the ending of matching as justification for many long-standing practices, including systematic depreciation and other allocations' (Miller, 1990: 27). SFAC 3 advocated the recognition of 'comprehensive income'. This was defined as follows: 'the change in equity (net assets) of an entity during a given period that results from transactions and other events and circumstances from nonowner sources. Comprehensive income includes all changes in equity during a period except those that result from investment by owners and distributions to owners'

(FASB, 1980b: xi). The driving force appeared to be user needs and enabling them to predict future cash flows, because

> it is very important from a forecasting point of view that the income you forecast is comprehensive, otherwise you are going to lose certain aspects of the valuation [of the firm]. . . . The focus is on indicating the creation of wealth to the shareholders, as opposed to the distribution of wealth, and in terms of valuation that future wealth creation, which is going to be booked in the accounts in the future, has to be on a comprehensive income basis. (Penman, 1999: 98)

The asset/liability approach suggests the use of 'current values'; however, '[b]ecause of the emotions that arose later in the project, the FASB staff adopted the term "current exchange price" instead of "current value" to avoid the subjectivity connoted by the word "value". It also allowed the Board to avoid the controversial choice between entry and exit values' (Miller, 1990: 26). Miller (1990: 23) considered that 'the first three concepts statements implied such radical changes that a counterreformation was created to turn FASB back onto a less disruptive track', and 'it became apparent that many preparers and [some] Board members had grown uncomfortable with the drift toward the ultimate reform of using current value as the measurement attribute for the primary financial statements' (Miller, 1990: 28). In SFAC 5 (FASB, 1984: para. 90), it was agreed that '[i]nformation based on current prices should be recognized if it is sufficiently relevant and reliable to justify the costs involved and more relevant than alternative information'. Miller considered (1990: 28) that '[b]y creating this higher threshold for acceptability, the FASB made it more difficult to accomplish the change to current value that the reformation had been heading toward'.

'Investors' desires to predict cash flows from the firm have led many decision-usefulness theorists to a cash flow orientation' (AAA, 1977: 13):

> Cash returns to investors depend upon the firm's capacity to pay, which, in turn, depends upon its present cash balance and its cash flow potentials. Present cash and positive cash flow potentials are assets; negative cash flow potentials are liabilities. When reliable evidence of future cash flows is available it should be used in the measurement of an asset or a liability. (AAA, 1977: 13–14)

In view of the importance of present values in decision making, in 1990 the FASB issued *Present Value-Based Measurements in Accounting* (FASB, 1990) though it was not until ten years later that it was included in a concepts statement (FASB, 2000).

In 1996, the FASB issued an exposure draft advocating that 'net income and comprehensive income be accorded equal prominence in either one or two statements of financial performance' (Zeff, 1999: 116).

> Strong resistance from preparers forced the board to accept a compromise, permitting a third option – to display comprehensive income in the statement of changes in equity [FASB, 1997]. Thus, the board enabled preparers to exclude such items as unrealised gains and losses from a statement of financial performance. (Zeff, 1999: 116)

The FASB has put a lot of effort into developing its conceptual framework; however, there has been sustained criticism throughout its existence. Indeed, 'there is a broad perception that they have failed' (Burton and Sack, 1990: 117). For example, Dopuch and Sunder (1980: 4) considered that the FASB's framework had used circular reasoning: 'How can a conceptual framework guide choices from among alternative principles and rules if elements of the framework are defined in these very same terms?' In 1990, Burton and Sack wrote:

> The accounting standard setting process is in deep trouble, possibly in such deep trouble that our present structure is irretrievably lost to us. After seventeen years, the Financial Accounting Standards Board lies in dead water beset by critics on all sides. Its own parent body, the Financial Accounting Foundation, has evidenced its lack of confidence by imposing a super majority voting rule on the Board, over the strong and unanimous protest of the Board members. And, the Foundation has established an oversight group to oversee, in some as yet undefined way, the technical activities of the Board. (Burton and Sack, 1990: 117)

Burton and Sack (1990: 117) suggested that the FASB had 'lost sight of the fundamental nature of its job'. They continued: 'To the founders of the FASB, the change in name from the Accounting *Principles* Board to the Financial Accounting *Standards* Board was significant: the Board was not expected to search for great fundamental truths in accounting but instead was to lead the financial community in establishing the standards which all would find useful in reporting financial results.' Archer's view was that 'the conceptual framework was not supposed to be a theory of financial accounting (for one hardly constructs a theory by public consultation); rather, some underlying theory of financial accounting was presupposed, in terms of which the methods used in the CF [conceptual framework] project could be seen to be appropriate' (1993: 73). However, given the state of accounting theory, this presupposition was presumably misplaced.

> Criticisms of Board standards and initiatives take many forms, but particularly those of preparers assert that proposals are too costly, or at least more costly than the perceived benefits would justify. Preparers also are critical of many proposals because they would increase the volatility in reported earnings. This criticism really falls in the category of 'we don't like the answer' and often does not address at all whether the proposal is sound in concept, whether it seems to flow from the conceptual framework. (Wyatt, 1990: 84)

A study by Mezias and Chung (1989) 'suggests that preparers could be more effective in their participation [in the consultation process] if their letters of comment emphasized the theoretical support for their positions rather than what might be perceived as issues of self-interest' (Wyatt, 1990: 84). This again brings us back to the state of accounting theory, and so it may be an unrealistic expectation.

> It can be argued that the FASB's decision-orientated approach contains the seeds of destruction of the whole process unless handled with great care. In accordance with the FASB's views, most generally accepted decision models involve considering the timing, amounts and uncertainty of potential net cash inflows (see Brealey and Myers, 1988). This supports arguments urging that enterprises should provide forecasts of cash flows and their risks, although the problems which the publication of such forecasts might bring in their wake would still need to be solved. Accounting reports that do not deviate radically from those conventionally issued are not obvious instruments for publishing such forecasts or the elements of such forecasts, even in an imprecise way. (Bromwich, 1992: 294)

Despite the reservations expressed regarding the FASB's work, its 'conceptual framework has been imitated in other countries and by the International Accounting Standards Committee (IASC)' (Zeff, 1999: 123). The IASC was formed in 1973 and is based in London, but has a membership of accountancy bodies from all over the world (in 2001, it was renamed the International Accounting Standards Board [IASB]). In 1989, the IASC published its Framework for the *Preparation and Presentation of Financial Statements*. It stated: 'The objective of financial statements is to provide information about the financial position, performance and changes in financial position of an enterprise that is useful to a wide range of users in making economic decisions' (IASC, 1989: para. 12). The framework acknowledged that 'financial statements do not provide all the information that users may need to make economic decisions since they largely portray the financial effects of past events and do not necessarily provide non-financial information' (para. 13). It continued:

> *Financial statements also show the results of the stewardship of management, or the accountability of management for the resources entrusted to it. Those users who wish to assess the stewardship or accountability of management do so in order that they make economic decisions; these decisions may include, for example, whether to hold or sell their investment in the enterprise or whether to reappoint or replace the management. (IASC, 1989: para. 14)*

The IASC's framework listed the accruals basis (para. 22) and going concern (para. 23) as its underlying assumptions. It specified four principal qualitative characteristics ('that make the information provided in financial statements useful to users' [para. 24]), namely, understandability, relevance, reliability and comparability. 'An essential quality of the information provided in financial statements is that it is readily understandable by users' (para. 25). 'To be useful, information must be relevant to the decision-making needs of users. Information has the quality of relevance when it influences the economic decisions of users by helping them evaluate past, present or future events or confirming, or correcting their past evaluations' (para. 26). 'Information has the quality of reliability when it is free from material error and bias and can be depended upon by users to represent faithfully that which it either purports to represent or could reasonably be expected to represent' (para. 31). Reliability required faithful representation, substance over form, neutrality, prudence and completeness (paras. 33–8). 'Users must be able to compare the financial statements of an enterprise through time in order to identify trends in its financial position and performance. Users must be able to compare the financial statements of different enterprises in order to evaluate their relative financial position, performance and changes in financial position' (para. 39). The IASC framework recognized the constraints on relevant and reliable information for decision making, namely, the timeliness of the data, the balance between costs and benefits, and a trade-off between the qualitative characteristics.

The essence of the IASC framework was very similar to that of the FASB, and it did not create much of a reaction when it was published, but this was not the case when the UK's Accounting Standards Board (ASB) issued its *Statement of Principles* only two years later.

THE UK STRUGGLE WITH THE 'OBJECTIVE' OF THE FINANCIAL STATEMENTS

In the UK, *The Corporate Report* was published in 1975 by the Accounting Standards Steering Committee (ASSC) – it adopted the decision-usefulness approach and required greater disclosure. It was controversial but was overshadowed by the accounting for changing prices debate (Peasnell, 1982: 246). It was a further 15 years, and following the establishment of the ASB in 1990, before the idea of a conceptual framework was back on the agenda. The Dearing Report (1988) had considered that the new ASB should:

- limit the abuses taking place in financial reporting
- harmonize with international accounting standards
- adopt a framework that was in line with those of other standard setters.

Consequently, the development of a *Statement of Principles* was given a high priority by the ASB, and Tweedie and Whittington (respectively, chairman and member of the ASB) (1990: 87), expressing their personal views, stated: 'Our approach to the selection of systematic principles is to accept the broad consensus on the purpose of financial reports that exists between the Trueblood Report (AICPA, 1973) in the USA and the Corporate Report (ASSC, 1975) in the UK, in the 1970s, and more recently, the conceptual framework projects of the Financial Accounting Standards Board (FASB) in the USA and of the International Accounting Standards Committee (IASC, 1989), the Solomons Report (Solomons, 1989), and the ICAS publication, *Making Corporate Reports Valuable* (McMonnies, 1988), in the UK.' They acknowledged there were differences in detail, but considered that all the above broadly agreed (p. 87) that:

1   Financial reports are intended to serve users.
2   The balance sheet and the profit and loss account, supplemented by a funds statement or a cash flow statement, are the 'fundamental financial statements'.

3   'Users are concerned with economic evaluation and decision-making. This implies that measurement should strive to reflect actual economic opportunities and steer us towards current valuation and the estimation of future prospects, rather than historical cost valuation and concentration on past transactions.'

The ASB's original drafts of the first two chapters of the *Statement of Principles* (ASB, 1991) were very similar to the IASC's 1989 framework. In fact, 'the Board proposes to use wherever possible the IASC text . . . [thus] the Board expresses its commitment to the IASC's work in promoting harmonisation in international accounting' (para. iv). The objective paragraph stated: 'The objective of financial statements is to provide information about the financial position, performance and financial adaptability of an enterprise that is useful to a wide range of users in making economic decisions' (para. 12). The ASB did acknowledge stewardship, but this was not included in the definition of the objective of the financial statements. Paragraph 14 of the original exposure draft stated:

> *Financial statements also show the results of the stewardship of management, that is, the accountability of management for the resources entrusted to it. Those users who wish to assess the stewardship of management do so in order that they may make economic decisions; these decisions may include, for example, whether to hold or sell their investment in the enterprise or whether to re-appoint or replace management.*

The ASB's list of users of the financial statements included 'present and potential investors, employees, lenders, suppliers and other trade creditors, customers, governments and their agencies and the public' (1991: para. 9). It continued: 'While all the information needs of these users cannot be met by financial statements, there are needs that are common to all users' (para. 10).

The emphasis on decision making was criticized by Page (1991: 31): 'In my opinion the ASB should acknowledge that the decision-usefulness concept gives meagre guidance and should concentrate on setting standards which enhance the stewardship or control function of accounting.' He continued:

> *It is the existence of financial reporting which limits the freedom of directors and companies to behave opportunistically. The knowledge that actions and their effects will be reported causes management to act differently than would otherwise be the case. Stewardship*

reporting is different in kind from mere provision of information for
decisions. (Page, 1991: 31)

Whittington (1991: 33) responded that the ASB was not neglecting the stewardship function and considered that:

> *The idea that stewardship is inconsistent with economic decisions was*
> *destroyed originally by the biblical parable of the talents. . . . Those*
> *users who wish to assess the stewardship of management do so in*
> *order that they make economic decisions [such as whether to hold or*
> *sell their investment in the enterprise or whether to re-appoint or*
> *replace the management]. . . . It would be a singularly ineffective form*
> *of stewardship which did not lead to a decision of this type.*

Possibly as a result of these and other criticisms (Page, 1992a and 1992b), in the revised *Statement of Principles* exposure draft (ASB, 1995: 35), stewardship was included in the definition of the objective of the financial statements: 'The objective of financial statements is to provide information about the financial position, performance and financial adaptability of an enterprise that is useful to a wide range of users for assessing the stewardship of management and for making economic decisions.' Stewardship was simply defined as 'the accountability of management for the resources entrusted to it' (para. 1.2). However, stewardship and accountability may not be synonymous:

> *'Stewardship' implies responsibility, but it implies nothing as to the*
> *nature of the responsibilities. . . . 'Accountability' too has pleasant*
> *connotations – at least to accountants – but the label does not*
> *answer the questions: Accountability to whom? Or accountability for*
> *what? (Devine, 1985, Vol. 1: 103)*

ASOBAT (AAA, 1966: 22) had already pointed out the various 'dimensions of stewardship', which 'range from the most elemental level of custodianship to responsibility for acquisition, utilization, and disposition of resources embracing the whole scope of management functions in a business entity'. According to Devine (1985, Vol. 2: 28): 'The concept of stewardship is difficult to define, but one of its characteristics is certainly responsibility for accomplishing objectives.' He went on to imply that '[u]nlike the Biblical story of the talents, modern stewards are likely to have definite commissions with the objectives clearly set forth and the criteria of accomplishment carefully defined'. Myddelton (1996) seemed to imply that simply complying with statutory requirements was sufficient to satisfy stewardship requirements.

A re-revised exposure draft was issued in early 1999 (ASB, 1999a). Despite the criticisms of the earlier exposure draft (Wilkinson-Riddle and Holland, 1997), 'the changes seem to me to be, in the main, changes of presentation rather than of substance' (Lennard, 1999). In December 1999, the ASB forced the closure of the debate with the issue of the final version of its *Statement of Principles for Financial Reporting* (ASB, 1999b: Chapter 1), which stated:

> Put simply, the objective of financial statements is to provide infor-
> mation that is useful to those for whom they are prepared. However,
> the objective needs to be expressed more precisely if it is to be of any
> use in determining the form and content of financial statements.

Chapter 1 continued: 'The objective of financial statements is to provide information about the reporting entity's financial performance and financial position that is useful to a wide range of users for assessing the stewardship of management and for making economic decisions.' Thus, the statement recognized financial 'performance' as opposed to 'performance' per se. It continued: 'Present and potential investors need information about the reporting entity's financial performance and financial position that is useful to them in evaluating the entity's ability to generate cash (including the timing and certainty of its generation) and in assessing the entity's financial adaptability.' With the emphasis on decision making, '[i]n deciding which information to include in financial statements, when to include it and how to present it, the aim is to ensure that financial statements yield information that is useful' (Chapter 3). The term 'financial statements' means 'general purpose financial statements' (para. 1.1).

It should be noted that '[t]he Statement of Principles is not an accounting standard, nor does it have a status that is equivalent to an accounting standard. It therefore does not contain requirements on how financial statements should be prepared or presented' (para. 5).

Although the ASB espoused the importance of decision making, it was very indecisive in specifying the objective of the financial statements. It is also interesting to note that if the objective paragraph could be changed so easily with apparently very little impact on the rest of the *Statement of Principles*, one has to wonder just how important it really was within the overall framework. After all, it should have been the key paragraph from which everything else would logically flow. Thus, in response to criticisms, the ASB had compromised – but had the *Statement of Principles* now been compromised?

INCONSISTENCIES WITH STATUTORY REQUIREMENTS

Decision usefulness and the focus on user needs were fundamental changes in the nature of the objective of financial accounting. It is interesting to note that the Companies Acts 1985 and 1989 appear to say very little about user needs, but instead concentrate on the duties of the directors in relation to the financial statements and the format of those statements.

In Appendix 1 to its *Statement of Principles* (ASB, 1999b), the Accounting Standards Board states that '[t]he Statement was not developed within the constraints imposed by law' and '[a]s a result, there was a risk that inconsistencies could arise between the Statement and the law that would invalidate the Statement as a frame of reference for standard-setting' (para. 1). One reason why the framework was not developed within statutory constraints was so that it could assist in the future development of the law (para. 2), but such an approach 'would not have been appropriate . . . if there had been many significant differences between the Statement and the various legal frameworks involved' (para. 3)!

Inconsistencies that have been identified include:

- 'One implication of the Act [Companies Act 1985] is that proposed dividends are required to be recognised as liabilities, although they would not usually fall within the Statement's definition of a liability' (ASB, 1999b, Appendix 1: para. 6)
- 'The Act states that only profits realised at the balance sheet date can be included in the profit and loss account. . . . The Act defines realised profits, but does so in a way that allows the precise meaning of the term to be capable of development' (para. 7). The next paragraph states: 'Although the Statement and the Act clearly adopt different approaches, the way in which the Act defines a realised profit means that the exact effect of this difference is not clear. The potential inconsistencies . . . – concerning the number and format of the statement or statements of financial performance – make the effect of the difference in approach even less clear' (para. 8)
- 'The Statement envisages that, if the current value basis of measurement is regarded as the most appropriate measurement basis for a particular category of assets, all assets within that category will be recognised at their current value', but 'for some assets the Act requires the use of measurement bases that may differ from those suggested by the Statement' (para. 9).
- The requirements of the Companies Act 1985 'may necessitate a presentation that differs in certain respects from what would be suggested by following the presentation principles set out in the Statement' (para. 11).

The ASB considered that these inconsistencies 'will tend to be temporary and that the law will not be a permanent impediment to the adoption of approaches consistent with the Statement' (para. 15). However, if the *Statement of Principles* (which is supposed to provide a rationale for the development of standards) is inconsistent with statutory requirements, there is a danger that the ASB's own standards may also be inconsistent. Concern has been expressed about FRS 12 (*Provisions, Contingent Liabilities and Contingent Assets*). Trevett and Maugham (2000: 94) considered that some of the requirements of FRS 12 contravene the Fourth Directive and the Companies Act 1985, and reported 'internal European Commission documents that examine the compatibility with the EU accounting regime of IAS 37, *Provisions, Contingent Liabilities and Contingent Assets* (the international standard FRS 12 was based on and which is drafted in substantially identical terms) has referred to inconsistency between the Fourth Directive and IAS 37'.

While the dynamism and complexity of business *may* result in legal requirements becoming out of date, there must be a concern when the conceptual framework which is supposed to underpin the development of financial reporting standards is inconsistent with legal requirements – especially considering that the *Statement of Principles* took eight years to produce.

POTENTIAL FACTORS DRIVING CONCEPTUAL FRAMEWORK DEVELOPMENTS

It should be readily apparent that the lack of interest in 'accounting theory' appears to be in stark contrast with the intensity of work undertaken on the conceptual framework projects, raising the question of why this has been the case.

The financial statements are influenced by the accounting and auditing standards chosen by the regulatory institutions. These institutions are, in their turn, influenced by the preferences expressed by users, preparers, accountants and government during the development of the standards. This can be viewed as the debate between the 'technical' and the 'political' view (Armstrong, 1977; Solomons, 1978, 1983; Zeff, 1978, 2002) of standard-setting. The term 'economic consequences' has been used to describe situations where interested parties (such as management) have sought to influence accounting standard setters, or where accounting policies have been selected on the basis of the impact they would have on financial statement users. Zeff (1978: 56) defined 'economic consequences' as 'the impact of accounting reports on the decision making behaviour of business, government, unions, investors and creditors. It is argued that the resulting behaviour of these individuals and groups could be detrimental to the interests of other affected parties.' Not until the 1970s was it conceded that accounting standard-setting bodies may actually take account of the economic consequences of a proposed standard on interested parties, and that '[t]he economic consequences argument represents a veritable revolution in accounting thought' (Zeff, 1978: 56). Previously, it had been assumed that accounting standard setting was neutral, that is, independent of the views of interested parties. Zeff (1978) classified management's interventions in the standard-setting process as follows:

1   arguments couched in terms of the traditional accounting model, where management is genuinely concerned about unbiased and 'theoretically sound' accounting measures
2   arguments couched in terms of the traditional accounting model, where management is really seeking to advance its self-interest in the economic consequences of the contents of published reports
3   arguments couched in terms of the economic consequences, in which management is self-interested.

Standard-setting bodies may bow to pressure from lobbying groups because they perceive that, otherwise, the power of the lobbyists is sufficient to undermine the authority of the standard-setters. Moreover, individual members of standard-setting bodies may, through their personal business connections, have a sympathy for a particular commercial interest. To observe that a standard-setting body cannot preserve its authority without some degree of responsiveness to 'economic consequences' is not to deny the importance of technical accounting considerations:

> The [FASB] board is thus faced with a dilemma which requires a delicate balancing of accounting and non-accounting variables. Although its decisions should rest – and be seen to rest – chiefly on accounting considerations, it must also study – and be seen to study – the possible adverse economic and social consequences of its proposed actions. (Zeff, 1978: 63)

Therefore, the conceptual framework projects could be seen as a means of countering these political pressures, as well as responding to criticisms: 'Accountants must give serious and careful thought to the theoretical underpinnings of financial reporting' (SEC, 1978: 279). The FASB considered that the function of a conceptual framework was 'to serve the public interest by providing structure and direction to financial accounting and reporting to facilitate the provision of even-handed financial and related information that is useful in assisting capital and other markets to function efficiently in allocating scarce resources in the economy' (FASB, 1980a: 1). Dopuch and Sunder (1980: 17) suggested that 'a body like the FASB needs a conceptual framework to boost its public standing'. They continued:

> *A conceptual framework provides the basis for arguing that: (1) the objective of its activities is to serve the users of the financial state-ments (it is easier to use the public-interest argument for the user group than for any other group), and (2) it selects among accounting alternatives on the basis of broadly accepted objectives and not because of pressures applied by various interest groups seeking a favorable ruling from the Board. (Dopuch and Sunder, 1980: 17)*

'Viewing CF projects as constituting a strategic manoeuvre to assist in socially constructing the *appearance* of a coherent differentiated knowledge base for accounting standards, thus legitimising standards and the power, authority and self-regulation of the accountancy profession, may help in explaining why CF projects are continually undertaken by the profession, notwithstanding that each project is an apparent failure from a functional or a technical view' (Hines, 1989: 85, emphasis in original). Miller (1990: 23) also 'rejected the idea that it [the conceptual framework] is primarily an integrated accounting theory and . . . adopted the premise that it is a set of political declarations expressed in the form of an accounting theory'. Sadly:

> *There is little evidence that official statements of objectives of financial accounting have had any direct effect on the determination of financial accounting standards. Whenever the APB [Accounting Principles Board] or the FASB has had to consider a financial account-ing standard, various interest groups present arguments to support the methods that each perceived to be in its own best interests. The standards issued had to be compromises among the contending interests. (Dopuch and Sunder, 1980: 18)*

The weakness also applies to the consultation process regarding the con-ceptual framework itself (Archer, 1993: 73). How can a theoretically sound conceptual framework be the product of conciliation and negotiation between parties with vested interests?

The public face of the IASC's *Framework for the Preparation and Presentation of Financial Statements* was that it had multiple functions. The purpose of the framework was to:

a)   assist the board of IASC in the development of future Inter-
     national Accounting Standards and in its review of existing
     International Accounting Standards;

b)   assist the board of IASC in promoting harmonisation of regu-
     lations, accounting standards and procedures relating to the
     presentation of financial statements by providing a basis for
     reducing the number of alternative accounting treatments per-
     mitted by International Accounting Standards;

c)   assist national standard setting bodies in developing national
     standards;

d)   assist preparers of financial statements in applying International
     Accounting Standards and in dealing with topics that have yet to
     form the subject of an International Accounting Standard;

e)   assist auditors in forming an opinion as to whether financial
     statements conform with International Accounting Standards;

f)   assist users of financial statements in interpreting the infor-
     mation contained in financial statements prepared in conformity
     with International Accounting Standards; and

g)   provide those who are interested in the work of IASC with
     information about its approach to the formulation of Interna-
     tional Accounting Standards. (IASC, 1989: para. 1)

The purpose of the ASB's *Statements of Principles for Financial Reporting* (1999b) (as stated in paras. 1–4) is essentially in line with the IASC document, but the ASB also goes on to state that 'the Statement is expected to provide direction to the development of the legal requirements concerning the form and content of financial statements' (ASB, 1999b, Appendix 1: para. 15). As has been seen, this has resulted in inconsistencies between the ASB's *Statement of Principles* and the law.

Therefore, there may be a number of potentially conflicting drivers in the development of a conceptual framework:

- *theoretical importance*: to help standard setters produce consistent and coherent accounting standards
- *practical importance*: to assist practitioners in solving accounting problems

- *political importance*: to maintain control over accounting developments and to present the public face of accounting to the outside world
- *educational importance*: to underpin what is taught to accountants, users (of the financial statements) and students about the nature and limitations of financial statements
- *importance to auditors*: the auditors' report presumably implies that the financial statements are fit for the purpose
- *to highlight future developments*: to provide a lead in the future development of legal requirements.

These drivers may help to explain the often hostile reactions to conceptual framework projects. Indeed, the need for a conceptual framework has been challenged.

ARGUMENTS AGAINST THE DEVELOPMENT OF A CONCEPTUAL FRAMEWORK

Although there appears to be strong support for the development of a conceptual framework, opinion is not unanimous. The arguments against such a development were summarized by Anthony (1983: 11–15) as follows:

- The project is infeasible: 'Some who doubt the feasibility of developing an acceptable conceptual framework point out that none of the attempts by various persons or organizations has succeeded' (p. 12). Anthony considered this to be a defeatist attitude.
- Another problem 'is the assertion that the purpose of financial accounting is to measure "true income" and the claim that this goal cannot be achieved because no one knows what true income is' (p. 12). However, while it may not be possible to calculate one true income figure, Anthony thought that some ways would be more useful than others.
- The conceptual framework should be delayed until it has been established by research 'why accounting is what it is, why accountants do what they do, and what effect these phenomena have on people and resource utilization'. Anthony considered that the problem here was that the 'proponents are unwilling to settle for anything less than perfection, whereas accounting needs a conceptual framework, even if imperfect, as a guide in resolving important outstanding issues' (pp. 12–13).
- As the resolution of issues in accounting 'is essentially a political process . . . advocates with the strongest clout have issues resolved in their favor. In these circumstances, a conceptual framework is irrelevant, and its

development is a waste of time' (p. 13). However, the counter to this would be that a conceptual framework may help the standard setters to stand up to any political pressures.

- It has been suggested that users are able to 'see through' various accounting adjustments, and therefore it is problematic whether accounting standards are required. While users may be able to adjust for dramatic changes in accounting practices, it is problematic as to what they would make of the data if there were no standards.
- There is a concern that 'the development of a conceptual framework is undesirable because it would lead to too much rigidity in accounting' (p. 14). Anthony considered that 'this danger is less grave than the alternative of attempting to develop standards without a framework' (p. 15).
- It has been suggested (Butterworth, 1972; Colantoni et al., 1971) 'that entities should report essentially raw data, and users could then arrange these data in whatever way they found most useful' (p. 14). If raw data was being reported, this would obviate the need for a conceptual framework. In 1983, Anthony concluded:

> It seems unlikely that users have the time, the inclination, or the ability to construct their own financial statements from disaggregated data. They expect accountants to do this. Assuming only 10 items are reported on an operating statement, with three alternative numbers for each item, approximately 1,000 'bottom lines' would be possible. The result would be chaotic. (p. 14)

It is interesting that with the advances in technology, the database approach is again being taken seriously.

So, while there have been strong arguments against the development of a conceptual framework, these have not prevailed. However, they may help to explain some of the reasons why conceptual framework projects appear to have had limited practical impact.

REAL-TIME REPORTING IN A KNOWLEDGE ECONOMY

Technological advances have given rise to the discussion of real-time reporting (Elliott Committee, 1997) and proposals for users to have access to raw accounting databases. Such moves would presumably have implications for the conceptual framework projects – if users have access real-time to company data, this would presumably erode the 'usefulness' of the financial statements. If the financial statements are really about satisfying user needs, and the users (in particular investors and analysts) say they are irrelevant to decision making, does this mean that the standard-setters would abolish the financial statements? This question arises because if one takes the argument to its logical conclusion, if users do not find the financial statements useful, the question is then, 'Why have them?' However, the traditional response has been to try to 'make' the financial statements useful, but with alternative sources of data (particularly real-time data) this strategy may not continue to work. Obviously, it would not be possible for the standard-setters to unilaterally abolish the financial statements because of statutory requirements – but would this result in the government and the tax authorities having a greater say about the purpose of the financial statements (and hence influence on the contents of the financial statements)?

If the communication process is about establishing a message and then communicating it, will real-time access destroy the communication process? Would users really be able to extract a message from this raw data? Littleton (1953) considered that the role of accounting is to make a mass of facts intelligible by compressing the data in order to make it intelligible – the importance of this should not be underestimated. Auditors may be able to issue up-to-date 'audit reports' on whether the information systems are working (see Chapter 7), but the meaning of such real-time raw accounting data may be unclear.

CONCLUSION

The globalization of world commerce has intensified the drive for the international harmonization of accounting standards. The standard-setters are the parties most involved with the production of conceptual frameworks for financial reporting. The main bases appear to be IASB and FASB; however, these frameworks have not been without criticism. If a conceptual framework is an attempt to operationalize the accounting theory, the first stumbling block is the lack of agreement on the nature and scope of this theory. So, rather than having a common starting point and then a disagreement about which direction one should go, there appear to be many different starting points, each with its own set of future avenues. Indeed, given the state of 'accounting theory' and the political nature of standard setting, it could be argued that the foundations of the conceptual framework projects have been built on shifting sands – those of user needs and desires. Hence the debates as to what the conceptual frameworks are trying to achieve and about the objective of the financial statements. Indeed, the direction of the conceptual framework projects may be leading to disenchantment with the standard-setting process:

> There is . . . more interest in alternatives to the GAAP [Generally Accepted Accounting Principles], basically on financial statements prepared in accordance with other comprehensive bases of accounting (OCBOA). The impulse to switch to the OCBOA came from changes in the tax laws made by the Economic Recovery Act of 1981 and the increasing separation of tax accounting from the GAAP accounting, the increase in the number of partnerships, the subchapter S corporations and other entities that prefer to present tax or cash-basis financial statements, and the tentative conclusions of the AICPA accounting standards overload-study special committee in favor of the increased tax basis of accounting. (Riahi-Belkaoui, 2000: 42)

The chameleon nature of accounting may do much to hide its limitations, but it is unlikely to help the standard-setters produce consistent and coherent accounting standards. It may be appropriate to question whether the standards setters are the right bodies to construct the conceptual frameworks. The political and consensual approaches to the development of recent conceptual frameworks may have undermined their potential usefulness. It must be asked whether conceptual frameworks are really conceptual.

DISCUSSION QUESTIONS

1   What is the objective of the financial statements? Do you think this is clear/achievable?

2   Financial reporting standard-setters emphasize user-needs. What are the main problems associated with this stance?

3   In the dynamic business world of the twenty-first century, do you agree that the past earnings of a firm is the most important single item of information that is relevant to predicting future earnings?

4   Do you think that conceptual frameworks are conceptual? Set out a reasoned argument to justify your stance.

5   In view of the controversies stirred up by the conceptual framework debates, who regulates the regulators (that is, the standard-setters)?

REFERENCES

Accounting Principles Board (APB) (1970) APB Statement No. 4: *Basic Concepts and Principles Underlying Financial Statements of Business Enterprises*. New York: AICPA.

Accounting Standards Board (ASB) (1991) *The Objective of Financial Statements and the Qualitative Characteristics of Financial Information, Exposure Draft – Statement of Principles*. London: ASB.

Accounting Standards Board (ASB) (1995) *Statement of Principles for Financial Reporting – Exposure Draft*. London: ASB.

Accounting Standards Board (ASB) (1999a) *Statement of Principles for Financial Reporting, Revised Exposure Draft – Statement of Principles*. London: ASB.

Accounting Standards Board (ASB) (1999b) 'Statement of principles', reproduced in *Accounting Standards and Guidance for Members 2001*. London: ICAEW.

Accounting Standards Steering Committee (ASSC) (1975) *The Corporate Report – A Discussion Paper*. London: ASSC.

American Accounting Association (AAA) (1936) 'A tentative statement of accounting principles underlying corporate financial statements', *The Accounting Review*, June: 187–91.

American Accounting Association (AAA) (1966) Committee To Prepare a Statement of Basic Accounting Theory, *A Statement of Basic Accounting Theory*. Sarasota, FL: AAA.

American Accounting Association (AAA) (1977) Committee on Concepts and Standards for External Financial Reports, *Statement on Accounting Theory and Theory Acceptance*. Sarasota, FL: AAA.

American Institute of Certified Public Accountants (AICPA) (1973) (Trueblood Report) *Objectives of Financial Statements*, Report of the Accounting Objectives Study Group. New York: AICPA.

Anthony, R.N. (1983) *Tell It Like It Was: A Conceptual Framework for Financial Accounting*. Homewood, IL: Richard D. Irwin Inc.

Archer, S. (1993) 'On the methodology of constructing a conceptual framework for financial accounting', in M.J. Mumford and K.V. Peasnell (eds), *Philosophical Perspectives on Accounting: Essays in Honour of Edward Stamp*. London: Routledge.

Armstrong, M. (1977) 'The politics of establishing accounting standards', *The Journal of Accountancy*, February: 76–9.

Beattie, V., Brandt, R. and Fearnley, S. (1999) 'Perceptions of auditor independence: U.K. evidence', *Journal of International Accounting, Auditing and Taxation*, 8 (1): 67–107.

Brealey, R. and Myers, S. (1988) *Principles of Corporate Finance*. New York: McGraw-Hill.

Bromwich, M. (1992) *Financial Reporting, Information and Capital Markets*. London: Pitman Publishing.

Burton, J.C. and Sack, R.J. (1990) Editorial: 'Standard Setting Process in Trouble (Again)', *Accounting Horizons*, 4 (4): 117–20.

Butterworth, J.E. (1972) 'The accounting system as an information function', *Journal of Accounting Research*, Spring: 1–27.

Canning, J.B. (1929) *The Economics of Accountancy*. New York: Ronald Press Company.

Chambers, R.J. (1996) 'Ends, ways, means and conceptual frameworks', *Abacus*, 32 (2): 119–32.

Colantoni, C.S., Manes, R.P. and Whinston, A. (1971) 'A unified approach to the theory of accounting and information systems', *The Accounting Review*, January: 90–102.

Davidson, R.A., Gelardi, A.M. and Li, F. (1996) 'Analysis of the conceptual framework of China's new accounting system', *Accounting Horizons*, March: 58–74.

Davies, M., Paterson, R. and Wilson, A. (1999) *UK GAAP*. London: Butterworths Tolley.

Dearing Report (1988) *The Making of Accounting Standards*. London: ICAEW.

Devine, C.T. (1985) *Essays in Accounting Theory*. Sarasota, FL: AAA.

Dopuch, N. and Sunder, S. (1980) 'FASB's statement on objectives and elements of financial accounting: a review', *The Accounting Review*, 55: 1–21.

Elliott Committee (1997) Special Committee on Assurance Services, *Report of the Special Committee on Assurance Services*. New York: AICPA.

Financial Accounting Standards Board (FASB) (1974) *Discussion Memorandum on the Conceptual Framework for Accounting and Reporting: Consideration of the Report of the Study Group on the Objectives of Financial Statements*, FASB Discussion Memorandum. Stamford, CT: FASB.

Financial Accounting Standards Board (FASB) (1976a) *Tentative Conclusions on Objectives for Financial Statements of Business Enterprises*. Stamford, CT: FASB.

Financial Accounting Standards Board (FASB) (1976b) *Discussion Memorandum on the Conceptual Framework for Accounting and Reporting: Elements of Financial Statements and Their Measurement*. Stamford, CT: FASB.

Financial Accounting Standards Board (FASB) (1978) Objectives of Financial Reporting by Business Enterprises (SFAC No. 1). Stamford, CT: FASB.

Financial Accounting Standards Board (FASB) (1980a) *Qualitative Characteristics of Accounting Information* (SFAC No. 2). Stamford, CT: FASB.

Financial Accounting Standards Board (FASB) (1980b) *Elements of Financial Statements for Business Enterprises* (SFAC No. 3). Stamford, CT: FASB.

Financial Accounting Standards Board (FASB) (1984) *Recognition and Measurement in Financial Statements of Business Enterprises* (SFAC No. 5). Stamford, CT: FASB.

Financial Accounting Standards Board (FASB) (1990) *Present Value-Based Measurements in Accounting*. Norwalk, CT: FASB.

Financial Accounting Standards Board (FASB) (1996) *Exposure Draft: Reporting Comprehensive Income*. Norwalk, CT: FASB.

Financial Accounting Standards Board (FASB) (1997) *Reporting Comprehensive Income*. Norwalk, CT: FASB.

Financial Accounting Standards Board (FASB) (2000) *Using Cash Flow Information and Present Value in Accounting Measurement* (SFAC No. 7). Stamford, CT: FASB.

Gore, P. (1991) *Conceptual Frameworks for Financial Reporting: An Examination and Explanation*. London: ICAEW.

Gore, P. (1992) *The FASB Conceptual Framework Project 1973–1985: An Analysis*. Manchester: Manchester University Press.

Gore, Pelham (1994) *The Practical Use of Conceptual Frameworks for Financial Reporting*, Department of Accounting and Finance, Lancaster University Management School, Working Paper No. 94/012.

Grady, P. (1965) *Inventory of Generally Accepted Accounting Principles for Business Enterprises*. New York: AICPA.

Hines R.D. (1989) 'Financial accounting knowledge, conceptual framework projects and the social construct of the accounting profession', *Accounting, Auditing and Accountability Journal*, 2 (2): 72–92.

Hines, R.D. (1991) 'The FASB's conceptual framework, financial accounting and the maintenance of the social world', *Accounting, Organizations and Society*, 16 (4): 313–31.

International Accounting Standards Committee (IASC) (1989) *Framework for the Preparation and Presentation of Financial Statements*. London: IASC.

Joyce, E.J., Libby, R. and Sunder, S. (1982) 'Using the FASB's qualitative characteristics in accounting policy choices', *Journal of Accounting Research*, 20 (2 II): 654–75.

Lennard, A. (1999) 'The revised draft statement of principles', in M.J. Mumford and M.J. Page, *Try Again: Proceedings of the ACCA Conference on the ASB's 1999 Revised Draft Statement of Principles*. London: ACCA.

Littleton, A.C. (1953) *Structure of Accounting Theory*, American Accounting Association Monograph No. 5. Sarasota, FL: American Accounting Association.

Macve, R. (1981) *A Conceptual Framework for Financial Accounting and Reporting: The Possibilities for an Agreed Structure*. London: ICAEW.

Mathews, M.R. and Perera, M.H.B. (1996) *Accounting Theory and Development* (3rd edn). Melbourne: Nelson.

McMonnies, P. (ed.) (1988) *Making Corporate Reports Valuable*. Edinburgh: ICAS/Kogan Page.

Mezias, S.J. and Chung, S. (1989) *Due Process and Participation at the FASB*. Morristown, NJ: Financial Executives Research Foundation.

Miller, P.B.W. (1990) 'The conceptual framework as reformation and counter-reformation', *Accounting Horizons*, June: 23–32.

Moonitz, M. (1961) *The Basic Postulates of Accounting*, Accounting Research Study No. 1. New York: AICPA.

Myddelton, D.R. (1996) 'Orthodox versus revolutionary accounting', *Journal of Applied Accounting Research*, 3 (2): 17–36.

Page, M. (1991) 'Now is the time to be more critical', *Accountancy*, October: 31.

Page, M. (1992a) 'The ASB's proposed objective of financial statements: marching in step backwards? a review essay', *British Accounting Review*, March: 77–85.

Page, M. (1992b) 'Turn again Professor Whittington', *Accountancy*, February: 30.

Paton, W.A. (1922) *Accounting Theory – with Special Reference to Corporate Enterprise*. New York: Roland Press Company.

Paton, W.A. and Littleton, A.C. (1940) *An Introduction to Corporate Accounting Standards*. Chicago: AAA.

Peasnell, K.V. (1982) 'The function of a conceptual framework for corporate financial reporting', *Accounting and Business Research*, Autumn: 243–56.

Penman, S. (1999) 'The value of reporting comprehensive income', in M.J. Mumford and M.J. Page, *Try Again: Proceedings of the ACCA Conference on the ASB's 1999 Revised Draft Statement of Principles*. London: ACCA.

Power, M.K. (1993) 'On the idea of a conceptual framework for financial reporting', in M.J. Mumford and K.V. Peasnell (eds), *Philosophical Perspectives on Accounting: Essays in Honour of Edward Stamp*. London: Routledge.

Riahi-Belkaoui, A. (2000) *Accounting Theory* (4th edn). London: Business Press Thomson Leaning.

Sanders, T.H., Hatfield, H.R. and Moore, U. (1938) *A Statement of Accounting Principles*. USA: American Institute of Accountants.

Schroeder, R.G. and Clark, M. (1995) *Accounting Theory: Text and Readings* (5th edn). New York: Wiley.

Securities and Exchange Commission (SEC) (1978) *Report to Congress on the Accounting Profession and the Commission's Oversight Role*. Washington, DC: US Government Printing Office.

Solomons, D. (1978) 'The politicization of accounting', *The Journal of Accountancy*, November: 65–72.

Solomons, D. (1983) 'The political implications of accounting and accounting standard setting', *Accounting and Business Research*, 13 (50): 107–18.

Solomons, D. (1989) *Guidelines for Financial Reporting Standards*. London: ICAEW.

Sprague, C.E. (1923) *The Philosophy of Accounts* (5th edn). New York: Ronald Press Company.

Sprouse, R.T. and Moonitz, M. (1962) *A Tentative Set of Broad Accounting Principles for Business Enterprises*, Accounting Research Study No. 3. New York: AICPA.

Stamp Report (1980) *Corporate Reporting: Its Future Evolution*. Toronto: Canadian Institute of Chartered Accountants.

Sterling, R.R. (1972) 'Decision oriented financial accounting', *Accounting and Business Research*, Summer: 198–208.

Storey, R.K. (1964) *The Search for Accounting Principles*. New York: AICPA.

Storey, R.K. and Storey, S. (1998) *The Framework for Financial Accounting Concepts and Standards*. Norwalk, CT: FASB.

Taylor, P. and Turley, S. (1986) *The Regulation of Accounting*. Oxford: Basil Blackwell.

Trevett, P. and Maugham, J. (2000) 'FRS 12's legal obstacles', *Accountancy*, June: 94.

Tweedie, D. and Whittington, G. (1990) 'Financial reporting: current problems and their implications for systematic reform', *Accounting and Business Research*, 21 (81): 87–102.

Vatter, W.J. (1947) *The Fund Theory of Accounting and Its Implications for Financial Reports*. Chicago: University of Chicago Press.

Wheat Report (1972) *Establishing Financial Accounting Standards*. New York: AICPA.

Whittington, G. (1991) 'Good stewardship and the ASB's objectives', *Accountancy*, November: 33.

Wilkinson-Riddle, G.J. and Holland, L. (1997) 'An analysis and discussion of the responses to the ASB's Statement of Principles for Financial Reporting', *Journal of Applied Accounting Research*, 3 (3): 3–46.

Wyatt, A. (1990) 'Accounting standards: conceptual or political?' *Accounting Horizons*, September: 83–8.

Zeff, S.A. (1972) *Forging Accounting Principles in Five Countries: A History and Analysis of Trends*. USA: Stripes Publishing Co.

Zeff, S.A. (1978) 'The rise of "economic consequences"', *The Journal of Accountancy*, December: 56–63.

Zeff, S.A. (1999) 'The evolution of the conceptual framework for business enterprises in the United States', *Accounting Historians Journal*, 26 (2): 89–131.

Zeff, S.A. (2002) '"Political" lobbying on proposed standards: a challenge to the IASB', *Accounting Horizons*, 16 (1): 43–54.

5   Developments in Auditing and Assurance

Facts as facts do not always create a spirit of reality, because
reality is a spirit.

– G.K. Chesterton

I n view of the diversity of theories about accounting and the problematic
nature of the conceptual frameworks, this chapter aims to examine the
development of the external audit to see if it can help clarify the scope
and nature of financial accounting.

The external audit has evolved in line with changes in the auditor's role, the
auditing environment, and auditing technology. Today, '[t]he annual audit is
one of the cornerstones of corporate governance' (*Cadbury Report*, 1992: 36).
However, in the nineteenth century, the primary objective of the corporate
audit was the detection of fraud. As the complexity of business developed so
came the realization of the impossibility of such a proposition. Therefore, the
role of the auditor has changed over time (e.g., Beck, 1973; Bird, 1970; Brown,
1962; Carmichael and Whittington, 1984; Flint, 1971; Lee, 1986), is still
changing, and will probably continue to change (Panel on Audit Effectiveness,
2000). Audit approaches have been forced to change in order that a commercially viable service could be provided. Five 'generations' of audits are
identified, culminating in the 'continuous audit'. The pressures for this latest
generation of audit have arisen from developments in information technology
(IT) and the perceived needs of the users of external financial data. This can be
linked directly to the current emphasis on the provision of assurance services,
which may be viewed as an extension of the statutory audit function.

EARLY AUDITS

Littleton (1933: 260) was of the view that early auditing 'was designed to
verify the honesty of persons charged with fiscal, rather than managerial
responsibilities'. He identified two types of early audits; firstly, public hear-
ings of the results of governmental officials, and, secondly, the scrutiny of the
charge-and-discharge accounts (as discussed in Chapter 3). 'Both types of

audit were designed to afford a check upon 'accountability' and nothing more. It was in effect a case of examining and testing an account of steward-ship' (Littleton, 1933: 264). In the nineteenth century, the role of the auditor may have been directly linked to management's stewardship function (Flint, 1971) – with stewardship being regarded in the narrow sense of honesty and integrity. However, Littleton (1933: 264–5) considered that, as a consequence of commercial developments, this had changed:

> With the advent of business, there came, instead of 'accountability', the accounting problems attendant upon the ownership of property and the calculation of profits or losses. Auditing, no longer an auditory process of checking another's stewardship, now began to lay increas-ing emphasis upon the visual scrutiny of written records and the testing of entries by documentary evidence.

It was this that would lay the foundations for the basis of today's audits. The Joint-Stock Companies Act of 1844 introduced the requirement for an annual audit for companies formed under it. This Act did not confer the protection of limited liability on the shareholders. Therefore, this lack of limited liability for the owners of the business, together with the requirement of an audit, could lead one to conclude that the audit was intended to protect the stockholders from unscrupulous managers. However, it is the opinion of Lee (1969: 14) that:

> the main objective of company auditing was exactly the same as that of company accounting – to portray a picture of solvency for the benefit of creditors who might otherwise lose confidence, panic and cause the downfall of the particular company owing them money. . . . It was thought, at least in the 1840s and 1850s, that such measures served to protect the shareholder best.

The enactment of the Company Clauses Act 1845 (Section CII) required auditors to have at least one share in the company. The next major change came ten years later with the enactment of the Limited Liability Act 1855. It appears that the audit on its own was not enough to encourage wealthy investors to become members in unlimited joint-stock companies.

> If there were no provision for limited liability, every firm (in a private enterprise economy) must have just one owner, or it must have a small

group of owners. It would have to be a small group of owners when each was liable for the debts of the firm, if it ever came to be wound up, to the full extent of his wealth, his personal wealth. So it would be most unwise to invest in a firm, as part-owner, unless one was prepared to keep in close touch with its affairs, so as to see that one was not ruined by the mistakes it made. (Hicks, 1982: 11)

The consequence of unlimited liability had been that the capital of an unlimited joint-stock company was still restricted to what could be raised by a small group of individuals. This defect in the 1844 Act was, therefore, rectified by the Limited Liability Act 1855. In the following year, there was a further liberalization of the law, for the Joint-Stock Companies Act 1856 abandoned the statutory requirement for a compulsory audit. There appears to be no clear consensus on why the audit was made optional. The introduction of limited liability status for companies registered under the Limited Liability Act 1855 meant that shareholders had less to lose if their company went into liquidation, and so this is a possible reason for the relaxation of the law. Hein (1963: 509), however, quotes Robert Lowe, who was Vice-President of the Board of Trade in 1856, on the topic of limited liability companies, as saying that, 'having given them a pattern, the State leaves them to manage their own affairs and has no desire to force on these little republics any particular constitution'. On the change in legislation, Lee (1969: 16) concluded that '[t]he reason for this move is not apparent from writings on the subject but presumably was because of a general feeling by legislators of the day that the audit was not beneficial enough to necessitate a compulsory provision – in other words, the "solvency" of the company could be established from the balance sheet without the need for an audit of that document'.

Another innovation contained in the Joint-Stock Companies Act 1856 was the provision that the auditor of a company did not have to be a member of it. The same article, Article 76, also forbade directors to take up the post of auditor, along with anyone else who might have a business interest in the company. The implications of this article are twofold. Firstly, it was a break from the original concept of shareholders that were not involved in the day-to-day running of the company checking on those that were, and, secondly, it was the introduction of the concept of independence. All in all, it was opening the way for the employment of professional accountants as auditors.

The Companies Act 1900 reintroduced the statutory requirement for a compulsory audit of all limited companies. This was basically how the legal position remained until the enactment on the Companies Act 1948. During the intervening period, the role of lending credibility to the accounts emerged as the auditor's primary objective (Lee, 1986).

THE DETECTION OF FRAUD AS AN AUDIT OBJECTIVE

During the nineteenth century and the early part of the twentieth century fraud detection was seen as an important part of the audit. Although the Joint-Stock Companies Acts remained silent on the subject of fraud, the Punishment of Frauds Act 1857 strengthened the law against fraud, making it an offence for a director or officer of a company to alter falsely a company's accounting records in order to defraud a creditor or shareholder. The judgement in Nichol's Case (1859) stated that it was part of an auditor's duty to discover fraudulent misrepresentations. Thus, the detection of fraud was laid down as being one of the top priorities of an audit and generally remained so well into the 1920s (Lee, 1986). The Victorian view on the detection of fraud can be seen from a contemporary comment: 'The object of an audit is a two fold one, the detection of fraud where it has been committed, and its prevention by imposing such safeguards, and devising such means as will make it extremely difficult of accomplishment, even if the inclination is in that direction' (Bourne, 1887: 330).

The decline in the importance of fraud as an audit objective started towards the end of the nineteenth century. This is reflected in the judgement in the *Kingston Cotton Mill Case* (1896). Auditors did not have to approach their work with the foregone conclusion that something was wrong, however, once something untoward was discovered, the auditor should investigate it to ensure that the error or defalcation was not so material as to affect the view given by the accounts. This case gave rise to the famous saying, 'an auditor is a watchdog but not a bloodhound'. In *Irish Woollen Co. Ltd.* v *Tyson and Others* (1900), it was held that an auditor is liable for any damages sustained by a company by reason of falsification which might have been discovered by the exercise of reasonable care and skill in the performance of the audit. So, instead of having to detect all frauds, it was becoming clear that it was the auditors' duty to exercise reasonable care and skill in the conduct of their work.

THE CONCEPTUAL BASIS OF AUDITING

The AAA's Committee on Basic Auditing Concepts (1973: 9–11) identified four conditions which it considered created the demand for an independent audit of accounting data. These can be summarized as follows:

1 *The potential or actual conflict of interest.* This conflict may exist between the user of the information and the preparer.
2 *Consequence.* The user may require the information for decision-making purposes; therefore, the user needs to be confident of the quality of the accounting information.

3 *Complexity.* The processes of producing the accounting information are so complex that the user has to rely on someone else to examine its quality.

4 *Remoteness.* Even if the user had the ability to reach a conclusion on the quality of the accounting information, it is unlikely that the user would have access.

This committee considered that '[t]hese four conditions (conflict of interest, consequence, complexity, and remoteness) interact in such a way that as they increase in their intensity they make it both increasingly important that an informed, independent conclusion be reached by the user as to the quality of the accounting information being received and increasingly difficult for the user of the information to reach such a determination without outside assistance' (AAA, 1973: 10).

In 1993, Pratt and Van Peursem considered that '[a]uditing has developed in a very practical way over the last 3,000 years, but it is only in the last 30 years that much consideration has been given to the discipline's underlying theoretical foundations'. This could be seen to have started in 1961 with Mautz and Sharaf's attempt to formulate a theory of auditing. They intended to try to bring together 'the bits of theory now in the literature' (p. 4), the objective being that such a framework would ensure that problems facing the auditor would be dealt with in a rational and consistent manner. Altogether, eight tentative postulates of auditing were formulated by Mautz and Sharaf:

1 *Financial statements and financial data are verifiable.*

2 *There is no necessary conflict of interest between the auditor and the management of the enterprise under audit.*

3 *The financial statements and other information submitted for verification are free from collusive and other unusual irregularities.*

4 *The existence of a satisfactory system of internal control eliminates the probability of irregularities.*

5 *Consistent application of generally accepted principles of accounting results in the fair presentation of financial position and the results of operations.*

6 *In the absence of clear evidence to the contrary, what has held true in the past for the enterprise under examination will hold true in the future.*

7 *When examining financial data for the purpose of expressing an independent opinion thereon, the auditor acts exclusively in the capacity of an auditor.*

8 *The professional status of the independent auditor imposes commensurate professional obligations. (Mautz and Sharaf, 1961: 42)*

Lee (1972) developed Mautz and Sharaf's work by categorizing auditing postulates into three divisions, to form 'justifying', 'behavioural' and 'functional' postulates. Sherer and Kent (1983: 19) described this categorization as 'a rational and comprehensive basis upon which to base an examination of auditing theory'. The justifying postulates set out the reasons for the existence of the external audit function. Gwilliam (1987: 45) describes these justifying postulates as 'the most significant extension of the postulate approach'. This was because Mautz and Sharaf were more concerned with whether an audit was in fact feasible, and not with whether it was necessary.

Lee's justifying postulates (1972: 53–6) can be summarized as follows:

1   Without a formal audit, the accounting information contained in a company's financial statements lacks credibility to be used confidently by external users.
2   The most important requirement of the external audit is to increase the credibility of the financial statements.
3   The best way to enhance the credibility of the financial statements is by means of the external audit.
4   It is assumed that the credibility of the financial statements can be established by the external audit process.
5   Users of the financial statements are not able to satisfy themselves as to the credibility of the accounting information in the financial statements.

The behavioural postulates support the assumption that the external auditor can enhance the credibility of the financial statements. Therefore, the assumptions (Lee, 1972: 56–60) are that:

1   The audit is not impeded by unnecessary conflicts of interest between the external auditor and company management.
2   The work of the external auditor is not impeded by any unreasonable legal restrictions.
3   The auditor is independent both mentally and physically.
4   The auditor has sufficient skill and experience to carry out the duties required.
5   The auditor is accountable for the quality of the work performed and the opinion expressed thereon.

The functional postulates relate to the actual work performed by the auditor (Lee, 1972: 60–3):

1   It is assumed that there is sufficient reliable evidence available to enable the external auditor to carry out an audit within a reasonable time and at a reasonable cost.

2   The accounting information in the financial statements, largely due to the existence of internal controls, is free of major fraud and error.
3   There exists generally accepted and recognized accounting concepts and bases which, when used consistently, result in a true and fair presentation of the accounting information in the financial statements.

Flint (1988: 9) considered there was 'a place for theory to explain the responsibility of the audit function and the basis of its evolution, and to assist in resolving the unanswered questions which have been posed – not a theory built up on a piecemeal basis from a series of solutions to particular questions, but a set of comprehensive propositions making up an overall theory from which the solutions to all these questions can be derived'. Flint's basic postulates view the audit in its wider setting and can be summarized as follows:

1   A relationship of accountability exists.
2   An audit is required because the subject matter is too remote, too complex or too important.
3   The distinguishing characteristics of audit are independence, and freedom from investigatory and reporting constraints.
4   The subject matter for audit 'is susceptible to verification by evidence' (p. 31).
5   The standards for accountability can be set and actual performance can be compared by known criteria – 'the process of measurement and comparison requires special skill and the exercise of judgement' (p.32).
6   'The meaning, significance and intention of financial and other statements and data which are audited are sufficiently clear that the credibility which is given thereto as a result of audit can be clearly expressed and communicated' (p. 38).
7   'An audit produces an economic or social benefit' (p. 39).

Flint (1988) viewed audit as 'a social control mechanism for securing accountability': 'The onus is on auditors and audit policy-makers constantly to seek to find out what is the societal need and expectation for independent audit and to endeavour to fulfil that need within the limits of practical and economic constraints, remembering at all times that the function is a dynamic, not a static one' (p. 17).

Although the Companies Acts set out the responsibilities of the auditor, they do not specify, in any great detail, how they are to be accomplished. The first UK auditing pronouncement (*General Principles of Auditing*) was issued in 1961. This was the first of the *Statements of Auditing*, which were replaced by the *Auditing Standards and Guidelines* during the 1980s. Following the recommendations of the Dearing Report (1988), the Auditing Practices Board (APB) was established in 1991, and it introduced the *Statements of Auditing Standards (SASs)*. The *SASs* contain the basic principles and essential procedures with which auditors are required to comply. The objective of an audit of financial statements was defined by *SAS 100* as being 'to enable auditors to give an opinion on those financial statements taken as a whole and thereby to provide reasonable assurance that the financial statements give a true and fair view (where relevant) and have been prepared in accordance with relevant accounting or other requirements' (para. 1). It then sets out the auditor's responsibilities in relation to the conduct of an audit. They are required to:

(a) *carry out procedures designed to obtain sufficient appropriate audit evidence, in accordance with Auditing Standards contained in SASs, to determine with reasonable confidence whether the financial statements are free from material misstatement;*

(b) *evaluate the overall presentation of the financial statements, in order to ascertain whether they have been prepared in accordance with relevant legislation and accounting standards; and*

(c) *issue a report containing a clear expression of their opinion on the financial statements. (para. 2)*

SAS 210 goes on to state that '[a]uditors should have or obtain a knowledge of the business of the entity to be audited which is sufficient to enable them to identify and understand the events, transactions and practices that may have a significant effect on the financial statements or the audit thereof' (para. 2). This can be derived from knowledge of the industry in which a client operates and the related legislation. Knowledge of a specific client can be obtained through past experiences with them, recent discussions with management and visits to the site(s) of the client's operations. The findings then need to be related back to what is known about the industry. This knowledge can then be used to assist in the assessment of risk.

SAS 300 requires the auditor to 'use professional judgment to assess the components of audit risk and to design audit procedures to ensure it is reduced to an acceptably low level'. It defines audit risk as being composed of three components: inherent risk, control risk and detection risk. In developing an audit approach, an auditor must assess the likelihood of inherent risk ('the susceptibility of an account balance or class of transactions to material misstatement, either individually or when aggregated with misstatements in other balances or classes, irrespective of related internal controls' [para. 4]). Therefore, inherent risk would include the integrity of the directors and management (and pressures on them), and the nature of the business and the industry in which it operates. Lower down the organizational structure, inherent risk would include the quality of the accounting system, the complexity of transactions, adjustments involving a high degree of estimation and unusual transactions.

A control risk is the risk that a material error or misstatement may go undetected by an accounting or internal control system (note that 'inherent risk and control risk are highly interrelated' [para. 32] because in situations where high inherent risk is likely to exist, management often counters this by its accounting and internal control systems), whereas detection risk is the risk that auditors' substantive procedures will not detect a material misstatement. *SAS 300* defines the internal control system as 'the control environment and control procedures' (para. 8) – thus highlighting the distinction between the two. The control environment is the overall philosophy and operating style of the directors and management in relation to their company's internal controls, while control procedures relate to specific policies and procedures. Therefore, the internal control system 'includes all the policies and procedures (internal controls) adopted by the directors and management of an entity to assist in achieving their objective of ensuring, as far as practicable, the orderly and efficient conduct of its business, including adherence to internal policies, the safeguarding of assets, the prevention and detection of fraud and error, the accuracy and completeness of the accounting records, and the timely preparation of reliable financial information' (para. 8).

'Auditors should obtain sufficient appropriate audit evidence to be able to draw reasonable conclusions on which to base the audit opinion' (*SAS 400*, para. 2). Audit evidence is gathered by carrying out tests of control or substantive procedures. The reliability of audit evidence is stated to be influenced by its source (*SAS 400*, para. 16):

- *audit evidence from external sources . . . is more reliable than that obtained from the entity's records,*
- *audit evidence obtained from the entity's records is more reliable when the related accounting and internal control system operates effectively,*
- *evidence obtained directly by auditors is more reliable than that obtained by or from the entity,*
- *evidence in the form of documents and written representations is more reliable than oral representations, and*
- *original documents are more reliable than photocopies, telexes or facsimiles.*

In relation to fraud, the current position is as follows: 'Auditors plan, perform and evaluate their audit work in order to have a reasonable expectation of detecting material misstatements in the financial statements arising from fraud or error' (*SAS 110*, para. 18).

DEVELOPMENTS IN AUDIT APPROACHES: FROM AUDIT EFFICIENCY TO AUDIT EFFECTIVENESS?

In relation to the external audit, perhaps the only constant thing is change. In the 1980s, audit efficiency was probably the major driving force behind audit developments (Burton and Fairfield, 1982). Accountancy firms were quite open about this, and Turley and Cooper (1991: 23), following their interviews with senior auditors, were able to conclude that '[t]he most important criterion for making the choice of [audit] strategy is the notion of efficiency'. However, there have been concerns about audit effectiveness (e.g. *Cadbury Report*, 1992: 36) and while there is no doubt that auditors are still very much concerned with efficiency, there is now evidence (Davis, 1996) that things have changed. Given the litigious atmosphere in which the auditors have to operate, they are starting to reassess the objective of the audit and, consequently, how this should be accomplished. So, rather than simply concentrating on how to do their work more efficiently (that is, the same level of confidence at lower cost), they are now starting to question what, as auditors, they are trying to achieve and thus, what sort of work this requires (what is required to achieve their objectives; that is, effectiveness). Therefore, there appears to have been a move by some firms to reconsider the overall effectiveness of their audit approaches in the light of a re-evaluation of the risks (both audit and commercial) that they face (Pincus et al. [1999] examined audit effectiveness in comparison with audit efficiency, but, essentially, this was just in relation to the auditor's responsibility for fraud detection). The nature of the changes implemented by some firms is such that the developments could almost be classified as an example of 'process re-engineering'. This is likely to have a dramatic impact on what people consider auditing is all about, and could indicate a need for the reassessment of the external auditor's function.

> The benefits of more effective audits include improving the reliability of financial statements, enhancing the credibility of and investors' confidence in those financial statements, improving management decision making, lowering entities' cost of capital, and increasing the effectiveness of capital markets in allocating resources. (Panel on Audit Effectiveness, 2000: 8)

Davis (1996: 6) considered that the first-generation audit could be described as 'verifying transactions in the books'. In relation to the audits of large companies, the first generation of audits probably ended during the late 1960s; however, the attempted verification of transactions probably continued in relation to the audit of very small companies until the abolition of their statutory audit requirement in 1994. Davis described the second-generation audit as 'relying on systems'. This approach involved the auditor's ascertaining and documenting the accounting system, with particular regard to information flows and the identification of internal controls. It required the evaluation of the usefulness to the auditor of these controls, and then compliance tests were required if the auditor wished to rely on them. If this work showed that the controls were effective, this would enable a reduction in the level of detailed substantive testing (although, in the early days this was not always the case, and thus there was a concern about overauditing). Though the early 1970s were the high point of the systems-based approach to auditing, this was never really appropriate for the audit of small companies due to the lack of controls that would be required to give audit assurance to external auditors.

The early 1980s saw a readjustment in auditors' approaches. The assessment of these systems was an expensive process, and so auditors began to cut back their systems work and make greater use of analytical procedures. Linked with this, was the development during the mid-1980s of risk-based auditing (Turley and Cooper, 1991), which Davis has termed 'the third-generation audit'. The significance of the application of the concept of risk to the audit approach 'is that its concern is not with the choice of a particular strategy for collecting evidence per se, but rather with providing a criterion for making that choice and determining the overall direction of audit work' (Turley and Cooper, 1991: 15).

Though risk-based auditing may have dominated auditors' approaches during the first half of the 1990s, by 1996 Davis considered that the fourth-generation audit had arrived. This he termed 'the investigatory audit', but it has also been called 'the business risk approach' (Bell et al., 1997; KPMG, 1999; Lemon et al., 2000; Winograd et al., 2000):

> *It means audit people making judgements about audited people. With integrated business and accounting systems, most system failures in larger companies are now detected long before the audit. Things go wrong from human abuse of the systems and of trust. The motives are usually personal protection in seeking to conceal poor profits, or personal gain through theft. The whites of the eyes test is worth hundreds of words in an audit programme. (Davis, 1996: 6)*

'[D]uring the 1990s, several of the major international accounting firms have developed their methodologies on the basis of business risk analysis, and this has led to claims that a new generation of audit approaches, conceptually different from previous approaches, has arrived' (Lemon et al., 2000: 1). Lemon et al. report that business risk audit approaches 'emphasize a "top-down" approach to the audit, starting from the business and its processes and working through to the financial statements, rather than in the opposite direction, where the business is essentially defined by the financial statements' (p. 11). With the business risk approach, 'emphasis is placed on understanding the risks the entity is subject to, in its environment, operations, and control processes' (p. 15).

The business risk approach appears to be moving the auditor's focus even further away from the detail of the entries in the accounting system and on to the people who manage the business. This is almost a recognition that external auditing could be regarded as the audit of motivations (this will be discussed further in the next chapter). Though the Accounting Standards Board (ASB) has made great efforts to limit management's discretion regarding the preparation and presentation of its financial statements, it must be recognized that the production of any set of financial statements requires the employment of judgement. Therefore, the honesty and motivations of management are important; however, there is a debate as to how much audit emphasis should be placed on these things rather than on the detail of the accounting records, and the risk-based approaches have been criticized (Hatherly, 1998).

In view of the limited amount of information about auditors' approaches to their audits, this chapter reports the results of eighteen interviews (including one pilot interview) which were conducted (in late 1995 and early 1996) with senior audit partners and managers. Consequently, the findings probably tend to reflect audit developments in larger firms and on larger audits, but they do illustrate issues which are of concern to auditors.

Most of the firms had moved towards a risk-based audit approach in the late 1980s; since then, there have been a number of developments, though most of these may be described as 'incremental' – building on what was already there. One person considered that over the previous decade, the increased emphasis on risk has been 'out of all proportion' to how it was used originally. A number of the larger firms do appear to have made significant alterations to their audit approaches. These approaches now place much greater emphasis on high-level risk (or business risk). This is the risk to the auditors themselves; that is, it is not just audit risk (the risk of a wrong opinion), but also commercial risk (the adverse consequences of an audit failure). This has led to a reassessment of the fundamentals of the audit: 'Do we need to do all this work? What are the risks?' Therefore, there is evidence that audit effectiveness is being questioned. Effectiveness could be defined as an assessment of whether the auditor's approach is achieving its objective (as opposed to efficiency, which relates inputs to outputs). Therefore, 'audit effectiveness' leads to the auditor questioning whether something really needs to be done in order for an audit opinion to be formulated, whereas it could be argued that 'audit efficiency' (in the literal sense of the phrase) is about whether an existing procedure can be done in a more cost-effective manner. Consequently, some auditors are placing considerably greater emphasis on high-level risk, concentrating much more on the individuals who comprise the management team. There has been a greater emphasis on the understanding of management's control of business risk and its overall control of the information systems. This has involved examining management's attitude to controls and the strength of its control environment (that is, controls over the detection of errors and controls aimed at preventing fraud and manipulation). A couple of the interviewees stated that it was now their firms' policies to resign or refuse reappointment as auditors if they had doubts about the integrity of any of their clients.

A number of interviewees (speaking about other firms' approaches) were concerned about this emphasis and reliance on high-level risks and controls. One person stated that as part of the risk assessment, his firm would look at management, but he perceived a problem: 'I don't think we have enough information about the individual people.' Another person concluded that: 'The Big 6 [as it was then] can risk away with impunity.' Therefore, it can be seen that a debate exists regarding how much assurance auditors should be seeking from their assessment of the levels of risk. *SAS 400* requires that '[a]uditors should obtain sufficient appropriate audit evidence to be able to draw reasonable conclusions on which to base the audit opinion' (para. 2), and as one person stated: 'It all comes back to judgement at the end of the day.'

Central to the conduct of an audit is the development of a strategy aimed at achieving the audit objective, followed up by a specific plan to implement the strategy. Auditors are required to 'obtain an understanding of the accounting and internal control systems sufficient to plan the audit and develop an effective audit approach' (*SAS 300*, para. 3). It is a requirement of *SAS 200* that auditors plan and document their work. Thus, the overall plan should describe the expected scope and conduct of the audit. All those interviewed considered that the time spent on these parts of the audit had increased, some admitting to a significant increase. The planning stage was seen as an opportunity for auditors to consolidate their knowledge of the client; it 'enables the identification of problem areas at the start of the audit, and not at the end'. However, other factors appear to have been the JMU (Joint Monitoring Unit) visits as well as the *SAS* on planning.

Auditors' approaches now tend to emphasize the overview of the control flows, and 'the top level controls are more and more important'. The auditors are now interested in 'how managers manage the business', or, as another person described it, 'a top-down' approach to controls – 'historically, people worked up from the bottom (e.g. transactions controls and compliance)'. As a consequence, there has been 'far less compliance testing by low level junior staff'. It was considered that the auditing disasters of the early 1990s had illustrated the threats posed by things going wrong at the top of an organization. Another reason given for this switch from concentrating on the low-level, detailed controls was the changes in the nature of clients' systems. One person stated that auditors 'hardly ever find controls work picking up errors'. The greater use of IT by clients was cited as being particularly important in this respect. Until the 1970s, most systems were clerically based, whereas now IT predominates; consequently, the auditor needs to obtain a different type of evidence. Management's use of IT means that auditors are now encountering much fewer clerical errors – 'there has been a drastic reduction in the number of errors found'. Therefore, auditors tend to consider that the client's use of standard software packages has contributed to a reduction in control risk. Obviously, they need to consider the individual environments and the potential for any unauthorized adjustments to the systems, but, generally, it was considered that 'the vast majority of companies do not have people with the necessary expertise'. This person stated that 'fraud in a computerised environment is not extensive – big frauds do not happen as a result of a manipulation of software'; as a consequence, this interviewee considered that 'computerised systems were less risky than manual systems'. It appears that auditors are most concerned when management make alterations to its systems – one person stated that 'change equals risk'. A few types of audits are of necessity systems-based (as in the financial sector), but, in general, one can now report the 'death' of the old systems-based audit (that is, the second-generation audit). One person considered that the move away from systems work was 'a shame because of a loss of quality in what we can provide'; consequently, the auditor's comments were not as helpful to management.

It was suggested that the systems audit can often be done by internal audit, and then the external auditors can review this work. The existence of an internal audit function does depend very much on the nature and size of the company being audited. It still tends to be the largest companies which make extensive use of them. As a result of the *Cadbury Report*, more companies have reassessed their use of the internal audit function. One development has been the outsourcing of this function – some companies have started to use external agencies, rather than set up their own departments. Though external auditors try to make as much use as possible of the internal auditor's work, its value to them is often limited. This is because of the varied nature of the internal auditor's work. It is just as likely to relate to operational issues (such as economy, efficiency and effectiveness) as to the operation of the financial controls which are of most interest to the external auditors. Where possible, more use was being made of internal audit departments. A number of auditors made favourable comments regarding the quality of the people in such departments and the clarification of their reporting lines. Generally, the auditors' views of internal audit departments appeared to be much more positive than in the mid-1980s. However, one person made it clear that he did not want to comment on the usefulness of the few internal audit departments that he had encountered!

In general, auditors have continued to make greater use of analytical review. *SAS 410* defines analytical procedures as the analysis of relationships:

> (a)   *between items of financial data, or between items of financial and non-financial data, deriving from the same period; or*
>
> (b)   *between comparable financial information deriving from different periods or different entities. (para. 3)*

Analytical review is now an extremely important part of the audit. As one person stated, 'the whole thing is about reducing [detailed] substantive testing – justifiably'. Another person stated: 'If you want reduced costs but the same coverage, analytical review was the answer.' Analytical review was regarded as 'very important . . . and very powerful'. The main perceived advantages were that it enabled the reduction in other types of work, it was relatively cheap to perform, it should force the auditor to think about the implications of the results, and it focused the auditor on problem areas. Although analytical review is mandatory at the planning and review stages of an audit (*SAS 410*), one person considered that it was 'nonsense in relation to the beginning of the audit – if analytical review is an attempt to predict an account balance'. The intention of using it at the start of the audit was to identify unusual variations and subsequently direct audit attention to them; however, this person was concerned that at the commencement of an audit it was often very difficult to attempt to make a prediction of what the relationship should be.

Another person was concerned about the lack of management accounting information available to auditors in some businesses. This person considered that the limited use of management accounting was 'one of the most disappointing things about British business'. Thus, there was a concern that the data necessary for an analytical review may not be available. Other drawbacks were stated as being the difficulty of interpreting the results and determining when something was unusual. One interviewee considered that analytical review was 'strong regarding completeness . . . [but] there is a question as to how effective it is'. Another person considered that 'in many cases the quality of analytical review leaves much to be desired . . . the quality has improved and it needed to!' The general view was that analytical review was now of a better quality and performed more thoughtfully than in the past. It was considered that auditors were now better trained in its use. However, one view was that 'it was a constant struggle to use more analytical review', and that 'slow progress' was being made, because 'it was difficult to get people to relate it intelligently to the audit'. Other reservations about the usefulness of analytical review, have come from the Panel on Audit Effectiveness:

> *The entities with the most sophisticated frauds often were concerned about concealing them from the auditors and particularly about making the numbers and relationships among them 'look right' to the auditors when they performed their analytical procedures. A favorite technique for accomplishing this was to 'play around' with the numbers, often through the use of non-standard entries, until they 'looked right'. (Panel on Audit Effectiveness, 2000: 85)*

Therefore, there are concerns regarding the effectiveness of analytical review, and there is a question over the amount of assurance that it gives.

Perhaps the key thing to come out of the interviews is how greatly the detailed substantive testing of transactions appears to have declined. The early 1980s saw a swing away from reliance on internal controls and towards more substantive testing (analytical review and testing of transactions). This was because audit partners required a heavy level of detailed substantive testing in order for them to feel comfortable about forming the audit opinion. An examination of audit manuals in the mid-1980s found that a number of firms then considered that substantive tests of detail were the most reliable source of evidence. At least one firm considered that direct substantive testing of transactions and balances could provide high, easily measurable levels of assurance, and in many cases the bulk of their evidence was derived from this source. Thus, it can be seen that detailed substantive testing used to be a fundamental type of audit procedure.

However, there was a perception at the time that overauditing was taking place. The rise of analytical auditing procedures during the 1980s resulted in a justification for reductions in detailed substantive testing. The implementation of risk-analysis approaches continued to move auditors even further away from detailed substantive testing. This trend has continued. The interviews made it clear that during the 1990s less and less audit assurance was being sought from detailed substantive testing. All firms were developing their audit approaches so as to be able to justify reductions in detailed substantive testing – 'we have moved a long way from gaining assurance from detailed substantive assurance'. Another person described the trend as 'a waning of heavy substantive tests'. The risk-evaluation approach adopted by some of the larger firms has had the impact of eliminating a number of areas of work. The justification was that if a company had good internal controls and there was a good analytical review, the auditor 'may not do any tests of detail in many cases'.

Clients' use of IT was also considered to have contributed to the decline in detailed substantive testing. Reliance on this has enabled auditors to concentrate on analysing what is produced – to the extent that 'the need to check transactions is much reduced – if not eliminated'. In view of these comments, it is interesting to note that '[t]he advent of the computerized systems has increased the improper manipulation of input or transaction data, application programs, data files, and computer operations. Embedded fraud is often hard to detect' (Vanasco, 1998: 62). Despite this, the effect of the developments in the audit approaches is such that, in some large firms, one can almost pronounce the demise of detailed substantive testing, as, increasingly, 'sampling is a test of last resort'.

The changes identified here are profound, and it can be concluded that the nature of some audits (particularly those of large companies) has been completely revolutionized. In the light of this development, one wonders whether the 'basis of opinion' paragraph in the current unqualified audit opinion really reflects the work that underpins the formulation of the auditor's view. This paragraph states: 'An audit includes examination, on a test basis, of evidence relevant to the amounts and disclosures in the financial statements' (APB, 1993, SAS 600, Example 2). Given the swing away from testing, and the additional emphasis being given to the assessment of risk and high-level controls, it may now be appropriate to reconsider this wording.

Not everyone is in agreement with the extent to which some of these developments have been taken. One person considered that 'transactions are key. If you ignore transactions you are getting away from your responsibilities. This is taking risk too far, which is what we are not prepared to do.' It is clear that each firm has had to formulate its own view in deriving an audit strategy to obtain sufficient appropriate audit evidence, and it is clear that there is a debate within the profession regarding the nature and extent of the audit evidence required by the auditor.

The decrease in the reliance on detailed substantive testing also has implications in relation to statistical sampling. The 1970s saw the growth in statistical sampling and statistical approaches to auditing – recent developments mean that these have now been almost eliminated. Even with the reductions in sample sizes which occurred in the 1980s, firms would claim that there was an underlying statistical basis for their samples. Now, with most firms, there is little pretence at the statistical approach to auditing. One person whose firm did use 'an essentially statistical method' considered that they 'tend to find statistical theory more helpful in planning sample sizes and choosing the sample, rather than in the evaluation process . . . [as] you do need judgement for this'. Even this person considered that 'statistical evaluation was not that useful at the end of the day'. The main advantages of a statistical approach were seen as 'ensuring comparability across the firm', and that it 'makes some people think about what they should be thinking about when selecting a sample'. Another person stated: 'If we resort to sampling it is only on a statistical basis.' However, this 'was relatively infrequently used. Often enough confidence comes from the controls and analytical review.' When samples were conducted, most interviewees considered that efforts were made to ensure that they were representative of the whole population – though this did not necessarily mean that they were selected on a statistical basis. In general, there appears to have been a swing away from quantitative approaches to auditing. Without a statistical basis, it would now be very difficult for auditors to try to specify any sort of confidence levels to underpin their opinions – this may reflect the essentially judgemental nature of the external audit, and, in one person's view, that 'auditing is an art form'. Another reason for abandoning a claim to a statistical approach could be the current litigious atmosphere. After all, if, under scrutiny, a 'statistical' approach was found to be faulty, this would obviously damage an auditor's defence.

With tighter and tighter reporting deadlines (especially with major companies), the auditors have had to rethink the timing of their work. Market pressures mean that directors want to report their results as soon after their year end as possible. In order to cope with this, auditors have tended to adopt a 'hard-close' approach. Therefore, if a company has a 31 December year end, the auditors essentially carry out their detailed audit work on the figures at the end of November and then roll forward the accounting data to the end of December. This enables results to be published earlier than otherwise would be possible. In this situation, timeliness appears to be taking priority over 'precision'.

Overall, it can be seen that a number of fundamental changes have been identified as having occurred in recent years. Underlying all this has been a growing sense of crisis. The ever-present pressures on auditors have meant, in the words of one interviewee, that 'developments have been accelerated by market forces, driving auditors into more and more desperate ways of increasing efficiency'. Another person expressed his unease as follows: 'My biggest concern is whether an audit, as currently designed, is appropriate. . . . The big problem with audit is, unlike other services, it is not for the benefit of the directors. . . . Therefore, a cost benefit analysis can never be done properly.' This comment was reinforced by another person who posed the question: 'Does the independent audit have a future?'

ASSURANCE SERVICES

In view of these concerns, auditors have been trying to 'add value' to the external audit (Steen, 1989). Initially, it seemed that auditors were trying to give themselves a competitive edge by trying to distinguish their services from those of the other firms. Examples of 'adding value' include bench-marking, keeping management informed about developments in their business sector, and advice on foreign currency management, treasury issues and stock management. Such developments did cause concern regarding auditor independence (Hatherly, 1989). Some auditors considered that this was simply a formalization of what had been happening in the past, but, strictly speaking, it was not part of the audit – it was part of the auditor–client relationship.

In a way, the emphasis on assurance services could be seen as an extension of this attempt to add value to the audit. Elliott (1994; 1995) advocated the recognition of customer needs and emphasized the decision usefulness of information. Whereas 'adding value' could be seen to be giving more to management, 'assurance services attempt to help decision makers (who might not be clients) arrive at optimum decisions' (Elliott Committee, 1997a: 7). The Elliott Committee defined assurance services as 'independent professional services that improve the quality of information, or its context, for decision makers' (p. 1). It contended: 'Assurance services help people make better decisions by improving information available to them' (p. 2). It would appear that the audit is trying to realign itself with the decision-usefulness approaches so espoused by the accounting standard-setters. The Elliott Committee identified the opportunity to provide assurance services in relation to:

- risk assessments (e.g. profiling an entity's business risk);
- business performance measurements (including both financial and non-financial); and
- information systems reliability – 'this service represents a major step in a migration path that will eventually lead to real-time assurance on on-line data base systems' (1997b: 3).

These services may seem very similar to the provision of the non-audit services that have given rise to the debate about the auditor's independence, but

> CPAs [Certified Public Accountants] presently are involved in limited aspects of these three assurance services in conjunction with the performance of an audit. The new services represent extensions (though substantial extensions) of current activities. And the

intersection of the three services represents a possibly new account-
ability domain into which today's financial reporting/auditing model
might migrate. (Elliott Committee, 1997b: 2–3)

Such an approach would require a customer focus (Elliott and Pallais, 1997a) and would also require the building of acceptance to such changes, the creation of measurement criteria, and the bringing of such products to the market place (Elliott and Pallais, 1997b). Kelly (1997: 10) reports an Ernst & Young partner talking of an 'assurance revolution', with auditors starting to look way beyond the statutory financial statements. These developments could eventually lead to the next generation of audit.

CONTINUOUS AUDIT – THE FIFTH-GENERATION AUDIT?

Traditionally, independent assurance was viewed as resulting from the conflict of interest between preparers and users, the consequence of information to users, the complexity of subject matter and audit process, and the remoteness of users from subject matter and the preparers (AAA, 1973: 11). The CICA (1999: 3) considered that '[t]hese conditions will continue to prevail in the digital economy, and will spur the growth of opportunities for independent auditors to provide assurance on new information needs'. As a result of the technological revolution, there is now talk of 'continuous audit' and 'continuous assurance'. The Elliott Committee (1997) discussed 'a set of real time financial and non-financial information accompanied by continuous assurance (to clients and possibly to the public)' (cited in ASB [US], 1997, Initiative A: 1).

Information technology is making the continuous performance of audit
procedures more practical and cost effective than in the past.
Performance of continuous audit procedures will permit auditors to
obtain evidence to support more timely and eventually continuous
assurance on information. (ASB [US], 1997, Initiative A: 1)

'A continuous audit is a methodology that enables independent auditors to provide written assurance on a subject matter using a series of auditors' reports issued simultaneously with, or a short period of time after, the occurrence of events underlying the subject matter' (CICA, 1999: 5). The CICA continued, 'a continuous audit is defined by both the desire to release audited information at frequent intervals and by the short length of time between the availability of the completed subject matter for audit and the release of related information with the auditors' report on it' (CICA, 1999: 10):

> In some cases, management may want audited information to be released on a real-time basis. In these situations, there would be virtually no delay between the occurrence of events underlying the subject matter, the availability of the complete subject matter for audit, the performance of the audit and the release of the information and the auditors' report on it. (CICA, 1999: 11)

In order for 'continuous audit' to be effective, the client would have to have a highly automated process that would require only the minimum of human intervention (CICA, 1999: 12) (that is, hard data rather than soft data, which is dependent on assumptions and judgements). 'Continuous audit' would also be dependent on the reliability of clients' systems and effective controls. Auditors may be able to monitor their clients' systems on a real-time basis with embedded audit modules (EAMs) – subroutines set up by the auditors. 'The EAMs work within an entity's application programs to perform audit procedures concurrently with normal application processing' (CICA, 1999: 54). Exception reports could then highlight unusual transactions, such as errors and anomalies. The CICA considered these developments to be a long-term goal.

The development of 'continuous audit' does raise a number of questions. Firstly, who should be responsible for continuous assurance? Is it the internal auditors or the external auditors? If the external auditors are trying to 'add value' to their audit, it is understandable that they would want to be involved with the 'continuous audit'. However, given the nature of the work, it would have seemed natural for the internal auditors to have adopted it as part of their work. Secondly, what sort of assurance can be given? 'The performance of more continuous audit procedures also is related to the trend toward testing effectiveness of processes rather than testing the results' (ASB [US], 1997, Initiative A: 1). Therefore, the auditors could monitor the working of the system on a real-time basis. Whether real-time figures per se would have much meaning is problematic; this issue is discussed further in Chapter 8. Thirdly, if the focus is very much on the contents of the real-time system, where does that leave the financial statements and all the effort and debate relating to the inclusion of current values and net present values?

CONCLUSION

The refocusing of auditors on assurance services could almost be classified as an audit revolution. The recognition of the limited usefulness of the financial statements for decision making appears to have resulted in the auditors trying to extend the remit of their work. Whether this is to provide a service to the stakeholders in general or simply to protect their position is problematic: 'assurance services will help accountants adapt to the evolving practice environment and sustain their contribution to society on into the future' (Elliott, 1998: 7).

For the past twenty years, auditors have been seeking less and less audit evidence from detailed substantive testing. Better accounting systems and the greater use of IT by clients has meant that very few material transaction errors are being discovered by external auditors. Therefore, audit emphasis is increasingly being switched away from the detailed examination of the routine processing of transactions and on to the corporate control culture and the potential of risk. Due to the pressure that auditors face, it appears that they have been reassessing what the audit is trying to achieve, and this has resulted in an extensive questioning of how it should be done. Therefore, it is suggested that it may be possible to view developments in terms of a change from audit efficiency to audit effectiveness. There has been a resurgence in the emphasis on judgement – judgement regarding the assessment of risks and controls, judgement regarding the interpretation of analytical review, and judgement in relation to any (limited) testing. The focus, by some firms, on the high-level risks and controls, together with the justification of very limited amounts of detailed substantive testing based on their risk analyses and analytical reviews, has completely altered previous conceptions of the external audit. It is clear that external auditors are going through a period of immense uncertainty; as to the outcome of this, only time will tell.

DISCUSSION QUESTIONS

1   The need for the external audit of limited companies is often questioned. What would you say are the factors that currently bring about the need for the external audit?

2   Can an auditor ever be fully confident of having done enough work to support an unqualified audit opinion?

3   In recent years, external auditors have placed much more emphasis on 'high-level' risks. What do you consider constitutes 'high-level' risks and why are they important?

4   How do assurance services differ from the traditional concept of the external audit? Are these services really compatible with the role of the external auditor?

5   What do you see as the advantages and disadvantages of the advent of the 'continuous audit'?

REFERENCES

American Accounting Association (AAA) (1973) Committee on Basic Auditing Concepts, *A Statement of Basic Auditing Concepts*. Sarasota, FL: AAA.

Auditing Practices Board (APB) (1993) *SAS 600 – Auditors' Reports on Financial Statements*, May. London: APB.

Auditing Practices Board (APB) (1995) *Statements of Auditing Standards (SAS 100: Objective and General Principles Governing an Audit of Financial Statements; SAS 110: Fraud and Error. SAS 200: Planning; SAS 210: Knowledge of the Business; SAS 230: Working Papers; SAS 240: Quality Control for Audit Work; SAS 300: Accounting and Internal Control Systems and Audit Risk Assessments; SAS 400: Audit Evidence; SAS 410: Analytical Procedures)*. London: APB.

Auditing Standards Board (ASB [US]) (1997) *Horizons for the Auditing Standards Board: Strategic Initiatives Toward the Twenty-First Century* (1997). New York: AICPA; http://www.aicpa.org/members/div/auditstd/horizon/inita.htm (viewed on 11/9/01).

Beck, G.W. (1973) 'The role of the auditor in modern society: an empirical appraisal', *Accounting and Business Research*, Spring: 117–22.

Bell, T.B., Marrs, F.O., Solomon, I. and Thomas, H. (1997) *Auditing Organizations Through a Strategic-Systems Lens: The KPMG Business Measurement Process*. KPMG Peat Marwick LLP.

Bird, P. (1970) 'The scope of the company audit', *Accounting and Business Research*, Winter: 44–9.

Bourne, H.J. (1887) 'Auditing', *The Accountant*, 4 June: 330–3.

Brown, R.G. (1962) 'Changing audit objectives and techniques', *The Accounting Review*, October: 692–703.

Burton, J.C. and Fairfield, P. (1982) 'Auditing evolution in a changing environment', *Auditing: A Journal of Practice and Theory*, 1 (2): 1–22.

Cadbury Report (1992) Report of the Committee on the Financial Aspects of Corporate Governance. London: Gee & Co.

Canadian Institute of Chartered Accountants (CICA) (1999) *Continuous Auditing*. Toronto: CICA.

Carmichael, D.R. and Whittington, R. (1984) 'The auditor's changing role in financial reporting', *Journal of Accounting and Finance*, 7: 347–61.

Davis, R. (1996) 'Serving the public interest', *True and Fair*, December 1995/January 1996: 6.

Dearing Report (1988) *The Making of Accounting Standards*. London: ICAEW.

Elliott Committee (1997) AICPA Special Committee on Assurance Services: *Report of the Special Committee on Assurance Services*. New York: AICPA. Found on websites: (a) http://aicpa.org/assurance/about/comstud/defncom.htm (viewed on 11/09/01), (b) http://aicpa.org/assurance/about/opportun.htm (viewed on 11/09/01).

Elliott, R.K. (1994) 'Confronting the future: choices for the attest function', *Accounting Horizons*, September: 106–24.

Elliott, R.K. (1995) 'The future of assurance services: implications for academia', *Accounting Horizons*, December: 118–27.

Elliott, R.K. (1998) 'Assurance services and the audit heritage', *Auditing: A Journal of Practice and Theory*, 17 (Supplement): 1–7.

Elliott, R.K. and Pallais, D.M. (1997a) 'Are you ready for new assurance services?', *The Journal of Accountancy*, June: 47–51.

Elliott, R.K. and Pallais, D.M. (1997b) 'To market, to market we go', *The Journal of Accountancy*, September: 81–6.

Flint, D. (1971) 'The role of the auditor in modern society: an explanatory essay', *Accounting and Business Research*, Autumn: 133–51.

Flint, D. (1988) *Philosophy and Principles of Auditing: An Introduction*. Basingstoke: Macmillan Education.

Gwilliam, D. (1987) *A Survey of Auditing Research*. London: Prentice Hall International/ ICAEW.

Hatherly, D.J. (1989) 'Discussion: adding value to the audit', *Auditing and the Future: Proceedings of an Auditing Research Conference*. Edinburgh: ICAEW/ICAS.

Hatherly, D. (1998) 'Is the risk-driven audit too risky?', *Accountancy*, August: 86.

Hein, L.W. (1963) 'The auditor and the British Companies Acts', *Accounting Review*, July: 508–20.

Hicks, Sir J. (1982) 'Limited liability: the pros and cons', in T. Orhnial (ed.), *Limited Liability and the Corporation*. London: Croom Helm.

Kelly, J. (1997) 'A niche in a risky business', *Financial Times*, 28 August: 10.

KPMG (1999) *The Financial Statement Audit: Why a New Age Requires an Evolving Methodology*. New York: KPMG LLP.

Lee, T.A. (1969) 'An inquiry into the nature and objectives relevant to the external audits of UK limited companies', unpublished MSc thesis, University of Strathclyde.

Lee, T.A. (1972) *Company Auditing: Concepts and Practices*. Edinburgh: ICAS.

Lee, T.A. (1986) *Company Auditing* (3rd edn). Wokingham: Van Nostrand Reinhold (UK).

Lemon, W.M., Tatum, K.W. and Turley, W.S. (2000) *Developments in the Audit Methodologies of Large Accounting Firms*. London: ABG Professional Information.

Littleton, A.C. (1933) *Accounting Evolution to 1900*. New York: American Institute Publishing Co.

Mautz, R.K. and Sharaf, H.A. (1961) *The Philosophy of Auditing*, American Accounting Association Monograph No. 6. Sarasota, FL: AAA.

Panel on Audit Effectiveness (2000) *Report and Recommendations*. Stamford, CT: Public Oversight Board.

Pincus, K.V., Bernardi, R.A. and Ludwig, S.E. (1999) 'Audit effectiveness versus audit efficiency: are the two in conflict?', *International Journal of Auditing*, 3: 121–33.

Pratt, M.J. and Van Peursem, K. (1993) 'Towards a conceptual framework for auditing', *Accounting Education*, 2 (1): 11–32.

Sherer, M. and Kent, D. (1983) *Auditing and Accountability*. London: Pitman Books.

Steen, D.M.C.E. (1989) 'Adding value to the audit', *Auditing and the Future: Proceedings of an Auditing Research Conference*. Edinburgh: ICAEW/ICAS.

Turley, S. and Cooper, M. (1991) *Auditing in the United Kingdom*. Hemel Hempstead: Prentice Hall/ICAEW.

Vanasco, R.R. (1998) 'Fraud auditing', *Managerial Auditing Journal*, 13 (1): 4–71.

Winograd, B.N., Gerson, J.S. and Berlin, B.L. (2000) 'Audit practices of PricewaterhouseCoopers', *Auditing: A Journal of Practice and Theory*, 19 (2): 175–82.

6 The Management–Auditor Relationship: Auditing Motivations

What people call impartiality may simply mean indifference, and what people call partiality may simply mean mental activity.

— G.K. Chesterton

B oth accounting and auditing are often considered to be technical subjects. However, this perception of technical precision tends to undermine the complexities of external reporting and the real nature of the management–auditor relationship. When businesses collapse soon after the publication of an unqualified set of accounts, or frauds go undetected by the auditors, the initial reaction is often that the auditors have failed in their duties and have thus been negligent. If accounting and auditing were simply technical subjects, each with a set of rules to prescribe what should be done, these reactions would be understandable. However, this totally ignores the subjective nature of the financial statements, the motivations of management and the multitude of judgements required by both management and auditors in the course of the preparation of the financial statements. Long gone are the days when auditors primarily concentrated on the accounting system and the accounting records. There is increasing recognition that to understand the figures in the financial statements it is necessary to attempt to understand what management is trying to achieve.

The crux of the management–auditor relationship is often viewed in terms of the independence and objectivity of the auditors. However, in order to form an independent and objective view of something, the auditors need to be aware of it. This chapter argues that external auditing should be viewed in terms of the audit of management's motivations. By appreciating this, it is then possible to understand the magnitude of the problems encountered by the auditors in the course of the audit.

INDEPENDENCE AND OBJECTIVITY

One would have thought that the independence of the auditor is central to the audit process. If an auditor is not independent, one would presume that the audit is a waste of time and that the figures in the financial statements may be meaningless. However, Antle (1984: 1) considered that 'the phrase "auditor independence" traditionally has had no precise meaning' and '[t]he academic literature on the subject also seems hopelessly ambiguous'. The AICPA (1993) considered that there were two elements to independence, namely, independence in fact and independence in appearance – the former being the mental attitude of the auditor and the latter referring to the perception of the auditor by a reasonable observer. The ICAEW, in its *Guide to Professional Ethics*, defines objectivity:

> *Objectivity is essential for any professional person exercising pro-*
> *fessional judgement. . . . Objectivity is the state of mind which has*
> *regard to all considerations relevant to the task in hand but no other.*
> *It is sometimes described as 'independence of mind'. (ICAEW, 2001,*
> *s.1.201: para. 2)*

Lee (1993: 98) considered that 'it is exceedingly difficult to give operational meaning to what is essentially a state of mind'. He continued, 'at least there is general agreement that independence is an attitude of mind which does not allow the viewpoints or conclusions of the corporate auditor to become reliant on or subordinate to the influences and pressure of conflicting interests'.

The ability of the auditors to remain independent has been challenged (Briloff, 1972, 1981, 1986, 1990; Mitchell et al., 1991; Sikka, 1997; Sikka and Willmott, 1995). In the competitive climate of the late 1980s, accountancy 'firms engaged in creative accounting and rule avoidance (Smith, 1992). . . . The chairman of Coopers and Lybrand was bold enough to state that "there is an industry developing, and we are part of it, in [accounting] standards avoid-ance" (*Accountancy Age*, 19 July 1990, p. 1)' (Sikka and Willmott, 1995: 566). Sikka and Willmott (1995) contended that the profession was more concerned with securing and keeping 'jurisdiction' over the audit than with 'inde-pendence'. This may raise a question about audit quality – 'the intensification of commercial pressures to take short cuts in the audit process coincided with major corporate frauds. . . . These collapses and scandals inevitably raised doubts about auditor independence and objectivity, especially as fraud had been suspected at BCCI, Maxwell, Polly Peck, International Signal and Control (ISC), Levitt and other cases' (Sikka and Willmott, 1995: 556).

Impediments to independence are often viewed in terms of financial considerations or personal relationships. Beattie et al. (1999: 68) identified four themes:

- economic dependence of the auditor on the client
- audit market competition
- the provision of non-audit services (NAS)
- the regulatory framework.

Beattie et al. (1999: 103) found that '[t]he principal threat factors relate to economic dependence and NAS provision'. The Elliott Committee (1997) conceded that it was not always easy to distinguish between consulting and assurance services, and stated:

> The difference between consulting and assurance services is based on the goal of the engagement: consulting services focus on outcomes; assurance services focus on decision-makers and the information they use. Consulting services are designed to improve the client's condition directly. Assurance services attempt to help decision makers (who might not be clients) arrive at optimum decisions. (p. 7)

Responses to the threat to the auditors' independence have included professional ethics guidance (for example, ICAEW, 2001: 1.201) and, through the corporate governance system, the greater use of audit committees. In 1997, the Independence Standards Board (ISB) was established in the USA as a joint effort between the SEC and AICPA. Its objective was to provide guidelines for improving the quality of audits – but its most significant aim was to develop a conceptual framework for auditor independence. The ISB produced three standards and much of this work was incorporated in November 2000 into the SEC's auditor independence rules; consequently, in July 2001, the ISB was abolished.

So while independence of mind is key to forming a judgement about the contents of the financial statements (both on individual items and overall), for these threats to independence to affect this judgement, auditors must first have identified something on which their view may be biased. This is not always as easy as it may seem. By definition, most criticisms of auditors come with hindsight. The complexity of modern corporations and thus their audit should not be underestimated.

AUDITING MOTIVATIONS

One of the most fundamental of all auditing skills is to anticipate the way that management is going to present the data in the financial statements. Not only does the auditor need to understand the client's business, industry and accounting system, but the auditor must also be aware of the motivations which drive management's actions – thus, external auditing could be viewed as the audit of motivations. Unless the auditors (and presumably users) understand why management has done something, it is probably not really possible to understand the financial statements themselves. Management's motivations provide the driving force behind the way the financial statements are prepared and presented. These motivations may range from the meeting of profit targets (so as to satisfy City expectations or the achievements of personal bonuses) to ensuring the survival of the business. Motivational aspects permeate the whole production of the financial statements. The financial statements are a function not only of the 'economic' activity of the business (such as sales, production and purchases) but also of motivations and the levels of discretionary expenditure allowed. It is important that users appreciate this.

If management intends to smooth profits, even auditors admit that this is very difficult for them to detect. The treatment of an item in the financial statements may be acceptable, questionable or unacceptable, depending on the motivations. For example, the imminent return at the year-end of faulty goods would require a provision. However, if by some good fortune, at a later date, the customer had been persuaded to keep the goods, then the following year the provision could be released and management would be applauded for having acted prudently. But if management had colluded with the external customer – encouraging him to threaten to return the goods, this would be very difficult for the auditor to detect. If this was because the directors had achieved their targets for the current year's bonuses and wanted to ensure the following year's bonuses, their actions would be regarded as unacceptable. However, what if they wished to smooth their profits in order to ensure the renewal of a loan and thus the continuation of the business? This action would certainly be questionable – even though the directors, if discovered, would claim that they were acting in the best interests of the shareholders. Yet, it is difficult for the auditor to establish management's motivations. It could be argued that a particular treatment should be trying to reflect the underlying reality (that is, representational faithfulness), but, given the subjectivities involved in the preparation of the financial statements, this may be problematic.

In recent years, greater prominence has been given to the recognition that financial statements contain inherent uncertainties and involve the use of accounting estimates. *SAS 420* gives the following as examples of accounting estimates:

- *allowances to reduce stocks and debtors to their estimated realisable value;*
- *depreciation provisions;*
- *accrued revenue;*
- *provision for deferred taxation;*
- *provision for a loss from a lawsuit;*
- *profits or losses on construction contracts in progress; and*
- *provisions to meet warranty claims. (APB, 1995c: para. 3)*

Given the subjective elements in the financial statements, the problem for the auditor is that bias is inextricably linked to a management's motivations. It may be argued that if bias exists, it is unlikely to be material. However, according to *SAS 220*, '[a] matter is material if its omission would reasonably influence the decisions of an addressee of the auditors' report' (APB, 1995b, para. 3). Therefore, as deliberate bias would be a complete waste of time and effort if it was not intended to influence users, by this definition, all deliberate bias would seem to be material.

With the adoption of risk-based audit approaches, auditors have increasingly concentrated on areas that pose the greatest danger of their arriving at an incorrect audit opinion. In recent years, some auditors have increasingly focused on the integrity of their clients. Auditors have always needed a healthy degree of scepticism; however, there is now a growing recognition that a major audit risk comes from a client's top management. Sudden company collapses (particularly those that result from fraud) have been seen to arise from the actions and motivations of senior executives, rather than through failures of low-level internal controls. Consequently, increasing audit emphasis is now being placed on the examination of senior management's attitude to control and the strength of a company's overall control environment. Therefore, central to the interpretation of a set of financial statements, is an understanding of the motivations behind the figures. Consideration has now started to be given to the possible assessment of management's motivations by external auditors (Panel on Audit Effectiveness, 2000: 87).

EARNINGS MANAGEMENT

As long ago as 1953, Hepworth suggested that companies may intentionally smooth the income figures that are reported in the financial statements. The reasons cited for this included reducing tax payments and the maintenance of good relations with investors and employees (if a corporation had a very good year, investors and employees would want a share of this and then they would be disappointed if this performance did not continue). Gordon (1964) maintained that smoothing was in fact an appropriate business objective. In 1973, Beidleman reported: 'Our results confirm smoothing of reported income as an observed practice and one that is engaged in by a majority of the sample firms' (p. 667). Givoly and Ronen (1981: 175) considered that '[c]onceptually, smoothing can be viewed as a form of signalling whereby managers use their discretion over the choice among accounting alternatives within generally accepted accounting principles so as to minimise fluctuations of earnings over time around the trend they believe best reflects their view of investors' expectations of the company's future performance'.

Eckel (1981) described two types of intentional management smoothing – 'real smoothing' and 'artificial smoothing'. Real smoothing 'represents management actions undertaken to control underlying economic events' (p. 29). In other words, management would undertake an actual transaction, or not as the case may be, based on the smoothing effect it would have on reported income. An area where this is possible is discretionary expenditure, such as the level of marketing expenditure incurred in a particular period. It can be seen that this type of smoothing is likely to affect the cash flows. Artificial smoothing 'represents accounting manipulations undertaken by management to smooth income. These manipulations do not represent underlying economic events or affect cash flows, but shift costs and/or revenues from one period to another' (Eckel, 1981: 29). This can come about because of the nature of accounting estimates.

The components of the financial statements can generally be classified as arising from accounting transactions or accounting estimates. Examples of accounting transactions would be purchases of raw materials or fixed assets, sales of finished goods, an expense for the leasing of a warehouse, etc. These transactions can be said either to happen or not. The subjectivity required to deal with such items is at a minimum. In fact, '[a]ccountants have always derived satisfaction from the fact that most of their measurements are transactions based' (Solomons, 1989: 34–5). Accounting estimates, however, require the exercise of a great amount of judgement and can be very subjective. Provisions for bad debts, return of sales, and stock write-downs are all examples of accounting estimates, or, to be more precise, management's judgement of the accounting estimates. It is the uncertainties associated with these accounting estimates that mean there is no one 'right' figure for the amount of profit reported in a particular accounting period (e.g., Parfet, 2000; APB, 2001).

The ASOBAT (AAA, 1966: 29) recognized that 'the influence of management on financial representations to external users may produce bias, since corporate management is naturally interested in representing itself to outsiders in as favorable a light as is possible'. However, management is probably a little more sophisticated than this implies. It is possible that directors consider it more important to be 'in control' of the figures than to present as favourable a picture as possible. Management not only manages the business, but it is also in a position to manage information about the business. Management has a keen interest in the picture that is presented to the outside world. 'Earnings management occurs when managers use judgment in financial reporting and in structuring transactions to alter financial reports to either mislead some stakeholders about the underlying economic performance of the company or to influence contractual outcomes that depend on reported accounting numbers' (Healy and Wahlen, 1999: 368). It is important to remember that bias can arise from the transactions that a business may or may not undertake and about which the auditors can do very little. Companies' reported earnings figures have become increasingly important to management:

> In recent years there have been numerous instances of the price of a company's stock dropping precipitously when the company failed to meet analysts' earnings forecasts by only a penny or two a share, or failed to meet their revenue forecasts. The Chairman and the Chief Accountant of the SEC, among others, have expressed concerns that some entities may have been 'managing' their earnings inappropriately (often referred to as 'earnings management') in order to meet analysts' forecasts and thereby avoid a precipitous drop in the share price of their stock. They also have expressed concern that auditors have not challenged these actions, but instead have 'waived' known potential misstatements of earnings or revenue because the amounts involved were quantitatively immaterial. (Panel on Audit Effectiveness, 2000: 56)

The Blue Ribbon Committee (1999: 1076) considered that 'some companies do respond to analysts and short-term market pressures by "managing" their earnings'; it continued, '[w]hilst earnings management is not necessarily inappropriate, it can become abusive when it obscures the true financial performance of the company'. This committee highlighted various earnings management practices:

- 'deliberately overstating one-time "big bath" restructuring charges in order to provide a cushion to satisfy future . . . [stock market] earnings estimates'
- misuse of acquisition accounting with improper write-offs so as to overstate future earnings
- overaccruals in good times in order to smooth out future earnings in bad times
- premature revenue recognition

- 'improper deferral of expenses to improve reported results'
- 'misuse of the concept of materiality to mask inappropriate accounting treatments'. (Blue Ribbon Committee, 1999: 1077)

Another factor that could induce management to smooth a company's reported earnings is the existence of a bonus plan. Watts and Zimmerman (1986: 208) report the bonus plan hypothesis: '*Ceteris paribus*, managers of firms with bonus plans are more likely to choose accounting procedures that shift reported earnings from future periods to the current period.' Bringing forward profit means that management receives the bonus earlier than it would otherwise. However, if the bonus plan has an upper limit, then once the company has achieved the profit to satisfy the highest bonus payment, there is an incentive to defer income to later periods and thus increase future bonuses. But if the company has made a loss, or has failed to reach the target figure for the payment of a bonus, there could be a temptation for managers to take a 'big bath', that is, recognize as many future losses and provisions as possible so that the company has one very bad year, and thus future earnings would be higher and allow for increased future bonuses.

Smith (1992) and Griffiths (1995) have discussed the ways in which companies have been able to manipulate their reported figures. Aggressive earnings management is now being recognized as a problem in the UK (APB, 2001), however, all this would seem to bring into question the neutrality concept espoused by the financial accounting standard-setters.

THE 'NEUTRALITY' CONCEPT

The concept of 'neutrality' or 'freedom from bias' is to be found in most discussions on the development of a conceptual framework for financial reporting. It can be traced from the American Accounting Association's '*A tentative statement of accounting principles affecting corporate reports*' (AAA, 1936) to the present day. This discussion of accounting conventions (AAA, 1936: 188) considered that '[i]t should still be possible to agree upon a foundation of underlying considerations which will tend to eliminate random variations in accounting procedures resulting not from the peculiarities of the individual enterprises, but rather from the varying ideas of financiers and corporate executives as to what will be expedient, plausible, or persuasive to investors at any given point of time'.

Paton and Littleton (1940) did not explicitly identify an accounting convention of neutrality, but did identify a range of important users of accounts as including investors, employers, government, and the general public. On the basis that '[t]he responsibilities of corporate administration extend widely in several directions' (p. 2), they argued that '[t]hrough bias in favour of one interest or prejudice against another, inequitable results may follow' (pp. 2–3). They went on to argue that the codification of accounting concepts (they use the term 'standards') was a means of reducing bias in the financial statements.

As was seen in Chapter 4, the AAA (1966: 7) used the term 'freedom from bias' as one of its accounting standards. As justification for this concept it is observed:

> The standard of freedom from bias is advocated because of the many users accounting serves and the many uses to which it may be put. The presence of bias which may serve the needs of one set of users cannot be assumed to aid or even leave unharmed the interests of others. It is conceivable that biased information could properly be introduced if it would aid one group without injuring the position of any other, but this conclusion cannot be reached with certainty in external reporting, where all potential users must be considered. (AAA, 1966: 11)

The Trueblood Report argued (AICPA, 1973: 58):

> While any information affected by judgments necessarily has some bias there should be no purposeful bias favoring any group. Absence of bias, which may be characterized as neutrality and fairness, has long been recognized in accounting, although the perception of what is neutral and fair has changed with the times and the needs.

The report goes on to argue that '[c]onservatism for its own sake may actually introduce bias' (AICPA, 1973: 59); furthermore:

> If financial statements do communicate information about varying degrees of uncertainty, about the judgements made and the interpretations applied, and about the underlying factual information, then the impact of surprises – pleasant or unpleasant – will diminish greatly. This should result in a substantial lessening in the belief that conservatism is essential.

Solomons (1989: 36) defined neutrality as 'the absence of bias intended to influence users to draw a pre-determined conclusion'. He argued that the credibility of financial reports would be diminished if it was known that some information was biased. It has been seen that the IASC considered neutrality to be a characteristic of reliability: 'Financial statements are not neutral if, by the selection or presentation of information, they influence the making of a decision or judgement in order to achieve a predetermined result or outcome' (IASC, 1989: para. 36). The ASB (1999) stated:

> The information provided by financial statements needs to be neutral – in other words, free from deliberate or systematic bias. Financial information is not neutral if it has been selected or presented in such a way as to influence the making of a decision or judgement in order to achieve a predetermined result or outcome. (para. 3.15)

While management may have an interest in issuing financial statements that will be credible, supported by both an audit opinion and by working within a recognized accounting framework, there are a range of factors within that framework that might create bias in management's choice of accounting practice. Examples include bonus plans based on accounting profits, debt covenants based on reported equity and borrowing figures, joint ventures where the published accounts are the basis for profit sharing agreements, and contracts where prices are based on a cost plus basis (Whittred et al., 1996). Prakash and Rappaport (1977) used the term 'information inductance' to describe the process by which the behaviour of individuals is affected by information they are required to communicate. Taylor and Turley (1986: 100) considered that 'management's choice of accounting policies may be based upon an anticipation of economic consequences: either in order to avoid undesirable consequences (on their remuneration or their firms' operations, for example) or in order to achieve desirable consequences (for example, a subsidy from government)'. Therefore, it seems that there is some evidence to indicate that management is not indifferent to the setting of accounting standards, and that it may not be neutral when it comes to choosing accounting policies.

The motives behind off-balance sheet financing were examined by Peasnell and Yaansah (1988: 17), who considered that the possible prime motivation was to misinform the capital markets: 'Misinformation is not meant to imply false information but rather "incomplete" information which might result in actions or non-actions by investors or creditors that are different from those which might have resulted had "complete" information been available.' They also suggested that misinformation may, in fact, be market induced; that is, if companies are judged by particular ratio benchmarks, and a business does not conform, managers may fear that their firm's share price will be under-valued. Management, therefore, faces pressure to conform to industry norms, and '[t]here can be little doubt that many managers worry about such matters' (p. 19). Indeed, Hines (1988; 1991) looked on accounting neutrality as a myth. Therefore, if management has ulterior motivations in the preparation and presentation of the financial statements, this can lead to conflict with the auditors.

MANAGEMENT–AUDITOR NEGOTIATIONS

As the discussions between the auditors and their clients are not in the public view, there is only limited evidence of the negotiations that take place:

> Under Generally Accepted Auditing Standards, the literal claim is that financial statements are the representation of management. Our view of the auditing process, however, focuses on its negotiated character. Financial statements should be read as a joint statement from the auditor and manager. The statement becomes a joint venture if the auditor is unwilling to provide an unqualified opinion on management's stated representations. At that point, the auditor and the client begin negotiations in which the auditor may offer a revised statement. (Antle and Nalebuff, 1991: 31)

As the result of a disagreement, the audit may be extended, and threats may be made by the client, but '[i]n the end, compromises are usually found, statements are revised, and the auditor issues an unqualified opinion on the revised statements' (Antle and Nalebuff, 1991: 31). Lev (1979: 166) points out that there is an implicit 'bargaining process' in audit conflict situations – about which very little is known.

> Much of the empirical auditor–client conflict research draws on the routinism argument developed by Nichols and Price (1976) based upon Emerson's (1962) power-dependency relationships. They assert that the more structured or routine an audit engagement, one in which either or both the accounting and auditing standards are more tightly specified, the better will be the auditor to resist client pressure to acquiesce. (Lindsay, 1992: 345)

Beattie et al. (2000; 2001) examined the discussions and negotiations between the auditors and the directors, finding 'the audit process [to be] . . . a

continuing co-operative and consensual process, where problems are identified and addressed as they arise' (2000: 198). They considered that generally
'[t]he process benefits from a good working relationship between the parties
which is based on mutual understanding of each other's role'. While commercial considerations were seen to be key for the directors, the auditors were
concerned with compliance with the regulatory framework – thus giving rise
on occasion to negotiations about accounting treatments and presentation.
Auditors were found to consult with their firm on difficult matters, and
'[a]udit committees are generally viewed as a valuable support mechanism
from within the company' (2000: 198).

AUDIT COMMITTEES

In the USA during the late 1970s and early 1980s, the efforts of the Securities
and Exchange Commission (SEC) and the New York Stock Exchange led to
widespread adoption of audit committees (Knapp, 1987: 579). The Cohen
Commission (AICPA, 1978: 106) envisaged a role for the audit committee, and
this was reinforced by the Treadway Commission (1987: 183), which stated:
'An audit committee consisting of independent directors is the primary
vehicle that the board of directors uses to discharge its responsibility with
respect to the company's financial reporting.' In the UK, following the
Cadbury Report (1992), the audit committee has become a key element in the
corporate governance structure – most public limited companies in the UK
now have one (Conyon, 1995). The *Cadbury Report* regarded 'the appointment
of properly constituted audit committees as an important step in raising
standards of corporate governance' (1992: 30). Reviewing the various definitions of an audit committee, Spira (1998: 30) considered that 'such definitions
agree that the audit committee is a board sub-committee of (predominantly)
non-executive directors (NEDs) concerned with audit, internal control and
financial reporting matters'. Audit committees may be thought to:

(a) *improve the quality of financial reporting, by reviewing the
financial statements on behalf of the Board;*

(b) *create a climate of discipline and control which will reduce the
opportunity for fraud;*

(c) *enable non-executive directors to contribute an independent
judgement and play a positive role;*

(d) *help the finance director, by providing a forum in which he can
raise issues of concern, and which he can use to get things done
which might otherwise be difficult;*

(e) *strengthen the position of the external auditor, by providing a channel of communication and forum for issues of concern;*

(f) *provide a framework within which the external auditor can assert his independence in the event of a dispute with management;*

(g) *strengthen the position of the internal audit function, by providing a greater degree of independence from management;*

(h) *increase public confidence in the credibility and objectivity of financial statements. (Cadbury Report, 1992: 68–9)*

The Blue Ribbon Committee (1999: 1070–1) stressed that 'it is not the role of the audit committee to prepare financial statements or engage in the myriad of decisions relating to the preparation of those statements'. The role of the audit committee was 'one of oversight and monitoring', and the division of responsibilities was specified as follows:

> *Management is principally responsible for company accounting policies and the preparation of the financial statements. The outside auditor is responsible for auditing and attesting to the company's financial statements and evaluating the company's system of internal controls. The audit committee, as the delegate of the full board, is responsible for overseeing the entire process. (Blue Ribbon Committee, 1999: 1084)*

The 1990s saw a growth in the number of companies (particularly larger companies) with audit committees. In the early days, audit committees 'didn't understand and didn't care' (this was the view expressed by one person who was interviewed as part of the study reported in the previous chapter). However, as a result of corporate collapses in the early 1990s, as well as the greater recognition of corporate governance, this person considered that they now 'take the job more seriously'. It is now usual for the auditor to have a meeting with the audit committee before the commencement of the audit. The objective of such a meeting is to discuss the audit strategy with the committee. The auditor would also have at least one other meeting before the financial statements were approved. It was considered that the audit committee had improved the auditor's ability to communicate with clients, but at a price. These meetings have resulted in more work for the auditor, as more effort was required to produce more documentation. Beattie et al. (2000: 178) found: 'Audit committees generally reduce the level of negotiation and increase the level of discussion, suggesting that the overall degree of confrontation declines.'

However, '[a] review of the literature suggests that the claimed advantages of audit committees are not always realized in practice and that the support for audit committees is based upon anecdotal information on their effectiveness rather than objective evidence' (Collier, 1997: 79). It must be remembered that 'a corporation having an audit committee as part of its governance structure and having an effective audit committee are, of course, different matters' (Sommer, 1991: 91). Kalbers and Fogarty (1993: 24) reported that 'little empirical research has been conducted to investigate the effectiveness of audit committees and the factors associated with effectiveness'. In a later study, Kalbers and Fogarty (1998: 145) suggest 'that changes in the structure of corporate governance may be primarily symbolic'. Collier (1997: 81) suggests why audit committees may not be effective:

- Their establishment may be merely to provide the appearance of monitoring.
- Non-executive directors may not, in fact, be independent.
- There may be deficiencies in their operation.
- The whole idea may be flawed.

Given these concerns, the usefulness of the audit committee in assisting with auditor independence may be questionable. They may be able to support an auditor's stance once something has been discovered. However, as it is not the audit committee's role to produce the financial statements, it also needs to be aware of the motivations of management that may be behind the figures.

AUDITORS AND FRAUD

While the detection of management fraud may have been a primary objective of the external audit in Victorian times, the current position is that the auditors plan their work in such a way as to have a reasonable expectation of detecting material frauds (*SAS 110*). Porter (1997: 45) points out that '[t]he Companies Act 1985 does not mention auditors having a duty to detect fraud'. She considered that 'it may be presumed that any responsibility the auditor may have for detecting corporate fraud relates to his or her duty to form an opinion on the truth and fairness of the financial statements and/or on the adequacy of the accounting records and information and explanations received'.

However, there is a problem regarding what is meant by the word 'fraud'. Huntington and Davies (1994: 3) point out that 'English law does not define fraud', but on the basis of Buckley J's comments in *Re London and Globe Finance Ltd*, they considered that any fraud would have two essential elements, namely, deception or concealment, and deprival or loss to the victim. This is in line with French's (1985: 128) definition of 'fraud' as: 'Deception, either by stating what is false or by suppressing what is true, in order to induce a person to give up something of value.' Comer (1985: 439), however, considered fraud to be '[a]ny behaviour by which one person intends to gain a dishonest advantage over another', and that '[a] fraud may not be a crime'. This would seem to be a somewhat wider interpretation of the meaning of the word 'fraud'.

In terms of external auditing, the Auditing Practices Board viewed fraud as comprising 'both the use of deception to obtain an unjust or illegal financial advantage and intentional misrepresentations affecting the financial statements by one or more individuals among management, employees, or third parties' (*SAS 110*, para. 4). It considered that fraud could involve:

- *falsification or alteration of accounting records or other documents;*
- *misappropriation of assets or theft;*
- *suppression or omission of the effects of transactions from records or documents;*
- *recording of transactions without substance;*
- *intentional misapplication of accounting policies; or*
- *wilful misrepresentation of transactions or of an entity's state of affairs. (SAS 110, para. 4)*

SAS 110 (APB, 1995a: para. 3) also pointed out: 'It is for the court to determine in a particular instance whether fraud has occurred.' This emphasizes the importance of remembering that until a case has been proven, one is dealing with suspicions and allegations of fraud. As there is not a criminal offence of 'fraud' in English law, any prosecutions have to be brought against a specific offence – 'the most common being theft under s1 of the Theft Act 1968, obtaining property by deception under s15 of the Theft Act 1968, and false accounting under s17 of the Theft Act 1968; carrying on business with the intent to defraud under s458 of the Companies Act 1985 and the common law offence of conspiracy to defraud' (Huntington and Davies, 1994: 3). The word 'fraud' is commonly used as an umbrella term to cover a multitude of offences which may differ markedly in size; that is, they can be relatively small (such as a false expense claim) or very large (such as a fictitious overseas subsidiary). Whether all of these should be classified in the same way is problematic.

Another problem encountered relates to the actual identification of something as a 'fraud'. It is conceivable that victims may not even realize what has happened or that they have lost money. Burns (1998: 38) asked: 'At what point does sharp practice become fraud?' This does seem to imply that the dividing line between the two, in certain circumstances, may at the very least be very fine. Indeed, the classification of an action as being fraudulent may depend on the motivation behind it (was it deliberate or accidental?) (see case study 6.1).

How did that happen?   CASE STUDY 6.1

During the audit of a small manufacturing company, the auditors were carrying out their examination of the client's stock schedules. Total stock amounted to £72,000; however, the auditors noticed that the single largest stock item (amounting to £12,000) had been included on the stock sheets twice. As a result, stock and profits were each overstated by £12,000. When this was brought to the attention of the managers, they were naturally surprised and wondered how it could have happened. An adjustment was made to reduce the stock figure and thus the profit. Was this an attempt to boost profit in a lean year and thus a fraud, or was it a genuine accident? In this instance, the difference between a fraud and an accident would seem to be the motivation behind the event. What would have happened if this 'error' had been undetected and three months after the end of the audit the company had gone into liquidation? If the liquidator had spotted this in the wreckage of the business, no doubt the conclusion would have been that it was a fraud. [This is based on an actual incident.]

The *Cadbury Report* (1992: 27) points out that the directors are responsible under s.221 of the Companies Act 1985 for maintaining adequate accounting records, and in order to do this they need to maintain a system of internal control over the financial management of the company, including those procedures designed to minimize the risk of fraud. There was a concern about the non-reporting of fraud, and consequently there was a suggestion that external auditors should have a duty to report fraud to the appropriate authorities. The report did not recommend that a statutory duty to report fraud should be extended beyond the regulated sector; however, it did see scope for extending to the auditors of all companies the statutory provisions applying to auditors in the regulated sector which enable them to report a reasonable suspicion of fraud freely to the appropriate investigatory authority.

SAS 110 sets out the external auditors' current responsibilities regarding the reporting of fraud. If they discover a fraud, 'auditors should as soon as practicable communicate their findings to the appropriate level of management, the board of directors or the audit committee' (para. 41), but '[w]hen a suspected or actual instance of fraud casts doubt on the integrity of the directors, auditors should make a report direct to a proper authority in the public interest without delay and without informing the directors in advance' (para. 52). *SAS 110* (para. 53) states that in certain exceptional circumstances auditors are not bound by the duty of confidentiality and have the right or duty to report matters to a proper authority in the public interest. In this respect, the auditors need to weigh the public interest in maintaining confidential client relationships against the public interest in disclosure to a proper authority. These 'exceptional circumstances' include where the auditors 'suspect or have evidence that the directors are aware of such fraud and, contrary to regulatory requirements or the public interest, have not reported it to a proper authority within a reasonable period' (para. 54). However, there is one weakness: '"Public interest" is a concept that is not capable of general definition' (para. 56).

A common expectation of the external auditors is that they are there in order to detect fraud (Humphrey et al., 1992; Steen, 1990), and great pressure has been put on auditors to take more responsibility for the detection of fraud (Humphrey et al., 1993). The auditors' position relating to fraud has been set out (AICPA, 1997; APB, 1995a), but the expectations have persisted, and consequently the Panel on Audit Effectiveness (2000: 88) has advocated that auditors should incorporate a 'forensic-type fieldwork phase' into their work:

> During this phase, auditors should modify the otherwise neutral concept of professional skepticism and presume the possibility of dishonesty at various levels of management, including collusion, override of internal control and falsification of documents. The key question that auditors should ask is 'Where is the entity vulnerable to financial statement fraud if management were inclined to perpetrate it?' [footnote omitted] (Panel on Audit Effectiveness, 2000: 88–9)

While this approach may seem reasonable, it may be problematic as to what it will achieve. Auditors are already concentrating on high-level business risks. Beasley et al. (2000: 443) report that fraudulent financial reporting seems to be concentrated in certain industries (such as high technology, computer-related industries, manufacturing, business services, finance/insurance, and whole-sale and retail trade industries [for a discussion of these, see Bell and Carcello, 2000; Beneish, 1997; Bonner et al., 1998; Dechow et al., 1996; Loebbecke et al., 1989]). Therefore, when reviewing the risk of fraud, Beasley et al. suggested that the auditors should consider the industry characteristics and compare the clients' corporate governance mechanisms to no-fraud industry benchmarks

(2000: 441). In a 'forensic-type fieldwork phase', auditors would presumably focus on material areas, and so it would still be unreasonable to expect them to detect all frauds.

Mrs Smilie is dead   CASE STUDY 6.2

In the back office of a DIY shop, a little old lady was responsible for recording the petty cash. Mrs Smilie was always very helpful to the auditors. Following her sudden death, the accountant had to take over her job. On writing up the petty cash book, he found that some £400 was missing. In order to protect her good name (as she could not defend herself), he decided to make up some expenses in order to offset the missing money. When the auditors arrived, they found that the accountant had inadvertently recorded one week's cash takings twice in the petty-cash book and thus had overstated cash by £400. When approached by the auditors, he explained that he made the mistake in the chaos following the petty cashier's death and he explained to them what he had done. The auditors then asked him to identify the false expenses – the only problem was that the accountant could not identify these items because over the years he had had so much experience at making up expenses that he had become very good at covering his tracks. So even though the fraudster knew how much he was looking for and the time period in which this incident had occurred, even he was unable to identify his own false expenses. The accountant left the business soon after this. [This is based on an actual incident.]

Thus, the fact that fraudsters themselves cannot detect false accounting entries (see case study 6.2) highlights the problem facing the auditors. The auditor is not just auditing the accounting records (as required by statute) but is also faced with the audit of management's motivations.

CONCLUSION

This chapter has argued strongly that the external audit should be viewed in the context of the audit of management's motivations. Management is keenly interested in the picture that is portrayed in the financial statements. The very nature of financial reporting means that a whole multitude of judgements and estimates have to be made during the compilation of the financial statements – hence the potential for bias. But bias can arise from the transactions under-taken (over which the auditor has no say), as well as from the way the figures in the financial statements are compiled and presented (which the auditor may be able to influence if the matter is material). Therefore, it is necessary to ask whether the financial statements are really free from bias. Is it really the duty of the auditor to eliminate bias? Indeed, is this really feasible? If it is unrealistic to expect the auditors to eliminate bias, at what point does management bias become fraud? After all, there is a great clamour for auditors to detect fraud. Bearing in mind the definition of materiality (something likely to influence the decision of a user of the financial statements), deliberate bias would be a waste of time and effort if it was not designed to influence the users and so it would seem that, according to the definition, all deliberate bias is material.

While it is easy to criticize auditors for failing to detect a fraud, it is impossible to quantify the deterrent effect of the external audit. It may be cold comfort that if things are bad now with the external audit, they would probably be much worse without it.

DISCUSSION QUESTIONS

1   What are the impediments to auditor independence?

2   Who has the responsibility of ensuring that the financial statements are free from bias?

3   To what extent would you agree with the view that external auditing could be regarded as the audit of motivations?

4   Do audit committees have the necessary knowledge of the business in order to be independent?

5   Outline the difficulties encountered in identifying a fraud.

REFERENCES

Accounting Standards Board (ASB) (1999) Statement of Principles, reproduced in Accounting Standards and Guidance for Members 2001. London: ICAEW.

American Accounting Association (AAA) (1936) 'A tentative statement of accounting principles affecting corporate reports', The Accounting Review, June: 187–91.

American Accounting Association (AAA) (1966) A Statement of Basic Accounting Theory. Sarasota, FL: AAA.

American Institute of Certified Public Accountants (AICPA) (1973) (Trueblood Report) Objectives of Financial Statements, Report of the Accounting Objectives Study Group. New York: AICPA.

American Institute of Certified Public Accountants (AICPA) (1978) Commission on

Auditors' Responsibilities: Report, Conclusion and Recommendations (Cohen Commission). New York: AICPA.

American Institute of Certified Public Accountants (AICPA) (1993) *Professional Standards, Vols 1 and 2*. New York: AICPA.

American Institute of Certified Public Accountants (AICPA) (1997) *Consideration of Fraud in a Financial Statement Audit*, Statement on Auditing Standards No. 82. New York: AICPA.

Antle, R. (1984) 'Auditor independence', *Journal of Accounting Research*, Spring: 1–20.

Antle, R. and Nalebuff, B. (1991) 'Conservatism and auditor–client negotiations', *Journal of Accounting Research*, 29 (Supplement): 31–59.

Auditing Practices Board (APB) (1995a) *SAS 110 Fraud and Error*. London: APB.

Auditing Practices Board (APB) (1995b) *SAS 220 Materiality and the Audit*. London: APB.

Auditing Practices Board (APB) (1995c) *SAS 420 Audit of Accounting Estimates*. London: APB.

Auditing Practices Board (APB) (2001) *Aggressive Earnings Management* Consultation Paper. London: APB.

Beasley, M.S., Carcello, J.V., Hermanson, D.R. and Lapides, P.D. (2000) 'Fraudulent financial reporting: consideration of industry traits and corporate governance mechanisms', *Accounting Horizons*, 14 (4): 441–54.

Beattie, V., Brandt, R. and Fearnley, S. (1999) 'Perceptions of auditor independence: UK evidence', *Journal of International Accounting, Auditing and Taxation*, 8 (2): 67–107.

Beattie, V., Fearnley, S. and Brandt, R. (2000) 'Behind the audit report: a descriptive study of discussions and negotiations between auditors and directors', *International Journal of Auditing*, 4: 177–202.

Beattie, V., Fearnley, S. and Brandt, R. (2001) *Behind Closed Doors: What Company Audit is Really About*. Basingstoke: Palgrave.

Beidleman, C.R. (1973) 'Income smoothing: the role of management', *The Accounting Review*, 48 (4): 653–67.

Bell, T.B. and Carcello, J.V. (2000) 'A decision aid for assessing the likelihood of fraudulent financial reporting', *Auditing: A Journal of Practice and Theory*, Spring: 169–84.

Beneish, M.D. (1997) 'Detecting GAAP violation: implications for assessing earnings management among firms with extreme financial performance', *Journal of Accounting and Public Policy*, Fall: 271–309.

Blue Ribbon Committee (BRC) on Improving the Effectiveness of Corporate Audit Committees (1999) *Report and Recommendations of the Blue Ribbon Committee on Improving the Effectiveness of Corporate Audit Committees*. New York: NYSE and NASD.

Bonner, S.E., Palmrose, Z.-V. and Young, S.M. (1998) 'Fraud type and auditor litigation: an analysis of SEC accounting and auditing enforcement releases', *The Accounting Review*, October: 503–32.

Briloff, A.J. (1972) *Unaccountable Accounting*. New York: Harper and Row.

Briloff, A.J. (1981) *The Truth About Corporate Accounting*. New York: Harper and Row.

Briloff, A.J. (1986) 'Standards without standards/principles without principles/fairness without fairness', *Advances in Accounting*, 3: 25–50.

Briloff, A.J. (1990) 'Accountancy and society, a covenant desecrated', *Critical Perspectives on Accounting*, 1: 5–30.

Burns, S. (1998) 'Easy money', *Accountancy*, August: 38.

Cadbury Report (1992) *The Financial Aspects of Corporate Governance*. London: Gee.

Collier, P. (1997) 'Corporate governance and audit committees', in M. Sherer and S. Turley (eds), *Current Issues in Auditing* (3rd edn). London: Paul Chapman.

Comer, M.J. (1985) *Corporate Fraud*. Aldershot: Gower.

Conyon, M. (1995) 'Cadbury in the boardroom', *Hemmington Scott Corporate Register*, April: 5–10.

Dechow, P.M., Sloan, R.G. and Sweeney, A.P. (1996) 'Causes and consequences of earnings manipulations: an analysis of firms subject to enforcement actions by the SEC', *Contemporary Accounting Research*, Spring: 1–36.

Eckel, N. (1981) 'The income smoothing hypothesis revisited', *Abacus*, 17 (1): 28–40.

Elliott Committee (1997) AICPA Special Committee on Assurance Services: *Report of the Special Committee on Assurance Services*. New York: AICPA.

Emerson, R. (1962) 'Power-dependence relations', *American Sociological Review*, February: 32–41.

French, D. (1985) *Dictionary of Accounting Terms*. London: ICAEW.

Givoly, D. and Ronen, J. (1981) '"Smoothing" manifestations in fourth quarter results of operations: some empirical evidence', *Abacus*, 17 (2): 174–93.

Gordon, M.J. (1964) 'Postulates, principles and research in accounting', *The Accounting Review*, April: 251–63.

Griffiths, I. (1995) *New Creative Accounting*. London: Macmillan.

Healy, P.M. and Wahlen, J.M. (1999) 'A review of earnings management literature and its implications for standard setting', *Accounting Horizons*, December: 365–83.

Hepworth, S.R. (1953) 'Periodic income smoothing', *The Accounting Review*, January: 32–9.

Hines, R.D. (1988) 'Financial accounting: in communicating reality, we construct reality', *Accounting, Organizations and Society*, 13 (3): 251–62.

Hines, R.D. (1991) 'The FASB's conceptual framework, financial accounting and the maintenance of the social world', *Accounting, Organizations and Society*, 16 (4): 313–31.

Humphrey, C., Moizer, P. and Turley, S. (1992) *The Audit Expectations Gap in the United Kingdom*. London: ICAEW Research Board.

Humphrey, C., Turley, S. and Moizer, P. (1993) 'Protecting against detection: the case of auditors and fraud', *Accounting, Auditing and Accountability Journal*, 6 (1): 39–62.

Huntington, I. and Davies, D. (1994) *Fraud Watch: A Guide for Business*. Milton Keynes: Accountancy Books.

Institute of Chartered Accountants in England and Wales (ICAEW) (2001) *Members' Handbook*. London: ICAEW.

International Accounting Standards Committee (IASC) (1989) *Framework for the Preparation and Presentation of Financial Statements*. London: IASC.

Kalbers, L.P. and Fogarty, T.J. (1993) 'Audit committee effectiveness: an empirical investigation of the contribution of power', *Auditing: A Journal of Practice and Theory*, 12 (1): 24–49.

Kalbers, L.P. and Fogarty, T.J. (1998) 'Organizational and economic explanations of audit committee oversight', *Journal of Managerial Issues*, 10 (2): 129–50.

Knapp, M.C. (1987) 'An empirical study of audit committee support for auditors involved in technical disputes with client management', *The Accounting Review*, 62 (3): 578–88.

Lee, T. (1993) *Corporate Audit Theory*. London: Chapman & Hall.

Lev, B. (1979) 'Discussion of the predictive power of limited information in preliminary analytical review: an empirical review', *Journal of Accounting Research*, Supplement: 166–8.

Lindsay, D. (1992) 'Auditor–client conflict resolution: an investigation of the perceptions of the financial community in Australia and Canada', *International Journal of Accounting*, 27: 342–65.

Loebbecke, J.K., Eining, M.M. and Willingham, J.J. (1989) 'Auditors' experience with material irregularities: frequency, nature, and detectability', *Auditing: A Journal of Practice and Theory*, Fall: 1–28.

Mitchell, A., Puxty, T., Sikka, P. and Willmott, H. (1991) *Accounting for Change: Proposals for the Reform of Audit and Accounting*, Discussion Paper No. 7. London: Fabian Society.

Nichols, D. and Price, K. (1976) 'The auditor-firm conflict: an analysis using concepts of exchange theory', *The Accounting Review*, April: 335–46.

Panel on Audit Effectiveness (2000) *Report and Recommendations*. Stamford, CT: Public Oversight Board.

Parfet, W.U. (2000) 'Accounting subjectivity and earnings management: a preparer perspective', *Accounting Horizons*, 14 (4): 481–8.

Paton, W.A. and Littleton, A.C. (1940) *An Introduction to Corporate Accounting Standards*. American Accounting Association.

Peasnell, K.V. and Yaansah, R.A. (1988) *Off-Balance Sheet Financing*, Chartered Association of Certified Accountants' Research Report 10. London: Certified Accountant Publications Limited.

Porter, B. (1997) 'Auditor's responsibilities with respect to corporate fraud – a controversial issue', in M. Sherer and S. Turley (eds), *Current Issues in Auditing* (3rd edn). London: Paul Chapman.

Prakash, P. and Rappaport, A. (1977) 'Information inductance and its significance for accounting', *Accounting Organizations and Society*, 2 (1): 29–38.

Sikka, P. (1997) 'Regulating the auditing profession', in M. Sherer and S. Turley (eds), *Current Issues in Auditing* (3rd edn). London: Paul Chapman.

Sikka, P. and Willmott, H. (1995) 'The power of "independence": defending and extending the jurisdiction of accounting in the United Kingdom', *Accounting, Organizations and Society*, 20 (6): 547–81.

Smith, T. (1992) *Accounting for Growth: Stripping the Camouflage from Company Accounts*. London: Century Business.

Solomons, D. (1989) *Guidelines for Financial Reporting Standards*. London: ICAEW.

Sommer, A.A.J. (1991) 'Auditing audit committees: an educational opportunity for auditors', *Accounting Horizons*, 5 (2): 91–3.

Spira, L.F. (1998) 'An evolutionary perspective on audit committee effectiveness', *Corporate Governance: An International Review*, 6 (1): 29–38.

Steen, M. (1990) *Audits and Auditors – What the Public Thinks*. London: KPMG Peat Marwick McLintock.

Taylor, P. and Turley, S. (1986) *The Regulation of Accounting*. Oxford: Basil Blackwell.

Treadway Commission (1987) *Report of the National Commission of Fraudulent Financial Reporting*. National Commission on Fraudulent Financial Reporting.

Watts, R.L. and Zimmerman, J.L. (1986) *Positive Accounting Theory*. New Jersey: Prentice Hall.

Whittred, G., Zimmer, I. and Taylor, S. (1996) *Financial Accounting – Incentive Effects and Economic Consequences* (4th edn). Sydney: Harcourt Brace.

Far better an approximate answer to the right question, which
is often vague, than an exact answer to the wrong question,
which can always be made precise.

                                                    – J.W. Tukey

As the audit report is the means by which an auditor communicates
the results of the audit to the users of the financial statements, it is
the public face of the external audit. It may be the only contact the
auditor has with the vast majority of financial statement users. Therefore, a
key aspect of the auditor's role is that of communication. In fact, the Auditing
Practices Board (APB) (1992: 7) was of the view that '[t]he essential requirement to be met by auditors when reporting is that any report issued should
achieve clear communication with its readers'. So, it could be argued that if
the meaning of the auditor's report is not clear, the value of the audit could,
quite rightly, be questioned.

In the USA, as a result of criticisms of the profession by the Cohen Commission (AICPA, 1978), the Auditing Standards Board reviewed the wording
of the audit report with the intention of giving a clearer indication of the
nature of an audit and of the responsibilities of the auditors. The objective of
the changes was to reduce the perceived expectations gap relating to auditing.
A revised US audit report was introduced in 1988. The UK audit report was
expanded by the Auditing Practices Board in 1993 (and revised in 2001).
Fundamental to these changes is the clear identification of the auditor's
message. Lee (1986: 49) considered that 'it is vitally important that the meaning of the audit report is fully understood by all concerned in its preparation
and use'. However, what is the auditor trying to say?

EXPLORING THE AUDITOR'S MESSAGE

Though much work has been conducted on the audit report, it has often been
confined to interpreting the meanings of various styles of reports (Hatherly et

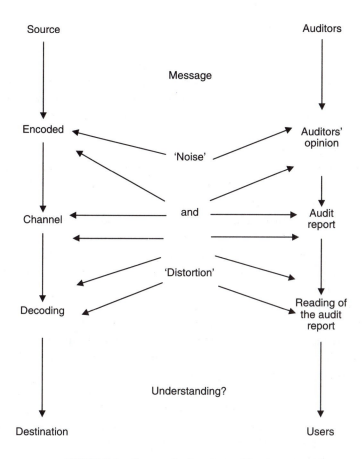

FIGURE 7.1   Communicating the auditors' message

al., 1991; Holt and Moizer, 1990; Houghton and Messier, 1991; Innes et al., 1997). Conceptually, the approach adopted in this chapter differs from most other work in that it attempts to establish the auditor's message, by asking auditors not to interpret the wording of a given audit report, but rather to state what they were trying to communicate at the end of an audit. Following on from the earlier discussion (in Chapter 2) of communication theory (which splits the communication process into the message, the means of communication, and whether the message is understood) and the nature of information, it is only when the auditor's message is correctly incorporated in the wording of the audit report and then interpreted and understood by the reader that the user receives the message that the auditor is trying to convey (Figure 7.1) and thus information is conveyed.

At the time of the proposed expansion of the UK audit report in the early 1990s, interviews were conducted with twenty-five technical partners and managers of the largest accountancy firms in the UK in order to try to clarify the auditor's message. The interviews commenced with these practitioners being asked what they thought was the essence of the message the auditor was trying to convey in an unqualified audit report. The intention was to start broadly and then focus on individual potential components of the message.

The most frequently made comment (mentioned by eight people) was that the auditor was trying to communicate compliance with legal or professional requirements. In fact, one person thought the auditor's message was, quite simply, that 'he has carried out his statutory duties'. Another who expanded on this point stated: 'The auditor is declaring that on the basis of his inspection of the records . . . the results and the financial position are all within the terms of reference of statutes, accounting standards and best practice, and that the disclosures required under these various headings have been satisfactorily met and provided.' One person described the audit report as 'a legal document which complies with the legal requirements'. Therefore, the notion that the auditor had done what was required came over strongly in the auditors' messages.

The words 'fair' or 'fairly' were contained in the second most frequently made response. Six people used these words to represent their views on the picture portrayed by the financial statements (the word 'fair' in this category was not used in terms of 'true and fair' – though three people did use this phrase in describing their messages). One person's message was that 'within reasonable bounds of accuracy the financial statements convey a fair record of what has taken place', and another person stated: 'I think he [the auditor] is trying to convey a message of some sort of credibility – that the financial statements have been fairly prepared.' One view was this: 'The auditor is trying to say that he, as an independent third party, has reviewed the accounting records, transactions and the resulting financial statements and believes that they fairly show what has gone on over the past year in that business, and at the end of the year, the financial statements give a reasonable view of the assets and liabilities that are attaching to that business.' Another view was that 'the financial statements taken as a whole are, I prefer to use the word, "fair" – I am a bit worried about the word "true".'

Five people stressed the limitations and imperfections of the financial statements. One view was: '[I]f I have my preference, my audit message would be the imperfection of the information to begin with, and therefore, the inherent limitations of the audit reports which flow therefrom and the fact that these are primarily management's statements as opposed to the auditor's statements – then how he [the auditor] goes about the audit, seems to me, to be of a lesser importance.' Other messages were that the audit report implied the financial statements were 'alright' or 'are about right' (four people), the audit report was simply 'trying to convey some message about reasonableness' (three people), the financial statements were 'OK' (two people), or they were 'not misleading' (one person).

A key comment made by one of these senior practitioners related to the objective of the financial statements. A clear definition of this was required because 'the audit report effectively is saying whether they do it [that is, achieve this objective]'. Therefore, an implication of an unqualified audit report is that the financial statements are fit for their purpose. The fact that there is a debate about the purpose of the financial statements may in itself contribute to a lack of clarity about the auditor's message. Interestingly, it can be seen that none of the auditors offered the view that part of their message was that the financial statements were appropriate for decision making.

Regarding the responsibilities of the directors, eighteen people were in agreement with stressing management's responsibility: 'It is probably a useful area that we could get over to them [management] – the extent we are responsible for certain things and what they are responsible for, but it may be perceived as negative.' Another person said: 'I certainly have always regarded it as implied, but maybe it ought to be said.' Four people were against the stressing of management's responsibilities – one of these stated: 'I don't think it is the auditor's responsibility to do that.' Another was concerned at the image that it would create: 'I think it should be expressed publicly; on the other hand, it would look awfully defensive.' Two interviewees, although in favour of stressing management's responsibility, questioned whether this should be in the audit report. Thus, there was support for stressing management's responsibilities, but there was a debate as to whether the audit report was the most appropriate place to do it. In the subsequently published *SAS 600* (APB, 1993), the audit report states that 'the company's directors are responsible for the preparation of financial statements' (p. 28). This was revised in 2001 (APB, 2001a) and now states: 'The directors' responsibilities for preparing the Annual Report and the financial statements in accordance with applicable law and United Kingdom Accounting Standards are set out in the Statement of Directors' Responsibilities' (p. 5).

Probably the key quality of the external audit is that it is an independent examination of the financial statements. The revised US audit report stressed the external auditor's independence by having the heading 'Independent Auditor's Report'. When asked whether this was part of the UK auditor's message, nine of the people interviewed were in favour of its being mentioned, five were against it, and eleven had no strong opinions. One stated: 'I don't think people realise that auditors are independent.' However, a contrasting opinion was that 'everyone will assume the auditor is independent'. This was reiterated by another person: 'I think audit report readers take independence for granted. They just expect the auditor to be independent.' One person was not keen on stressing auditor independence: 'To actually say, yes, this is the report of the independent auditor you have got to have an agreed formula for being independent.' This person considered that the then current guidelines on independence did not go as far as they could, and therefore considered that they should be strengthened before greater emphasis could be placed on the auditor's independence. In the *SAS 600* audit report (APB, 1993: 28), the auditors stated: 'It is our responsibility to form an independent opinion'; however, the 2001 revision now means that the audit report is headed 'Independent Auditors' Report' (APB, 2001a: 5).

It is one thing to say that the auditor is independent, but the achievement of independence is another matter completely: 'You try your best, but are bound to be swayed where they [the issues] are marginal.' As to whether clients put pressure on auditors, one view was as follows: 'Of course they do, oh yes, all the time. I think it is a fact of life.' It is important to remember that because of the subjectivity involved in the production of the financial statements there is no one 'right' amount for the reported profit figure.

Shaw (1980: 7) suggested that a true and fair view implied the absence of bias. Lee (1981: 270) considered that the financial statements should give 'as objective a picture as possible, free from wilful bias'. Given these views and the importance of the neutrality concept in financial reporting, the external auditors were asked whether they considered that an unqualified audit report implied that the financial statements were free from bias. Twenty-four of the interviewees did not think that this was the case, and that 'one should not read into the audit report that the accounts are free from bias'. Someone else stated:

> I don't think that financial statements can ever be neutral. . . . There are many situations where management tend to decide what the market's expectations are and tries to live up to those expectations rather than necessarily reporting what is a totally neutral position.

It is important to remember that management's motivations drive its actions. One person stated: 'Unless you can actually understand why people are doing things, you will never really understand the accounts.' Another said: 'It is inevitable that there will be elements of bias in-built – it is very difficult for auditors to argue against management's judgements'; 'I think it would be almost impossible to put together a set of accounts in a neutral fashion unless the whole of the preparation was done by someone who had no contact whatsoever with the management of the business.' This raises the question of the role of the auditor in relation to management bias: whether the role of the auditor is to eliminate bias, to minimize bias or to examine the reasonableness of management's justifications for its representations. Three people expressed the view that the auditor should eliminate bias. This was usually qualified in terms of material bias, in that the auditor is required to plan and conduct an audit with a reasonable expectation of detecting any material misstatements:

'We are trying to eliminate blatant bias.' Therefore, it can be seen that only a small minority were in favour of the idea of the auditor's being expected to eliminate bias. An opposing opinion was expressed as follows:

> *I really don't think we eliminate bias, I don't think, in fact, that we even consciously say that an unbiased set of financial statements this year will say this. I don't think we actually go there, and we would have to do that to eliminate bias.*

Bearing in mind, that technically, the auditor is merely required to express an opinion on the financial statements, one person stated: 'If the production of the financial statements is management's responsibility, then so is the elimination of bias!' Another person questioned whether it was possible to eliminate bias; 'I don't think that total elimination is possible because the accounts are subjective.' Six people thought that the role of the auditor might be to minimize bias – 'minimizing bias was probably the best we can hope for in the real world'. However, another view was this: 'I would like to think that they [the auditors] would minimize the bias, but I'm not sure how they do that.' Fourteen of the interviewees opted for the view that the role of the auditor was to examine the reasonableness of management's justifications for its representations. In fact, one person went as far as to say: 'I think management is entitled to bias the financial statements in favour of the general commercial good of the company.' This person termed it 'legitimate bias' as opposed to bias for personal gain. Another stated: 'I think, on balance, society is better served if we [the auditors] don't actually extenuate the peaks and troughs.' Two people thought the three categories were not mutually exclusive: 'I would be inclined to a combination of all three, with a fourth [category] which is to make sure that the bias is obvious.' This view was supported by another person, who stated that bias could be minimized 'by disclosing what management have done, so the effect is neutralized'.

The comments on bias are very interesting, especially in the light of the conceptual frameworks for financial reporting which employ the neutrality concept. The Committee on Basic Auditing Concepts (1973: 3) stated that, of the four standards (relevance, verifiability, freedom from bias, and quanti-fiability) used in evaluating potential accounting information, 'the audit function is most concerned with freedom from bias'. It continued: 'In general, the principal criterion towards which an audit will be focused is the control and/or disclosure of bias in communicated accounting information.' These comments seem to show that auditors prefer to view themselves as being required to examine management's justifications for its representations, rather than to eliminate or minimize management bias.

One of the major problems underlying the detection of bias and the interpretation of management's motivations is the subjective nature of many of the items that comprise the financial statements. The interviewees were asked whether the auditor should stress the subjective nature of the financial statements. Altogether, fifteen of the interviewees thought this was a valid part of the auditor's message. In fact, this question elicited some very strong responses. One person stated: 'I think that this is by far the most important thing to get over [to the users],' and another thought that the profession was 'not getting this point over to the general public'. Though a contradictory view was expressed by one person, who thought that it would not be particularly helpful to do so, as it could devalue the auditor's work. One view was that users did not appreciate the difference between accounting trans-actions and accounting estimates – 'people are coping with the first [that is, recording transactions] but have difficulty with the financial statements [incorporating the accounting estimates]'. Another person considered that even reference in the Companies Acts 'is very much homing in on the data-base' (that is, the accounting transactions contained in the accounting records) at the expense of the measurement and valuation issues. One person who questioned whether the audit report was the right place to tackle the topic of subjectivity stated that 'the best way of focusing on the subjective nature would be to refer to the accounting framework within which the accounts are drafted'. Thus, whether this point is made in the audit report or somewhere else, a clear majority of the people interviewed considered that the subjective nature of the financial statements was an important part of the message to be communicated to their users. The SAS 600 audit report did include reference to 'an assessment of the significant estimates and judgments made by the directors in the preparation of the financial statements' (p. 28). SAS 420, issued in March 1995, now covers the audit of accounting estimates.

The discussion of subjectivity raises the question of whether words such as 'verify', 'verifiable' and 'verification' should be used in relation to the finan-cial statements and auditing. Mautz and Sharaf (1961: 41–2) stated: 'Unless financial data are verifiable, auditing has no reason for existence.' They qualified this by conceding that 'verifiable' was not taken to mean 'beyond all doubt'; instead, verification was a process that 'carries one to a position of confidence about any given proposition'. It has already been seen that ASOBAT (AAA, 1966) considered that verifiability was one of its four standards which it used in evaluating potential accounting information, and Solomons (1989: 52) stated: 'All of the information given by the financial statements should be verifiable.' Given the widespread use of these words in the auditing literature, the interviewees were asked whether the auditor really verified the financial statement data and whether this was implied in the audit report. Four people had no objection to the use of the word 'verify'; however, fourteen of the interviewees were not happy with its use – 'a poor use of the term in auditing' was one view. Another comment was this: 'I am sure there are better words to use than verify – verbal sloppiness has crept in as part of the accepted code.' There was some agreement that it may be possible to verify a number of individual elements of the financial statements, but fourteen of the interviewees were unhappy at the implication that the auditor had verified all the data in the financial statements.

It is often said that the purpose of the external audit is to add credibility to management's representations. Lee (1986: 31) considered that the current primary objective of the external audit was 'attesting credibility of financial statements'. Therefore, the auditors were asked whether the audit was really adding to the credibility of the financial statements. Twenty-three of the twenty-five people interviewed considered that the role of the audit was to add credibility to the financial statements. In fact, there was very strong support for this notion: 'If you gave me one sentence to describe the whole audit process it is, that it adds credibility to the financial statements.' Again: 'We are selling a sort of standard of approval.' However, a slightly different view was put forward by another person: 'The accounts are a management representation and the fact that the audit report is attached to them, pre-sumably, that is to give credibility to them – but I think they ought to be credible documents on their own, without that happening.' Someone else wondered whether the audit was giving too much credibility to the financial statements.

The interviews then moved on to possible components of the auditors' message. Twelve of the interviewees had no objection to mentioning that the audit was conducted on a test basis. As one person said, it was 'a statement of fact'. However, 'users would be amazed how few transactions are examined'. One advantage of stating explicitly that the auditor's work was done on a test basis was that 'it should be part of the health warning'. However, six people had reservations about mentioning testing. One said: 'I think it would be something that would induce miscommunication.' Other views were that 'it is not adding to the positive message', and that it is 'defensive'. Therefore, reservations were again being expressed as to the appropriateness of the audit report for such a statement. The revised audit report (APB, 1993: 28) pointed out that the audit is conducted 'on a test basis'.

In the UK, companies are required to keep proper accounting records, and there is an implicit confirmation in an unqualified audit report that this has been the case. However, one person stated: 'Interestingly, this business about keeping proper books of account . . . one was inclined to, kind of, forget it all and, kind of, take it for granted.' When asked whether the auditor's message was specifically saying anything about a client's internal controls, only two of the people interviewed thought it was, whereas twelve thought it was not, and eleven did not have strong views on the topic. One opinion was this: 'I think it would be extremely difficult to communicate in any meaningful way on the adequacy or inadequacy of internal controls because it is a very grey area.' This was reiterated by someone else: 'I wonder about how many businesses we would actually be able to say anything desperately positive on their internal controls.' One of the main concerns expressed was regarding the spectrum of clients – very large to very small. Therefore, one person felt, 'we cannot impose the same set of rules [on them]'.

One person who was not keen on the idea of auditors having to report on a client's internal controls stated: 'Companies that go under, don't go under because of failures in control systems, but because they have made some very big decisions which have either gone against them through circumstances or because they were ill-informed at the time.'

Since the *Cadbury Report* (1992), the responsibility for establishing and maintaining a system of internal controls has been clearly stated to rest with the directors. Turnbull (1999) set out the internal control requirements of the Combined Code of the Committee on Corporate Governance. The auditors are required to '"review" the company's compliance with certain aspects of the Combined Code' (APB, 1999: para. 8). The auditors are required to review only the disclosures made in relation to Code provision D.2.1, which states:

> The directors should, at least annually, conduct a review of the effectiveness of the group's system of internal control and should report to the shareholders that they have done so. The review should cover all controls, including financial, operational and compliance controls and risk management. (quoted in APB, 1999: para. 33)

The APB (1999: para. 40) stresses: 'We are not required to consider whether the board's statements on internal control cover all risks and controls, or form an opinion on the effectiveness of the company's corporate governance procedures or its risk and control procedures.'

In recent years, the accounting profession has been trying to convey to the users of the financial statements that the role of the auditor does not encompass specifically looking for fraud. In view of this, the interviewees were asked whether this was part of the message contained in the audit report. There was very little support for this suggestion, with only two people in favour. Six people were against this idea, with one person stating, 'but we are not actually going out of our way to look for it'. However, fraud was seen to be an important issue facing the profession: 'I think fraud is an area that has to be tackled. . . . It's such a glaring loophole within the current structure.' The main problem was viewed as being how to communicate the auditor's responsibility; hence, the high number (seventeen) of people who did not express a strong view as to whether the auditors' message should say anything about fraud. One person stated: 'We have difficulty even explaining it to senior management – to the layman it would be an exercise in futility.' Another said: 'I think it [the auditor's role] is not appreciated at the moment, though whether the audit report or some other means of communication is the appropriate way of getting it across, I don't know.' Therefore, these people were not saying that the auditor's responsibility in relation to the detection of fraud was not part of the message, but rather that its explicit inclusion in the audit report was unlikely to do much good. Another admitted: 'My worry is, if you put all these things in, the message is so negative.' The view was expressed that some other place was probably more appropriate – possibly part of a general 'health warning' relating to the whole nature of the financial statements. The *SAS 600* audit report states: 'We planned and performed our audit so as to obtain all the information and explanations which we considered necessary in order to provide us with sufficient evidence to give reasonable assurance that the financial statements are free from material misstatement, whether caused by fraud or other irregularity or error' (APB, 1993: 28).

An auditor has to assess whether a company is a going concern before an unqualified audit report can be issued. Therefore, the interviewees were asked whether the auditor should specifically mention that the company is a going concern. Six people thought that this could be part of the message: 'He [the auditor] is not guaranteeing that it is a going concern but I suppose implicitly he is agreeing that the "going concern" concept is appropriate.' However, eight people were not keen on 'going concern' being highlighted; for example, one said, 'I would like to take that implication out of the audit report because it is misunderstood [by users].' Eleven people did not express strong views on the subject: 'When it comes to fundamental accounting concepts, I would rather that they were assumed.' The *SAS 600* unqualified audit report did not mention 'going concern', but 'the [Stock Exchange] Listing Rules now require the auditors to review the directors' statement on "going concern"' (Hampel Report, 1998: 50).

It can be seen that there was generally little support for the detailing of the scope of the auditor's work in the audit report. The main problems were the perceived negative message this would give and the crowding of the audit report (with the revisions of 2001 [APB, 2001a], the audit report will become even more crowded). It was questioned whether the audit report was the best place for some of these topics.

THE AUDITOR'S OPINION

In the European Union (EU), the auditor's report culminates with the expression of opinion on whether the financial statements show 'a true and fair view'. In the USA, the auditor's opinion is an expression of whether the financial statements 'present fairly' the results and financial position (AICPA, 1988). In 1970, the US Accounting Principles Board concluded:

> Financial statements 'present fairly in conformity with generally accepted accounting principles' if a number of conditions are met: (1) generally accepted accounting principles applicable in the circumstances have been applied in accumulating and processing the financial accounting information, (2) changes from period to period in generally accepted accounting principles have been appropriately disclosed, (3) the information in the underlying records is properly reflected and described in the financial statements in conformity with generally accepted accounting principles, and (4) a proper balance has been achieved between the conflicting needs to disclose important aspects of financial position and results of operations in accordance with conventional concepts and to summarize the voluminous underlying data into a limited number of financial statement captions and supporting notes. (Accounting Principles Board, 1970: 91)

Currently, the meaning of 'present fairly in conformity with generally accepted accounting principles' is set out in *SAS 69*:

> The auditor's opinion that financial statements present fairly an entity's financial position, results of operations, and cash flows in conformity with generally accepted accounting principles should be based on his or her judgment as to whether (a) the accounting principles selected and applied have general acceptance; (b) the accounting principles are appropriate in the circumstances; (c) the financial statements, including related notes, are informative of matters that may affect their use, understanding, and interpretation ... (d) the information presented in the financial statements is classified and summarized in a reasonable manner, that is, neither too detailed nor too condensed . . . and (e) the financial statements reflect the underlying transactions and events in a manner that presents the financial position, results of operations, and cash flows stated within a range of acceptable limits, that is, limits that are reasonable and practicable to attain in financial statements [footnote omitted]. (AICPA, 1992: para. 04)

As has been stated, in the UK, the aim of the external audit is to enable the auditor to express an opinion as to whether a set of financial statements gives 'a true and fair view'. The following two sections aim to give an overview of the background of this phrase and its interpretation by UK auditors.

THE DEVELOPMENT OF 'A TRUE AND FAIR VIEW'

The Joint-Stock Companies Act 1844 initiated the annual statutory audit for companies formed under its auspices. This Act required companies to prepare a 'full and fair' balance sheet; although it did not define this phrase, it 'was generally taken to mean that the balance sheet properly portrayed the company's solvency for the benefit of its bankers and creditors' (Lee, 1972: 22).

The Company Clauses Act 1845 altered the reporting requirements: 'The Directors shall cause full and true Accounts to be kept of all Sums of Money received or expended on account of the Company by the Directors and all Persons employed by or under them.' It is uncertain why the Act changed the words 'full and fair' to 'full and true', but Chastney considered that the change in wording was because the 1844 Act afforded more flexibility in the way financial information could be presented.

The model Articles of Association of the Joint-Stock Companies Act 1856 (Article 74) stated: 'The Accounts of the Company shall be examined and the Correctness of the Balance Sheet ascertained by One or more Auditor or Auditors to be elected by the Company in General Meeting.' The requirements of the auditor were set out in Article 84: 'The Auditors shall make a Report to the Shareholders upon the Balance Sheet and Accounts, and in every such Report they shall state whether, in their Opinion, the Balance Sheet, is a full and fair Balance Sheet, containing the Particulars required by these Regulations, and properly drawn up so as to exhibit a true and correct View of the State of the Company's Affairs.'

New requirements and duties of the auditors were set out in S.23 of the Companies Act 1900: 'In every such report [they] shall state whether, in their opinion, the balance sheet referred to in the report is properly drawn up so as to exhibit a true and correct view of the state of the company's affairs as shown by the books of the company; and such report shall be read before the company in general meeting.' The phrase 'true and correct' was generally taken to mean 'that he [the auditor] had verified the accuracy of the accounting data in the company's books etc., had found it to be free of fraud and error so far as he could tell from his examination, and had verified that it was adequately reported in the balance sheet in accordance with the best practices of the day' (Lee, 1972: 23–4).

The introduction of the phrase 'a true and fair view' was recommended by a UK government committee on company law (the Cohen Committee) to replace the requirement that the balance sheet should exhibit 'a true and correct view' of a company's affairs. This change was advocated by the ICAEW. The reason for the ICAEW's preference for the word 'fair' instead of 'correct' was explained in *The Accountant* of 1 July 1944 (p. 2):

> The word 'correct' has always been too strong because it implies that there is one view which is 'correct' as against all others which are incorrect. In published accounts there is no standard of absolute truth and the Institute's suggested amendment would recognise that the presentation of the figures can only be that which is, in the personal view of the auditor, a fair view.

This view of 'fair' as a more attainable standard than 'correct' is similarly articulated by McMonnies (1967: 73), who considered that:

> 'Fair' is possible, in a way that the 'correct' of the 1929 audit report never was, but 'true'? Any thinking accountant is almost certain to agree that no financial accounts present a true view in the sense that truth is normally understood by reasonable right-minded people. So, because the law tells him to, the auditor proceeds to say . . . something that he does not mean and which, in his heart of hearts, he can hardly believe.

To Lord Benson (1989: 45), 'true and fair' seemed a more demanding requirement than 'true and correct':

> Before the 1948 Act came into force it was not unusual for accountants to say 'Well it is on the right side'. In short, provided that the accounts as presented to shareholders and the public showed a worse position than was in fact the case they could be accepted. . . . The 1948 Act changed the whole situation. It required that the accounts should be 'true and fair'. This meant that the doctrine of 'correctness' or 'is it on the right side' went out of the window. In effect substance took precedence over form.

Lord Benson was one of those considered for the chairmanship of the committee which drafted the Companies Act 1947, which formed the basis for the 1948 Act (Bircher, 1988). The Companies Act 1948 required: 'Every balance sheet of a company shall give a true and fair view of the state of affairs of the company as at the end of its financial year, and every profit and loss account of a company shall give a true and fair view of the profit or loss of the company for the financial year' (S.149[1]). This was the first time that there was a specific requirement for the auditor to express an opinion on more than just the balance sheet.

There has been no explanation of the meaning of 'a true and fair view' in either UK company law or in the EC's Fourth Directive. In 1982, Flint argued that:

> For more than thirty years the directors of companies have approved and auditors have reported on accounts which have been claimed to have given a 'true and fair view' as required by law. It is reasonable to assume, therefore, that there must be some general understanding of what is required, although it is not explicitly recorded. (p. 8)

The meaning of true and fair has been examined (e.g., Houghton, 1987; Parker and Nobes, 1994; Rutherford, 1985; Walton, 1991). Nobes and Parker (1991) examined the actions taken by directors to ensure their financial statements showed a true and fair view, and subsequently (Parker and Nobes, 1991) the operational meaning to auditors of 'true and fair' was explored. A review of the literature reveals very few definitions of the phrase 'a true and fair view', possibly suggesting that few authors are willing to commit themselves to a definition of the 'general understanding' that Flint believed to exist.

Lee (1972: 31) suggested that 'the true and fair view of company profits and financial position should be regarded as the relevant and objective measurement and description of the company's economic progress and financial position, mainly for the benefit of its shareholders'. 'Relevant' means the appropriateness of the information contained in the financial statements to the economic activities and transactions that the statements purport to portray. 'Objective' means that the information is unbiased in relation to the financial interests and informational needs of the shareholders. Another interpretation is offered by Lee (1981: 270):

> Today, 'true and fair view' has become a term of art. It is generally understood to mean a presentation of accounts, drawn up according to accepted accounting principles, using accurate figures as far as possible, and reasonable estimates otherwise; and arranging them so as to show, within the limits of current accounting practice, as objective a picture as possible, free from wilful bias, distortion, manipulation, or concealment of material facts. In other words the spirit as well as the letter, of the law must be observed.

The UK courts have considered how to interpret the 'true and fair' concept. In the case of Re Press Caps Ltd (1949, ch. 434), a shareholder challenged the validity of a balance sheet where freehold property valued at £90,000 had been shown at cost less depreciation of £30,000. The Court of Appeal rejected the challenge. In doing so, Lord Justice Somervell observed that the accounting treatment was 'in accordance with what is very common practice'. The judgement is frequently cited as an indication that a true and fair view can be achieved by following normal accounting principles. However, Williams (1985) points out that the other two judges in the Court of Appeal decided the case on other grounds. A number of authorities have argued that the FRSs and SSAPs are a strong indicator of best professional practice and, therefore, that compliance is likely to ensure 'a true and fair view'. Counsel's opinion obtained by the Accounting Standards Committee expressed the view that 'the immediate effect of a SSAP is to strengthen the likelihood that a court will hold that compliance with the prescribed standard is necessary for the accounts to give a true and fair view' (Hoffmann and Arden, 1983: 156). One company law textbook (Mayson et al., 1989: 218) observed: 'If a court ever had to decide whether a set of accounts gave a true and fair view it is difficult to see what other criteria could be applied than whether the accounts are drawn up in accordance with the considered practice of accountants generally.' Arden (1997: 676) considered that courts would give 'true and fair' a 'contemporaneous interpretation'. She continued:

> The courts would not give it the meaning which it had or may have had when it was first introduced into English law or when the Fourth Directive was adopted. It will give it the meaning which it had when the accounting presentation under dispute was made. In this way the true and fair view is subject to continuous rebirth.

Rutherford (1985: 492–3) saw compliance with Generally Accepted Accounting Principles (GAAP) as the only credible interpretation of a true and fair view (TFV): 'The TFV doctrine as currently employed by the profession lacks a settled and widely accepted explication and is unlikely to achieve one in the near future, except by the adoption of compliance with GAAP as a technical definition.'

It should be noted that the legal interpretations are based on a perception of FRSs and SSAPs as an expression of the accounting profession's best technical judgement. In the USA, the weight of evidence that accounting rules emerge, in response to lobbying, on a 'political' rather than 'technical' basis has led to some questioning of the constitutional validity of accounting standards as privately produced quasi-legislation (Committe, 1990). It might be interesting to see the response of the UK courts to evidence that some of the accounting standards, at least, have emerged from a similarly politicized process (Hope and Gray, 1982).

Following an extensive study, Chastney (1975: 92) concluded: 'True and fair is what you make it.' However, it is from these foundations that the 'true and fair' concept was exported to all the member countries of the European Community (EC). The EC's Fourth Directive on company law, issued on 25 July 1978, has been described as the 'Kingpin of accounting harmonisation within the community' (van Hulle, 1990: 5). Nobes (1993) and Walton (1997) have examined the inclusion of 'true and fair' in the development of the Fourth Directive. All the member states of the then EC complied with the requirement that annual accounts should present a true and fair view. In translation, however, the phrase 'a true and fair view' may take on a different tone. Nobes (1993: 35) suggests that 'the origins of the concept of the pre-dominance of the "true and fair view" (TFV) are British, although the signi-fiers used in other European languages are, in general, not literal translations of this'. As to the Continental understanding of 'a true and fair view', Alexander (1993: 60) quotes French conference delegates as saying, '*Il faut demander aux Anglais* [we must ask the English]'. The following section reports the views of UK practitioners.

THE VIEWS OF UK PRACTITIONERS

In view of the lack of a definitive definition, the interviewees were asked, 'How well does the phrase "true and fair" reflect what the auditor is trying to say about the financial statements?' Given that it was the UK which pressed for this phrase to be included in the Fourth Directive, it was supposed at the outset of the study that there would have been strong support for it. How-ever, this was not the case. What support there was for it was hardly staunch, while a number of the interviewees did express major reservations about it, and in particular about the word 'true'.

It can be seen from Table 7.1 that ten people could be classified as being broadly supportive of the phrase. It was considered to be 'a useful phrase' and 'a powerful concept'. The interviewee most supportive of the phrase offered a combined definition and justification: 'Truth to me encompasses a notion of correctness . . . and fairness . . . is a very much broader concept that says in portraying this reality we have told the reader all that he is entitled to know in the circumstances of this particular business.' However, another firm supporter of the phrase appeared positively to relish the ambiguity: 'I think it is a pretty good phrase because it could mean all things to all men.' Two of its supporters were aware that the phrase was meaningful only to those with a good technical grasp: 'In our opinion it is a valid concept to use . . . [but] the

TABLE 7.1   Summary of auditors' opinions on 'true and fair'

Broad categories	No. of auditors	Spectrum of views	No. of auditors
		Strongly supportive	2
		Supportive but aware that the phrase might confuse non-accountants	3
Supportive	10		
		Broadly supportive but doubts regarding the word 'true'	4
		Broadly supportive but doubts regarding the word 'fair'	1
Largely indifferent	4		4
		Mildy opposed	2
		Opposed because 'true' was misleading	1
Negative	11	Opposed because the phrase was ambiguous	3
		Disliked it, but resigned to it	1
		General distaste for it	4
	25		25

subtlety is lost on a lot of readers'; 'I think it conveys quite a good message to a very informed reader.' Another person raised the specific issue of whether the users appreciated the subtle difference between 'a true and fair view' and 'the true and fair view'. Though there is only a slight difference in wording here, there is a massive difference in meaning. One person, while broadly supportive, was concerned that the word 'fair' was very subjective. Similarly, four interviewees expressed broad support for the phrase but disliked the word 'true'. One stated: 'The idea of truth . . . may be overstating the case a bit.' Another said: 'I'm not sure that true is the best word to use,' and a third stated: 'I think "true" is an unhelpful word.' The fourth person asked, 'What else would you have if you didn't have true and fair?' though he did consider that 'truth is the problem'. Of the ten supporters, only two could be said to be strongly in support.

Four interviewees appeared to accept the phrase but with a large measure of indifference. Their respective comments included: 'Nobody has come up with a better set of words'; 'I don't think there is anything to be gained from slinging it out of the window and starting again'; and 'I don't think the actual terminology matters.' These sorts of view were reflected in the respective comments of two interviewees who were mildly opposed to the phrase: 'The words are ingrained and at the end of the day they're just words'; 'It's jargon. . . . The trouble is there isn't a better substitute.'

Eleven of the interviewees could be classified as having negative views about the phrase. One interviewee who was opposed to the phrase was averse to the word 'true' because 'the two words are in conflict with each other . . . truth has an exactitude about it'. Three interviewees disliked the ambiguity of the phrase. One: 'I have never quite satisfactorily worked out in my own mind what "true and fair" means.' Another stated: 'I think it's a cop-out . . . if you can't define it you probably don't know what it means.' The third person thought 'it's such a sort of muddled statement'. One person who disliked the phrase seemed resigned to its continuance: 'I don't think it is likely to change in the near future.' Four interviewees expressed a general distaste for the phrase. Their comments included: 'I don't think it helps terribly much,' 'I don't think it reflects the results of the auditors' work,' 'It's a clumsy phrase,' and 'It's an apparent contradiction in terms.'

As Table 7.1 highlights, the auditors' comments on the phrase 'true and fair' covered a spectrum of views. The interviewees could be split roughly between fourteen who accepted the phrase and eleven who rejected it. However, a majority of those who broadly accepted it, expressed reservations about or indifference to the phrase. Therefore, this study has highlighted some concern as to whether the phrase 'a true and fair view' really reflects the message the auditor is trying to communicate. These findings contrast with those of Parker and Nobes (1991: 358), who concluded: 'It is auditors who continue to support the TFV [true and fair view] requirement and to make most use of it in practice.' However, the comments reported here appear to show that some senior auditors have major reservations regarding the phrase – most of those interviewed were unenthusiastic about 'a true and fair view'. This distaste was mainly because of the spurious precision implied by the word 'true' and the ambiguity of the formula of the words. It is from this base that it has now been exported to most of Western Europe.

FREE-FORM AUDIT REPORTS

Estes (1982) has called for a 'free-form' audit report – one that does not have standard wording. In terms of communication theory, one would still have to identify what the auditors were trying to communicate at the end of the audit and encode it in the wording of the audit report, and there would still be the problem of whether the message was understood. From a communication theory approach, it may be problematic whether the myriad of potential audit reports would enhance the communication process. If auditors struggle to agree on the general message they are trying to communicate at the end of the audit, it is likely that a message specific to a particular company would be even harder to formulate.

'EVERGREEN AUDIT REPORTS' FOR REAL-TIME REPORTING?

The drive towards 'continuous audit' and 'continuous assurance' has implications for the audit report – which is essentially produced once a year. 'A continuous audit, by definition, would result in the issuance of reports on a short interval basis (e.g., daily, weekly) or on an "immediate" basis, whereby a current report would be available whenever a user needed it' (CICA, 1999: 40). The CICA gave examples of two types of immediate or real-time auditors' reports:

- Evergreen reports. *An audit report, dated as at the time of user access, would be available whenever a user accesses an electronic site containing the subject matter of a continuous audit.*

- Reports on demand. *This type of immediate report would be similar to the evergreen report except that the user would need to specifically request access to the report, rather than it being automatically available. (CICA, 1999: 47)*

The traditional audit report has focused on the financial statements; however, 'when stakeholders want continuous assurance . . . it may make sense for auditors to report on the effectiveness of controls over systems/processes producing information, rather than on the information itself' (CICA, 1999: 71). Thus, the evergreen audit report could give some assurance that a company's systems and controls are operating effectively. The CICA study also gives an example of how an evergreen audit report could relate to a specific account item (such as total inventory costs [p. 49]), but it is likely that this would only be feasible where there is routine hard data.

The concept of an evergreen audit report (or a report on demand) opens up a whole new area for the investigation of the message to be communicated by such a report.

CONCLUSION

This chapter has highlighted differences of opinion on what auditors consider to be the message to be communicated at the end of the audit. If practitioners sending the message are not agreed on what they are trying to say, it is not surprising that users are confused by the audit report. The auditor is not implying that the financial statements are free from bias, nor that they have been verified, but the majority of the interviewees considered that the role of the auditor was to examine the reasonableness of management's justifications for its representations. Therefore, just as an auditor does not specifically look for fraud, it seems that neither does the auditor specifically test for bias. The auditor has to form an opinion on whether the financial statements show a true and fair view. On the basis of the opinions stated here, it would seem that the existence of bias would not necessarily mean that the financial statements did not show a true and fair view. There were concerns regarding the phrase 'a true and fair view', and it may be questionable whether it is communicating the message that the auditor is trying to send.

The publication of the financial statements via the Internet does not really alter the message the auditor is trying to communicate. The accompanying audit report is essentially the same as the hard-copy one (APB, 2001b), though there may be minor differences, such as page numbers. Consideration has to be given to the security of the website (and hence any threat of manipulation of the financial statements or the audit report), but, in terms of communication theory, the essence of the auditors' message will be the same. Evergreen audit reports which relate to continuous assurance will be very different from the traditional audit report. It is likely that their focus will be on the operation of a client's systems rather than their contents.

It is interesting to note that despite all the emphasis of the accounting standard-setters on the decision-usefulness of the financial statements, this seems to have had little impact on the auditors' message. The audit report presumably implies that the financial statements are fit for their purpose, but the audit report does not seem to say (or imply) much about the decision-usefulness of the financial statements.

DISCUSSION QUESTIONS

1   What do you consider to be the message that the auditor is trying to communicate at the end of the statutory external audit?

2   What is your view on whether or not the data in the financial statements have been 'verified' by the auditor?

3   'A true and fair view' is central to financial reporting in the EU. If auditors in the UK, where this phrase originated, have reservations about it, is it a help or hindrance in terms of international harmonization?

4   Part of the auditors' message appears to be that the financial statements are fit for the purpose – but this does not seem to include decision making. Given that, since the 1960s, most accounting standard-setters have been espousing the decision-usefulness of the financial statements, what are the implications of the auditors' views?

5   How useful do you think that 'evergreen audit reports' will be?

REFERENCES

Accounting Principles Board (1970) APB Statement No. 4: *Basic Concepts and Principles Underlying Financial Statements of Business Enterprises*. New York: AICPA.

Alexander, D. (1993) 'A European true and fair view?', *European Accounting Review*, 2 (1): 59–80.

American Accounting Association (AAA) (1966) *A Statement of Basic Accounting Theory*. Sarasota, FL: AAA.

American Institute of Certified Public Accountants (AICPA) (1978) *Commission on Auditors' Responsibilities: Report, Conclusion and Recommendations* (Cohen Commission). New York: AICPA.

American Institute of Certified Public Accountants (AICPA) (1988) *Reports on Audited Financial Statements*. New York: AICPA.

American Institute of Certified Public Accountants (AICPA) (1992) *SAS 69 The Meaning of Present Fairly in Conformity With Generally Accepted Accounting Principles*. AICPA: New York.

Arden, The Hon Mrs Justice (1997) 'True and fair view: a European perspective', *The European Accounting Review*, 6 (4): 675–9.

Auditing Practices Board (APB) (1992) *Auditors' Reports on Financial Statements*, Statement of Auditing Standards Exposure Draft. London: APB.

Auditing Practices Board (APB) (1993) *SAS 600 Auditors' Reports on Financial Statements*. London: APB.

Auditing Practices Board (APB) (1995) *SAS 420 Audit of Accounting Estimates*. London: APB.

Auditing Practices Board (APB) (1999) Bulletin 1999/5 *The Combined Code: Requirements of Auditors Under the Listing Rules of the London Stock Exchange*. London: APB.

Auditing Practices Board (APB) (2001a) Bulletin 2001/2 *Revisions to the Wording of Auditors' Reports and the Interim Review Report*. London: APB.

Auditing Practices Board (APB) (2001b) Bulletin 2001/1 *The Electronic Publication of Auditors' Reports*. London: APB.

Benson, H. (1989) *Accounting for Life*. London: Kogan Page with ICAEW.

Bircher, P. (1988) 'Company law reform and the Board of Trade', *Accounting and Business Research*, 18 (70): 107–19.

Cadbury Report (1992) *The Financial Aspects of Corporate Governance*. London: Gee.

Canadian Institute of Chartered Accountants (CICA) (1999) *Continuous Auditing*. Toronto: CICA.

Chastney, J.G. (1975) *True and Fair View – History, Meaning and Impact of the 4th Directive*. London: ICAEW.

Committe, B.E. (1990) 'The delegation and privatisation of financial accounting rule making authority in the United States of America', *Critical Perspectives in Accounting*, June: 145–66.

Committee on Basic Auditing Concepts (1973) *A Statement of Basic Auditing Concepts*. Sarasota, FL: American Accounting Association.

Cowan, T.K. (1965) 'Are truth and fairness generally acceptable?', *The Accounting Review*, October: 788–94.

Estes, R. (1982) *The Auditor's Report and Investor Behavior*. Lexington, MA: D.C. Heath.

Flint, D. (1982) *A True and Fair View in Company Accounts*. London: Gee and Co./ ICAEW.

Hampel Report (1998) *Committee on Corporate Governance: Final Report*. London: Gee Publishing.

Hatherly, D., Innes, J. and Brown, T. (1991) 'The expanded audit report – an empirical investigation', *Accounting and Business Research*, Autumn: 311–16.

Hoffmann, L. and Arden, M.H. (1983) 'The Accounting Standards Committee joint opinion', *Accountancy*, November: 154–6.

Holt, G. and Moizer, P. (1990) 'The meaning of audit reports', *Accounting and Business Research*, Spring: 111–21.

Hope, A. and Gray, R. (1982) 'Power and policy making: the development of an R and D standard', *Journal of Business Finance and Accounting*, 1982: 531–58.

Houghton, K.A. (1987) 'True and fair view: an empirical study of connotative meaning', *Accounting, Organizations and Society*, 12 (2): 143–52.

Houghton, K.A. and Messier, Jr, W.F. (1991) 'The wording of audit reports: its impact on the meaning of the message communicated', in S. Moriarty (ed.), *Accounting Communication and Monitoring*. University of Oklahoma Center for Economic and Management Research.

Innes, J., Hatherly, D. and Brown, T. (1997) 'The expanded audit report – a research study within the development of SAS600', *Accounting, Auditing and Accountability Journal*, 10 (5): 702–17.

Institute of Chartered Accountants in England and Wales (ICAEW) (1944) 'The institute of company law III', *The Accountant*, 1st July: 1–2.

Lee, G.A. (1981) *Modern Financial Accounting* (3rd edn). Walton-on-Thames: Nelson.

Lee, T.A. (1972) *Company Auditing: Concepts and Practices*. Edinburgh: ICAS.

Lee, T.A. (1986) *Company Auditing* (3rd edn). Wokingham: Van Nostrand Reinhold (UK).

Mautz, R.K. and Sharaf, H.A. (1961) *The Philosophy of Auditing*, American Accounting Association Monograph No. 6. Sarasota, FL: AAA.

Mayson, S.W., French, D. and Ryan, C.L. (1989) *Company Law* (5th edn). London: Blackstone Press.

McMonnies, P. (1967) 'The importance of being English', *The Accountants' Magazine*, February: 72–5.

Nobes, C.W. (1993) 'The true and fair view requirement: impact on and of the Fourth Directive', *Accounting and Business Research*, 24 (93): 35–48.

Nobes, C.W. and Parker, R.H. (1991) '"True and fair": a survey of UK financial directors', *Journal of Business Finance and Accounting*, April: 359–75.

Parker, R.H. and Nobes, C.W. (1991) '"True and fair": UK auditors' view', *Accounting and Business Research*, 21 (84): 349–61.

Parker, R.H. and Nobes, C.W. (1994) *An International View of True and Fair Accounting*. London and New York: Routledge.

Rutherford, B.A. (1985) 'The true and fair view doctrine: a search for explication', *Journal of Business Finance and Accounting*, Winter: 483–94.

Shaw, J.C. (1980) *The Audit Report: What It Says and What It Means*. London: Gee and Co.

Solomons, D. (1989) *Guidelines for Financial Reporting Standards*. London: ICAEW.

Turnbull Report (1999) *Internal Control: Guidance for Directors on the Combined Code*. London: ICAEW.

van Hulle, K. (1990) 'Status of the communities programme in the harmonisation of accounting standards', in *The Future of Harmonisation of Accounting Standards Within the European Communities*, Commission of the European Communities: 2–18.

Walton, P. (1991) *The True and Fair View: A Shifting Concept*, ACCA Technical and Research Committee Occasional Research Paper No. 7.

Walton, P. (1997) 'The true and fair view and the drafting of the Fourth Directive', *European Accounting Review*, 6 (4): 721–30.

Williams, D.N. (1985) 'Legal perspectives on auditing', in D. Kent, M. Sherer and S. Turley (eds), *Current Issues in Auditing*. London: Harper and Row.

In the land of the blind the one-eyed man is not king – he is
regarded as a jibbering idiot.

                                                              – Cherry

A t the moment, it appears that the accounting standard-setters believe
the objective of the financial statements is to enable users to predict
the future, take decisions, judge the stewardship of management
and assess the performance (past and potential) of the reporting entity. But
are all these things really possible or realistic, especially with just one set of
figures? A possible consequence of this is that '[a]nnual reports are expected
to be all things to all people' (*Financial Executive*, 1986: 26). So, has the failure
of accounting standard-setters to be clear about the objective of the financial
statements helped to exacerbate a financial reporting expectations gap? As
hypothesized in Chapter 1, it is suggested that there is a financial reporting
expectations gap composed of two elements – one being an expectations gap
relating to the financial statements and the other being the audit expectations
gap. There has been much discussion of the audit expectations gap; indeed, it
has been a driving force behind the expansion of the audit report and has
focused the debate about the responsibilities of the auditor. Compared to the
recognition given to the audit expectations gap, the possibility of a financial
statements expectations gap has almost been ignored. Yet, the possibility of a
mismatch of expectations regarding the financial statements should be taken
seriously (Figure 8.1); consequently, this will be explored.

THE AUDIT EXPECTATIONS GAP

Much has been written about the possibility of an audit expectations gap
(e.g., AICPA, 1978; CICA, 1988; Chandler and Edwards, 1996; Humphrey,
1997; Humphrey et al., 1992, 1993; Porter, 1993, 1996; Sikka et al., 1998). In
fact, 'the "expectations gap" is one of the most serious issues facing auditing
practitioners and regulators today' (Humphrey et al., 1992: 1). There is a

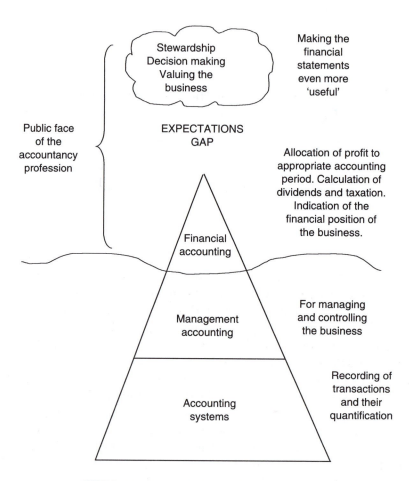

FIGURE 8.1   Uses and abuses of accounting data

debate as to whether it is as a role-perception gap (that is, an ignorance gap), or should be viewed more broadly 'as a representation of the feeling that *auditors are performing in a manner at variance with the beliefs and desires of those for whose benefit the audit is being carried out*' (Humphrey, 1997: 9, emphasis in original). Possible components of the overall audit expectations gap include 'auditors' fraud detection responsibilities, auditor independence, public interest reporting and the meaning of auditors' communications' (Humphrey et al., 1992: 5). Porter (1993: 50) defined 'the expectation–performance gap' as 'the gap between society's expectations of auditors and the auditors' performance, as perceived by society'. She suggested that this gap had two major components:

- a 'reasonableness gap' – the gap between what society expects of auditors and what it was reasonable to expect auditors to achieve

- a 'performance gap' – the gap between the reasonable expectations relating to auditors and the perception of their achievements. This could be subdivided into:
  - a 'deficient standards gap' (that is, potentially not enough was being required of the auditors)
  - a 'deficient performance gap' (that is, the auditors' performance was not as expected by society).

The *Cadbury Report* was concerned about the expectations gap, which it tended to view in terms of the audit expectations gap (1992: 37–40). It advocated clarity regarding the respective responsibilities of the directors and the auditors – the auditors' role did not include:

- the preparation of the financial statements
- providing absolute assurance that the figures were correct
- guaranteeing that the reporting entity will continue in existence.

The committee stressed that '[t]he prime responsibility for the prevention and detection of fraud (and other illegal acts) is that of the board, as part of its fiduciary responsibility for protecting the assets of the company' (p. 43). The detection of fraud was a key part of the early role of the audit, but, from the middle of the twentieth century, detection of fraud became a secondary objective. In Chapter 6, the difficulty of detecting fraud (and even defining it) was seen – if fraudsters cannot detect their own false accounting entries, how can an auditor be expected to find them? Yet, the detection of fraud is still a common expectation of the auditors (hence the call from the Panel on Audit Effectiveness [2000: 88] for auditors to include a 'forensic-type fieldwork phase' in their audits).

Part of the audit expectations gap may be due to the failure to view the external audit as the audit of motivations (Chapter 6). An item in the financial statements may be appropriate, inappropriate or questionable depending on the underlying motivations. So, rather than just thinking of the auditor as auditing the accounting systems and the records, it is necessary to remember that the auditor also has to try to understand management's motivations and their implications for the potential of bias in the financial statements. 'A true and fair view' is central to the auditor's opinion, yet as seen in the previous chapter, even senior auditors have major reservations about this phrase. If there is not a consensus among these people as to the usefulness of the phrase 'a true and fair view', what hope is there that the readers of the audit report will understand it? In the USA, the term 'present fairly' may also contribute to the audit expectations gap (Boyd et al., 2001).

Humphrey et al. (1992: v) considered that 'the auditing profession has reacted defensively to the expectations gap, stressing the need to educate the public as to the "true" nature of the auditors' duties' – but is this so unreasonable? Given the complexities of the financial statements and the limits on what can be expected of the auditors, education of the users would seem to be reasonable. However:

> *If the public expects that an audit provides a certain kind of assurance, whereas in fact it provides much less, then such an expectations gap can be managed as a resource for both parties as follows: auditors can help themselves to the high fees that correspond to high expectations and regulatory publics can help themselves to the appearance of high levels of assurance necessary to legitimate regulatory programmes. In short, the audit society routinely requires expectations gaps about the nature of audit, an imperative which is disturbed by crises where the gap becomes politically visible. (Power, 1994: 305)*

Power considered that 'such gaps are also political resources which preserve a discretionary space for professional action' (1994: 305). Although auditors have been vocal in publicizing some of the components of the audit expectations gap, this is often viewed in terms of self-interest; for example: 'Cynical users might also take the view that the expanded [audit] report containing extensive descriptions of the auditors' responsibilities, is so full of caveats and disclaimers that the opinion itself is both lost in the detail and devalued' (Chitty, 2001: 121). The audit report was expanded in the late 1980s in the USA, and in the UK in 1993 (and revised in 2001). The objective was to set out in more detail the work of the auditors, as well as the auditors' and directors' responsibilities, and thus help tackle the audit expectations gap. However, simply trying to tackle the audit expectations gap in isolation may not work if there is also a financial statements expectations gap. If users have unrealistic expectations about the financial statements themselves, this may lead them to have unrealistic expectations regarding the audit. So, although there has been much discussion of the audit expectations gap, there appears to have been little discussion of the possibility of a financial statements expectations gap. The rest of this chapter explores potential components of the financial statements expectations gap.

THE WIDER EXPECTATIONS GAP

If one can talk about an 'ignorance gap' in terms of auditing, it would seem appropriate to consider the possibility of one in relation to the complex financial statements. There is also the danger that false expectations have been raised regarding what the financial statements are capable of delivering.

Reference to the financial statements expectations gap is fairly limited (e.g., AAA, 1990; *Accountancy*, 1993: 1; ASCPA and ICAA, 1994; Deegan and Rankin, 1999; the Financial Reporting Commission, 1992: 53; Liggio, 1974; Stacy, 1987: 94). An American Accounting Association committee (1990: 383) was concerned that:

> *Less has been heard about an expectations gap in accounting – specifically in financial reporting. The FASB's conceptual framework might have been expected to address this matter, especially in its consideration of issues of recognition and measurement; but SFAC No. 5 was virtually silent on the subject. So was the International Accounting Standards Committee's* Framework for the Preparation and Presentation of Financial Statements *(July 1989) and the Canadian Institute of Chartered Accountants' statement,* Financial Statement Concepts *(September 1988).*

This committee held 'that concern about this expectations gap is widespread' (AAA, 1990: 384). It is interesting to note that David Tweedie (the Chairman of the Accounting Standards Board) was a member of this committee, but that the ASB's *Statement of Principles* was no more explicit in dealing with the financial reporting expectations gap than the earlier frameworks. This was despite a number of replies in the published responses (ASB, 1991a) to the ASB's initial exposure draft explicitly referring to the possibility of an expectations gap in terms of the financial statements (e.g., Arthur Andersen, p. 2; British Bankers' Association, p. 15; ACCA, p. 24; Ernst and Young, p. 39; ICAEW, p. 56; ICAI, p. 64; Higson, p. 77; Price Waterhouse, p. 152; Stoy Hayward, p. 165; Touche Ross, p. 167).

Another mention of a financial reporting expectation gap can be found in an Australian study:

> *The differing perceptions of the financial reporting and audit function – the so-called 'Expectations Gap' . . . goes to the very heart of financial reporting in this country [Australia]. It is vital that this important issue is given a frank and open airing to clear any misconceptions and ensure both preparers and users of financial reports fully understand the reporting and auditing process. (ASCPA and ICAA, 1994: iii)*

Though the Australian study's working party 'was given an unrestricted brief to investigate the "audit expectations gap"', they considered that 'the term "expectations gap" should be used to describe the difference between the expectations of users of financial reports and the perceived quality of financial reporting and auditing services delivered by the Accounting Profession' (1994: 3). The study 'acknowledges that there is, in reality, a difference between the expectations of users and the perceived quality of services' (p. 3) and considered that the gap consisted of 1. unreasonable expectations about what could be delivered and 2. inadequate performance by the accounting profession. Despite the apparent importance of the study, Porter (1996: 131) observed that the report appears to have been 'kept under wraps' and that the Australian bodies that published it were soon out of stock. So, though there is evidence that practitioners are concerned about a potential financial statements expectations gap, there is very little academic literature on this topic. The following sections set out some of the potential components of the financial statements expectations gap.

THE NATURE OF ACCOUNTING

One of the first discussions of an expectations gap relating to the financial statements was by Liggio (1974). He was concerned that since the late 1960s the accountancy profession had been under attack regarding the quality of its professional performance. Liggio (1974: 27) suggested two reasons for this – 'a greater willingness to hold others – especially professionals – accountable for perceived misconduct' and the expectations gap ('a factor of the levels of expected performance as envisioned by both the independent accountant and by the user of financial statements. The difference between these levels of expected performance is the expectation gap.'):

> Users view the financial statements, because of the use of numbers, as having a degree of exactness and certitude which, in fact, they do not have. From our earliest days in grammar school we are taught that two plus two equals four – an unalterable conclusion. Mathematics (and accordingly numbers) is scientific. Numbers are exact, precise and without error; thus, the core of the problem. Financial statements are a composite of numbers. Therefore, logically the reader (or user of financial statements) infers that they have that precision, accuracy and definitiveness. (Liggio, 1974: 28)

This view concurred with the opinions of Philip Loomis (a commissioner of the SEC) who was concerned about the 'widespread public misunderstanding of the function and limitations of accounting' (cited in Liggio, 1974: 29). Therefore, the perception of artificial precision could be an element in the financial statements expectations gap. Although Liggio was also concerned about users' expectations and knowledge of accounting, '[i]t is not fair to blame only the user of the financials for this misunderstanding – for this expectation is aided and abetted by the profession' (1974: 29), and he cites as an example the adoption in the 1930s in the USA of the word 'certificate' in relation to the audit report – '[t]he use of "certificate" and "certified" implied a degree of accuracy which is not inherent in financial statements'.

Communication theory could also help to explain part of the root cause of a financial statements expectations gap (Figure 2.1, Chapter 2). This highlights how the communication process could be disrupted by the use of technical accounting terms ('noise') and the misinterpretation of the meaning of the data in the financial statements ('distortion'). According to communication theory, 'information' is transferred only if the message sent is the message received by the reader. The financial statements contain 'data', and it is only if this data is appropriately interpreted that one can say that information has been received. If users do not understand the mechanisms and conventions behind the compilation of the financial statements, they will struggle to understand the figures. Indeed, Lee and Tweedie (1977) reported that unsophisticated readers of annual reports had difficulty in understanding them. In the case of the more sophisticated readers (that is, those with signi-ficant accounting backgrounds), although they had fewer problems, 'the level of understanding by respondents was not as high as might perhaps have been expected from financial experts' (Lee and Tweedie, 1981: 43). Edey (1971: 440) was also sceptical of the abilities of some potential users:

> To the man in the street, and one must include, I think, the financial journalist in the street, the words 'true and fair' are likely to signify that the accounts give a true statement of facts. He will be likely to associate 'facts' with 'actual profit' and 'actual values'. He does not realise that 'profit' and 'value' are abstractions.

With communication theory, it is important that the messages which both the directors and the auditors are attempting to send are clearly identified. If this is not achieved, it is very difficult to see whether the readers are receiving these messages – hence, the importance of establishing the objective of the financial statements (and the message the auditors are trying to communicate at the end of the audit).

THE USER DECISION-ORIENTED PERSPECTIVE

This perspective has dominated financial reporting standard-setting since the 1970s. Satisfying the needs of users and thus enabling them to take decisions has been the major objective of most recent conceptual frameworks for financial reporting. On a simplistic level, the decision-usefulness approach may be intuitively appealing, but it could also be conceptually flawed.

The strength of support for this decision-oriented approach has been such that Laughlin and Puxty (1981: 45) were very concerned that '[t]his criterion appears to be so widely accepted that it is not thought necessary to argue the fact: the literature tends to take it for granted'. Later, Puxty and Laughlin (1983: 543) feared that 'all extant accounting theory is based upon the usefulness of information to decision-makers, and that this basis has become so fundamentally ingrained that it is no longer considered problematic'. The ASB certainly appeared to endorse the decision-oriented approach with rather fewer reservations (1991b: para. iv): 'The Board considers that the amount of work already undertaken on the objective of financial statements and the qualitative characteristics of financial information has had the result that the substantive issues raised by these topics are now well known.' Therefore, in taking its initial stance on its *Statement of Principles*, the ASB was only following the precedent set by earlier frameworks and academic work – after all, there was no point in reinventing the wheel. However, the decision-usefulness orientation of the financial statements has repeatedly been questioned. Armstrong (1977) was surprised at the reaction to the Trueblood Report's specification that 'the basic objective of financial statements is to provide information useful for making economic decisions' (AICPA, 1973: 13):

> Could there be disagreement with a statement such as this? I am sure you will be astounded to learn that only 37 percent of our respondents were able to recommend the adoption of the objective. Twenty-two percent recommended that it be rejected out of hand; and 10 percent insisted that it needed further study. It is difficult to believe that only 37 percent can agree that the basic objective of financial statements is to provide information useful for making economic decisions. I think this suggests the problem quite clearly. (Armstrong, 1977: 7)

Solomons (1989: 9) stated that 'decisions must be based on estimates about the future, which backward-looking financial statements cannot directly provide'. The ASB's *Statement of Principles* (1999: para. 6) points out that the financial statements can at best provide only some of the information useful for taking economic decisions. Parker (1986: 17) makes the point that there may not be that much new information contained in the financial statements: 'Since this information will normally have been impounded from newspaper reports, stockbroker bulletins and investment circulars, it is argued that the annual report is issued too late to be of any use for shareholder decision-making.' In the case of *Caparo Industries plc* v *Dickman and Others* (1990), Lord Jauncey stated that 'the purpose of annual accounts so far as members were concerned was to enable them to question past management actions, to exercise voting rights, and to influence future policy and management. Investment advice to individual shareholders was no part of the statutory purpose' (quoted in Humphrey et al., 1992: 17). Therefore, at the moment, 'auditors have no liability to existing shareholders who rely on their report for investment decisions (e.g. to buy or sell shares), or actual creditors of the company who may make similar decisions about maintaining or withdrawing credit, or potential investors whether of equity or debt, or other potential creditors (e.g. trade creditors), who rely on the audit report for a view of the financial position of the company' (Company Law Review Steering Committee, 2001: para. 8.127). At the time of the Caparo judgement, there was an outcry, and there were calls for the position to be reviewed. The Company Law Review Steering Committee (2001: para. 8.128) did review the position and concluded:

> First, the question is really a wider one than auditors' duties. It is a question of who may place reliance upon, and sue in respect of, representations in the accounts. Logically, directors who prepare the accounts should have the same range of liability as auditors. Thus the extension of directors' duties and those of companies vicariously on their behalf, needs also to be taken into account. The other difficulty is the prevention of abusive exploitation by claimants of any such extension. . . . . If such difficulties could not be dealt with, it would be wiser to leave the Caparo rule in place, with the possibility of its development by the courts on a case by case basis.

In management accounting, the phrase 'different costs and benefits for different purposes' is well known; however, in the financial accounting area, there is the danger that one set of figures appears to suit all purposes. Clark (1923: 234) pointed out that:

> If cost accounting sets out determined to discover what the cost of everything is, and convinced in advance that there is one figure which can be found and which will furnish exactly the information which is desired for every possible purpose, it will necessarily fail, because there is no such figure. If it finds a figure which must be right for some purpose it must necessarily be wrong for others.

This emphasizes the point that it is important to know the reason why the costs and benefits are required because this influences the data that needs to be collected. For example (Drury, 2000: 22–33):

- In cost accounting, costs may be classified as direct or indirect (in relation to a cost objective).
- In decision making, the cost classification is relevant or irrelevant (to the decision) – with an emphasis on the future.
- In cost-volume-profit analysis, the distinction between fixed and variable costs is key.
- In responsibility accounting, costs are classified as controllable or non-controllable.

The point is that costs and benefits which are produced for one purpose may be totally misleading if used in another context. The financial statements (currently) contain predominantly historical costs, which presumably should be classified as sunk costs and thus would be irrelevant in terms of decision making (they certainly would be in a management accounting decision-making situation). It has been acknowledged that in order to enable users to take decisions the financial statements need to contain relevant costs; however, this has been used as justification for the adoption of current values (e.g., AAA, 1966: 34) (this debate is not helped by the phrases 'current costs' and 'current values' being used almost synonymously).

Decision making requires assessments about the future; therefore, future costs and benefits would be relevant. One should be interested in the best future course of action; therefore, decisions should be based on estimates about what is going to happen in the future – not on what has happened in the past. Opportunity costs are not used in cost accounting, but they are key in decision making – they are certainly not employed in financial accounting. In the management accounting context, obtaining costs and benefits for decision making is not just a matter of restating of the existing costs and revenues, but a whole different set of costs and benefits is required. This would not be the case with financial accounting if historical costs were simply replaced with current values. Analysts in particular have been prominent in supporting the adoption of current values; for example, Damant (1996: 30) considered that 'users need to forecast cash flows; that is what the capital markets (and the various frameworks of principle) are about – and for this we need up-to-date valuations' and, he continued, 'a wide range of users of accounts support current values'.

Although most recent conceptual frameworks relating to external reporting endorse the notion that financial statements are to enable users to take decisions, they seem to give scant regard to the data that would be required: 'I believe that accounting ought to supply the data specified by decision theories rather than the data desired by decision makers' (Sterling, 1970: 454). Sterling continued:

> *In my view, the accounting profession ought to devote some of its effort and resources to the education of the receivers. The profession ought to tell the receivers which decision theories are correct and then supply the data specified by those theories. Other professions have done this, e.g. the medical profession has gone to some lengths to convince the population that the germ theory of medicine is correct and that the demon theory of medicine is incorrect. (Sterling, 1970: 455)*

Ijiri (1975: 32) made the point that every transaction is recorded in the accounting system: 'If the objective of accounting is limited to providing useful information for decision makers, why is the practice not more selective in choosing the items to be recorded and reported?'

In the litigious climate of the business world, it is important that careful consideration is given to the implications of what is being stated. An emphasis on decision making may appear to make the financial statements 'useful' and enhance the status of the accountancy profession. As such, this may be an interesting theoretical approach; however, the implementation of a conceptual framework based on such ideas may be problematic. It would appear that the emphasis on decision making may be another element in the financial statements expectations gap. Laughlin and Puxty (1981: 45) questioned 'the unspoken assumption' that because the financial statements are produced for users therefore users' needs must be paramount. Perhaps it is also necessary to question the logic behind the argument that because users take decisions based on the financial statements the objective of the financial statements is to enable users to take decisions. Financial statements may provide a track record on which users may try to make forward-looking estimates; however, it would appear to be circular reasoning then to adopt decision making as the objective of the financial statements.

It was seen in the previous chapter that the external auditors did not offer the suggestion that the financial statements were fit for decision making as part of their audit message. One might conclude that this was because:

> *Most auditors had probably been educated to believe that accounting serves primarily a stewardship function, and that they would find it somewhat threatening to contemplate that accounting should have a more activist function in economic society. Such preconceptions and*

predispositions made it difficult for the board [that is, FASB] to impose
a decision usefulness objective on a profession that had been
accustomed to view accounting as basically a passive record-keeping
activity. (Zeff, 1999: 107)

However, an alternative view is that the auditors know more about the
financial statements than most users or other sections of society. Therefore,
when the implied message contained in an unqualified audit report is that the
financial statements are fit for their purpose but that this does not seem to
include decision making, this should be taken seriously.

THE IRRELEVANCE OF HISTORICAL COSTS?

The questioning of the use of historical costs in financial accounting is not a
new phenomenon; however:

Many accountants have deserted the historical cost camp upon
hearing a persuasive argument that historical cost is irrelevant to
economic decisions. Relevance to decisions is considered to be the
primary requirement of accounting information, and hence irrelevance
to decisions appears to be the most fatal weakness of historical costs.
(Ijiri, 1975: 85)

The perceived weaknesses of historical cost accounting (HCA) have been
listed as follows by the AAA report of the Committee on Accounting and
Auditing Measurement (1990: 394–5):

- There is 'a time lag in the matching of costs and revenues', thus leading to
  the overstatement of profit when prices are rising and its understatement
  when prices are falling.
- In times of changing prices, 'the value of resources to the enterprise is
  misrepresented if they continue to be carried at historical cost'.
- 'By showing only realized gains and ignoring unrealized gains (and some
  losses), the income statement misrepresents the performance of the enterprise and of its management, period by period.' An example cited was
  that of land; under HCA, 'the financial statements may fail to give credit
  for many years for a good decision to acquire the assets at an earlier time'.
- Therefore, the financial ratios may also be distorted.

- Due to the emphasis on realization, 'management can manipulate profits by judiciously timing the sale of assets or the redemption of liabilities that show gains or losses'.
- With HCA, 'information is lacking about purchasing power gains and losses on monetary assets and liabilities'.
- Comparison of results between time periods will be distorted by the changing purchasing power of money.
- Due to the 'changes in the value of money, and because financial statements contain a mixture of past costs and current values, they cannot claim to be truly additive'.

This committee considered that 'conceptually the superiority of financial reports based on current values is so self-evident, at least on the relevance dimension, that we cannot defend the maintenance of historical cost as the primary basis of measurement' (AAA, 1990: 397). But not all the members of the committee agreed with this – two members of the six-member team issued minority reports. One person was concerned that 'statements which say that historical cost have no value are too strong' (AAA, 1990: 407), and the other suggested:

> that the case has not been made for current cost/value measures for input assets, and that a productive direction for future investigation would be to examine the issues for a value-in-use perspective. Within this perspective, those advocating current values for input assets would need to put forward persuasive evidence that such values are representative of value in use – that is, that there is good cause to believe that changes in input values will lead to corresponding changes in output values. (AAA, 1990: 411)

The movement away from pure historical cost reporting presents a problem as to the *presentation* of any such adjustments in the financial statements. Traditionally, revaluations of fixed assets resulted in the adjustment to companies' reserves. As this was not always easy to detect, FRS 3 (*Reporting Financial Performance* first introduced by the ASB in 1992) advocated an additional statement:

> The range of important components of financial performance which the FRS requires reporting entities to highlight would often be incomplete if it stopped short at the profit and loss account, since certain gains and losses are specifically permitted or required by law or

an accounting standard to be taken directly to reserves. An example is an unrealised gain, such as a revaluation surplus on fixed assets. It is necessary to consider all gains and losses recognised in a period when assessing the financial performance of a reporting entity during that period. Accordingly, the FRS requires, as a primary statement, a statement of total recognised gains and losses [STRGL] to show the extent to which shareholders' funds have increased or decreased from all the various gains and losses recognised in the period. (ASB, 1992: para. 56)

In 1999, the G4 + 1 group of accounting standard setters (that is, standard-setters from *five* countries, namely, Australia, Canada, New Zealand, the UK and the USA, plus members of the IASC) issued a discussion paper (*Reporting Financial Performance: Proposals for Change*). 'The Group states that its proposals about reporting financial performance derive from a predictive ability or predictive value objective (para. 1.5 and para. 1.6) and takes as given that all gains and losses are useful for this purpose (para. 1.10)' (AAA, 2000: 366–7). Davies et al. (1999: 1547) stated: 'The crux of the proposal is that the profit and loss account and the statement of total recognised gains and losses should be combined into a single performance statement divided into three sections: operating (or trading) activities; financing and other treasury activities; and other gains and losses (comprising some of those shown as non-operating exceptional items under FRS 3 together with those formerly shown in the statement of total recognised gains and losses).' However, the use of the word 'performance' may be a weakness:

This paper is founded on the preconception that all the non-owner movements from one balance sheet to the next represent 'performance', and this is the fundamental problem. Although the ASB may regard the statement of total recognized gains and losses as a performance statement, this is not a view that is widely shared; this statement is rarely even discussed by either preparers or users of accounts. Revaluations that reflect changes in the replacement cost of operational fixed assets, or the effects of translating the opening balance sheet of foreign subsidiaries, are more in the nature of capital maintenance adjustments than performance measures. (Davies et al., 1999: 1551)

Following on from the G4 + 1 paper, the ASB (2000) issued FRED 22 (a revision of FRS 3 *Reporting Financial Performance*) – proposing that all gains and losses were to be reported in a 'Statement of Financial Performance'. This may be seen as an 'attempt to address the problem of accounts users ignoring the STRGL [Standard of Total Recognised Gains and Losses] and focusing only on the "bottom line"' (*Accountancy*, 2001: 7). The idea that the 'performance' statement as conceived could show the whole picture and that it does indeed show performance may be part of the financial statements expectations gap.

It may be thought that historical cost is more 'objective' than any other valuation basis, but, as Sterling (1970: 16) points out: 'Most writers outside the field of accounting consider that the word "cost" closes the discussion of objectivity. Nothing could be further from the truth.' There are subjective assessments even with historical costs – but the whole notion of splitting the life of the business into accounting periods is subjective, and it is valid to question what the figures mean. However, the idea that a quick fix can be supplied by using alternative accounting bases (current costs, replacements costs, current values, etc.) is problematic, because there would still be the question as to what the adjusted figures were supposed to mean:

> *This information is useless if accountants, financial analysts, and other users of financial statements are insufficiently trained and cannot properly interpret this kind of information. Indeed, this may be the primary reason why Beaver and Landsman (1983), in studying the reaction of statement users, came to the surprising conclusion that financial statements based merely on historical costs are at least as informative, or even more so, than those using current values or any other kind of price-level adjustment. (Mattessich, 1995: 98)*

It is therefore valid to question whether adjustments from historical cost to any another valuation basis would have a material impact on the financial statements. As has been seen, the operational definition of 'material' is if something would reasonably influence the decisions of an addressee of the auditors' report. In view of the above comment by Mattessich, it would seem that adjustments to the historical cost figures would not have a material impact on the financial statements – they may just give them the appearance of artificial precision and thus could be part of the financial statements expectations gap. Perhaps, we should remember:

> *If accounts are bound to be untruths anyhow . . . there is much to be said for the simple untruth as against a complicated untruth, for if the untruth is simple, it seems to me that we have a fair chance of knowing what kind of untruth it is. A known untruth is much better than a lie, and provided that the accounting rituals are well known*

and understood accounting may be untrue but it is not lies; it does not deceive because we know that it does not tell the truth, and we are able to make our own adjustment in each individual case, using the results of the accountant as evidence rather than as definitive information. (Boulding, 1962: 55)

In terms of decision making, even current values may be irrelevant. If current values were used and the associated unrealized gain was shown in the accounts, what would happen if there was a collapse in the current value after someone had taken a decision based on this data? The cry of 'Sue the accountant' would again go out. It would seem that the accountant cannot win. If there are unrealized gains that are not shown in the financial statements, it is argued that users may take the wrong decision; if the unrealized gains are shown, but they then disappear, it would again be argued that the users have been misled. Therefore, maybe users should be discouraged from taking decisions based on the financial statements irrespective of whether historical costs or current values are used.

PREDICTING FUTURE CASH FLOWS

It could be argued that many of the problems associated with financial reporting stem from the vagueness of accounting 'theory' (as discussed in Chapter 2), and the problems of specifying the objective of the financial statements (as discussed in Chapter 4). The use of theory adopted from economics, in which the prediction of the future tends to be a matter of course, may not have helped the situation. When accountants predict the future, it is almost expected that they will be accurate, though history should teach us that it is difficult enough to try to understand what has happened in a past accounting period, never mind what will happen in the future. Yet, from the 1970s onwards, more and more consideration has been given to the incorporation of future cash flows in the financial statements (e.g., AAA, 1971; FASB, 1990, 2000). Chambers considered that 'it is notorious that those who attempt to quantify future magnitudes may obtain vastly different results, as well as results which differ materially from what the magnitude turns out in due course to be' (1998: 43). This may present a problem in terms of the reliability of the data and its audit. It is also very unlikely that taxation or dividends will be paid on the basis of anticipated future cash flows, and so alternative disclosures will probably still be required.

The final version of the ASB's *Statement of Principles* (1999: para. 1.14) stated that '[i]nvestors require information on financial performance' because such information 'is useful in assessing the entity's capacity to generate cash flows from its existing resource base'. In 1996, the ASB's Technical Director at the Financial Accounting and Audit Research Conference (held at City University) seemed to imply that the objective of the financial statements was to enable users to make their own predictions of the future cash flows of an enterprise. However, the audience reaction to this was certainly not favourable, and many people were sceptical of the usefulness of even current values in predicting future cash flows. Most financial advertisements warn that past performance is not necessarily a guide to future performance; however, the standard-setters seem to be actively assisting users to make these predictions. In the current dynamic and volatile business environment, the prediction of future cash flows based on the financial statements may be part of the financial statements expectations gap.

FREEDOM FROM BIAS?

It has been seen that for accounting data to be 'useful' to users, it needs to be reliable: 'To be reliable, the information contained in financial statements must be neutral, that is, free from bias' (IASC, 1989: para. 36), but are the financial statements free from bias? Is it the role of the auditors to eliminate or minimize bias? If auditors view their role as being to examine the reasonableness of management's justifications for its representations, can it really be claimed that the financial statements are free from bias? If it is thought that the financial statements should be free from bias, what action must be taken to ensure this is the case? Simply to say that the financial statements comply with accounting standards will in itself not ensure that they are free from bias. It is the subjective nature of accounting estimates and ulterior management motivations, hidden by the complexity of modern business structures, that make bias so difficult to detect. It appears that some directors give a great deal of consideration to the composition of their financial statements. Reported profit is a function, not just of the economic activity of a business (sales, purchases, production, etc.), but also of its discretionary expenditure and the accounting estimates made by management. Just as 'the cost' of a particular item depends on the reason for wanting to know this information (that is, relative truth), so it could be argued that 'the profit' figure may be dependent upon management's (ulterior?) motivations.

DO THE FINANCIAL STATEMENTS REPRESENT GOOD STEWARDSHIP?

Though there are many controversial areas in financial accounting, one view that has not really been questioned is that financial statements are produced for stewardship purposes. However, Carsberg et al. (1974: 166) considered that '[t]he usefulness of this concept . . . has been blunted by a failure to make clear exactly what it means'; consequently, '[i]t may be useful, for the sake of clarity, to avoid the use of the word stewardship and to distinguish reporting on the legality of past behaviour on the one hand from reports on economic efficiency on the other' (pp. 166–7).

The parable of the talents (which is often used as an example of what is meant by stewardship [e.g., Pannell, 1978; Whittington, 1991]) clearly shows that the master knew what his stewards could achieve. As was shown in Chapter 3, this parable is probably better viewed in a management accounting context rather than a financial accounting one. This example of stewardship required the master to have the ability and expertise to formulate a judgement regarding the servants' actions. The complexity of modern businesses and the complete separation of ownership and management in large corporate organizations may mean that many shareholders have only a superficial knowledge of the business they own. This presumably makes it difficult for them to form a judgement, based on the financial statements, about management's stewardship abilities. Any such assessment is especially problematic if the financial statements are not free from bias. The financial statements may be used to attempt to judge performance, but this might actually be part of the financial statements expectations gap.

> Many a wise and desirable managerial decision is not reflected in the income statement until years after the decision was made. Often, the effects of various decisions are so mingled in a given income statement that the only result is an average of unknown weighting and of therefore dubious significance . . .
>
> Although there may be validity in the statement that entity income does in the final analysis represent a test of over-all management, this test is far too crude and much too vague and general to serve either as an appraisal of over-all managerial efficiency or as a guide for managerial decision. (Vatter, 1947: 34–5)

The ASC (1986: 11) considered that 'while historical cost information may appear adequate for stewardship purposes, it may provide unsatisfactory indicators for decision making'. This contrasts with Chambers' opinion (1966a: 354) that:

> Perhaps the most universal justification for holding this [cost] doctrine is the so-called stewardship notion, the import of which is that

> *business management are accountable for the money tokens that come into their hands. No doubt they are, but a cash account is all that would be required to serve this function. The superstructure of accounting processes and financial statements generally would have no justification if this were the primary function of accounting.*

Chambers (1966b: 451) expanded on this as follows: 'To hold management accountable in sums of money spent under conditions no longer prevailing, and in all likelihood spent by persons who are no longer managers, and sums which have no logical or discoverable relationship to a present monetary equivalent, is to fly in the face of the nature of things and to make accountability a ludicrous notion.'

It is important to remember that the auditor's report says nothing about *e*conomy, *e*fficiency and *e*ffectiveness (the three Es), yet if stewardship was really the objective of the financial statements, surely this would be necessary? The three Es were central to UK public sector 'value for money' audits during the 1980s and 1990s. The National Audit Office (1988) defined the three Es as follows:

> **Economy** *is concerned with minimizing the cost of resources acquired or used, having regard to appropriate quality . . .*
>
> **Efficiency** *is concerned with the relationship between the output of goods, services or other results and the resources used to produce them. How far is maximum output achieved for a given input, or minimum input used for a given output? . . .*
>
> **Effectiveness** *is concerned with the relationship between the intended results and the actual results of projects, programmes or other activities. How successfully do outputs of goods, services or other results achieve policy objectives, operational goals and other intended effects? (cited by Lapsley, 1996: 112)*

The difficulty of auditing the three Es should not be underestimated, especially in relation to effectiveness (that is, assessing whether an organization is achieving its goals and objectives: 'Purposeful goals/objectives are not easy to establish, particularly when they are required to be publicly stated' (Small, 1996: 132).

If the auditor says nothing about the three Es, how are the users expected to form their own opinions? This is especially problematic in the light of Lee and

Tweedie's empirical evidence (1977; 1981) regarding users' lack of compre-
hension of some fundamental aspects of accounting.

The meaning of stewardship has changed over time – to such an extent that
it is now such a confused notion that it has almost been rendered meaningless. Meanings attributed to it include honesty and integrity, custodianship,
accountability of management, good management, compliance with legal
requirements, control of management, earning a return, and corporate governance. Today, the word 'stewardship' is being used almost like a comfort
blanket – something to cling to in times of uncertainty. As a result of all this,
it would seem to be inappropriate to claim that stewardship is the objective of
the financial statements – to do so may merely contribute to the financial
statements expectations gap.

THE CALCULATION OF 'WEALTH'

During the *Statement of Principles* debate, there was a concern about the relative
importance of the balance sheet in comparison with the profit and loss account
(that is, the 'asset and liability view' in comparison with the 'revenue and
expense view'). Ron Paterson (of Ernst & Young) was particularly vocal in this
respect. Ernst & Young (1993) were concerned about the perceived focus of the
ASB on the balance sheet, and they feared that 'the balance sheet is to be the
focal point of the accounts, with the profit and loss account and other statements dependent upon it' (p. 2). Ernst & Young considered that this approach
had an intuitive appeal because '[l]aymen tend to think of a balance sheet as a
statement of a company's wealth, and on this basis it may seem sensible to
measure profits and other gains by measuring the increase in that wealth' (p. 2).
Rather than a process of valuation, Ernst & Young believed that financial
reporting 'is really an exercise in analysing and interpreting the transactions
undertaken by the company and allocating them to the years to which they
belong' (p. 3). Paterson's view (1995: 81) was that the ASB aimed to 'get the
balance sheet right'; this he then contrasted with the 'traditional' approach in
which 'transactions provide the starting point and the process is one of
matching them to accounting periods, with the balance sheet a statement of
residuals'. The allocation perspective does have a well-established history.
After all, it was the development of permanently invested capital which gave
rise to the need to divide the life of a business enterprise into arbitrary
accounting periods. In the 1936 version of the American Accounting Association's statement of accounting principles (AAA, 1936: 188–9), it was considered that '[a]ccounting is . . . not essentially a process of valuation, but the
allocation of historical costs and revenues to current and succeeding fiscal
periods'. Demski and Feltham (1976: 4–5) characterized this as the historical
communication approach:

> *[This] dominated the accounting literature until about 1960. Its dominance has faded, but it is still widely used and advocated. . . . The proponents of this historical communication approach maintain that the job of the accountant is to provide one type of clearly described data on a caveat emptor basis. The user should understand what the data represent and should proceed from that point. The major need is for an adequate set of standards, principles, definitions, or other guides to data collection.*

As was seen in Chapter 4, central to the *Statement of Principles* debate was the specification of what the financial statements were trying to achieve. Ernst & Young (1996: 4) considered that the ASB was attempting to use current values as a measure of an enterprise's wealth:

> *The Statement of Principles rejects historical cost accounting as the basis of British companies' accounts. . . . In its place, the ASB's vision of accounting is based on a simple economic model that involves measuring movements in a company's wealth from one year to the next.*

So, was there an attempt by the ASB to say that current values in the balance sheet represent the wealth of an enterprise? The *Statement of Principles* does not appear to use the word 'wealth', and if one consults Tweedie and Whittington (1990), one can probably conclude that the ASB did not imply that a current value balance sheet represents the wealth of the enterprise. Tweedie and Whittington preferred to seek 'economic relevance' (that is, relevance to decision making) rather than 'economic reality', which they considered 'has connotations of identifying "true" income or value, and the idea of identifying such single-valued summary measures of overall performance or worth seems to us to be inappropriate in a realistic setting of uncertainty and market imperfection or incompleteness' (1990: 88).

In an accounting context, there is the problem of what is meant by the word 'wealth'. In Chapter 2, it was seen that early accounting theorists had borrowed terms from economics. One of these was the word 'wealth', and 'accounting repeatedly has been regarded as the theory and practice of measurement of income and wealth' (AAA, 1971: 47). 'The undisputed definition of *income* is that it is the difference between wealth at two points in time after adjusting for consumption for individuals or investment for firms' (Sterling, 1979: 191, emphasis in original). As a consequence, Sterling concluded: 'Since income and wealth are inextricably entwined, an incorrect measure of one yields an incorrect measure of the other and vice versa' (1979: 196). In economics, 'wealth' is an extremely difficult concept to define and thus measure. Moonitz

(1961: 12) considered that accountants had 'translated the "wealth" of economics into the "assets" of accounting'. On this basis, it might be claimed that the balance sheet showed the 'wealth' of the business. However, 'Canning [1929] asserted that scarcely any two amounts representing asset classes in a balance sheet can be added, legitimately, to obtain a measure of the wealth of an entity in respect of those classes; and *a fortiori* a balance sheet total for assets cannot be taken as a measure of aggregate wealth' (Chambers, 1998: 42):

> It follows that, although accounting may be regarded as 'the theory and practice of measurement of income and wealth', accounting as it is done is not in fact an exercise in the measurement of wealth and income at all. For just as mistakes may be made in the simplest acts of measuring, mistakes may be made in the measurement of income and wealth. It is a mistake to consider the cost of an asset as a representation of or measure of the wealth (or part of the wealth) of its owner. And if mistaken representations of wealth are made at successive dates, the increment in wealth (income) during the interval will not be properly represented. The Committee [AAA, 1971] apparently does not see these things as mistakes. Yet they are just the kinds of mistakes which have led to the bankruptcy of many and to the costly litigation and settlements which have fallen on many professional accountants in the recent past. (Chambers, 1998: 42)

It is doubtful whether a balance sheet (even adjusted for current values) could ever represent a company's 'wealth', and so this connotation may be another example of the financial statements expectations gap.

CASE STUDY 8.1   Advertising the expectations gap

The directors of a dynamic advertising agency have just read that the balance sheet represents the wealth of their business. They are a little concerned about this. Because of the nature of their business, they rent their office and lease their photocopier, and the only assets are cash, debtors and stationery – therefore their balance sheet does not contain very much. They think that the performance of their business is based on the success of their past advertising campaigns, their client list and the creativity of their current employees. These non-tangible things are not really represented in their financial statements. The directors are a little confused as to why the accounting standard-setters seem to be preoccupied with the current value of their paper clips – presumably reported on a real-time basis.

The changes in the business environment (the growth of service industries, the development of the knowledge economy and the decline of the manu-facturing sector) are creating new problems (see case study 8.1). If accountants appear to be unable to appreciate the limitations of the financial statements in the old economy, it is unlikely that things will improve with the advent of the new economy.

HARNESSING THE FORCES OF TECHNOLOGY: REAL-TIME REAL PROBLEM?

The financial world is in the midst of a communications revolution, and no accountant can be unaware of the impact of this development. In response to changing business needs, financial reporting requirements have developed over the years – and will continue to develop. Perhaps the greatest challenge at the moment is to respond to the clamour, from analysts and other external parties, for real-time reporting.

> *Continuous reporting means making digitized information available through electronic channels simultaneously with its creation. To the extent that automated sensors create digitized data about business activities concurrent with those activities, continuous reporting means real-time reporting. To the extent that information about business activities is digitized later (for example, through human intervention), continuous reporting means availability through electronic channels immediately upon digitization. Such information does not change continuously, but it is continuously the freshest digital information available. (Elliott, 2002: 140)*

The argument put forward is that immediate access to and a greater quantity of data about a company must be a good thing and so should result in improved market efficiency. Therefore, on the face of it, this desire may seem justifiable. Such a move would obviously require the establishment of accounting standards to ensure consistency between companies. Elliott (2002: 141) considered that '[a]fter continuous financial reporting comes the next generation of business reporting: investor access to corporate databases'. But before all of this starts to happen, perhaps it would be useful to consider what the benefit of such a development would be.

There is a danger that this proposition is confusing the 'recording' aspect of accounting and the 'reporting' aspect of the financial statements. At a very basic level, 'raw' accounting data is simply a means of keeping track of the transactions undertaken by an organization. The periodic financial statements are an attempt, using this accounting data and related assumptions and conventions, to allocate profit to the appropriate accounting period and to state the financial position at a point in time. All this occurs after the necessary cut-off adjustments have been made. To report real-time or to allow outsiders access to the real-time 'raw' accounting data does raise the question of what they would do with this data and how exactly it would lead to greater market efficiency.

In fact, there could be very real dangers if analysts were able to gain access to the management accounting systems. Real-time reporting would not allow time for the investigation of variations and deviations, and the obtaining of resultant explanations. In any accounting system, mispostings (accidental or deliberate) may occur, and real-time access may mean that there would not be enough time for this to be spotted and corrected. There would also be problems with cut-off and period-end adjustments. Even if companies utilized computer programs to make these adjustments minute-by-minute or even day-by-day, would this really mean very much? An alternative could be simply to report real-time sales figures compared to budgets, but even here there would be problems with monthly peaks and troughs – maybe very little activity at the start of a month and bunching of sales towards the end. Therefore, instantaneous access to this data may not necessarily result in greater market efficiency, though greater volatility in share price movements could be a distinct possibility.

It is problematic how all this real-time data would be monitored by its intended users. There is a very real danger that even if such a development occurred, users could suffer from information overload. It is probable that even management is very wary about drawing conclusions from this unrefined data. If external users were granted real-time access to the internal management accounting data, how much more short-term could things become?

Though people may want this access, do they have a justifiable right to it? It is unlikely that management would favour such a development. Obviously, management would be concerned about the loss of confidentiality, though it has been suggested that companies would compete for capital and share price by making management accounting data available real-time. However, the paradox is that making real-time data available may actually increase company risk. All of this should lead to a questioning of the value of real-time access to internal accounting data even if it were to be made available. Surely, quality rather than quantity should take precedence in any future developments? Just the fact that people want such access does not necessarily mean that it will improve their decision-making procedures, and it would surely exacerbate the short-term culture which appears to be so prevalent at the moment. The way forward would appear to be the education of analysts and other external parties regarding the purposes of and the limitations of accounting data.

The benefit derived from external access to these internal systems would appear to be dubious and may even be detrimental to the running of public companies. It is probable that it would result in the amplification of movements in share prices and thus increase the threat of short-termism. Therefore, the development of such access could result in major problems for both management and the financial world.

CONCLUSION

This chapter has concentrated on identifying some of the potential components of the financial statements expectations gap. It is suggested that central to this has been the emphasis of standard-setters on the decision-usefulness of the financial statements. The history of the financial statements shows that the necessity to calculate profit came about as a result of the need to divide up the life of an enterprise into accounting periods following the development of permanently invested capital. The calculation of profit, dividends and taxation is probably as important today as at any time in the past. Such calculations may not be as exciting as predicting the future, but they would still appear to be useful.

While the expectations gap relating to the financial statements remains, mere changes in the audit report may not go very far towards eliminating the overall expectations gap. Twenty of the senior practitioners interviewed in Chapter 7 thought that an expectations gap relating to the financial statements did exist in the public's mind. One person stated: 'I think the expectations gap on the accounts is bigger than most people appreciate. The expectations gap on the audit report is perhaps less.' Therefore, simply changing the wording of the audit report may not be enough to overcome the audit expectations gap.

This chapter has suggested that a misinterpretation of the usefulness and limitations of the financial statements appears to have resulted in a financial statements expectations gap. Instead of a claim that the financial statements can be all things to all people, a greater recognition of the limitations of the financial statements may help to tackle the financial statements expectations gap. Only the recognition of these limitations and the clearer specification of the overall problem will enable the commencement of the real debate regarding the corporate communication of performance and risk.

DISCUSSION QUESTIONS

1 The phrase 'different costs and benefits for different purposes' is well known in management accounting. Contrast the management accountant's approach to costs and benefits for decision making with the stance taken by the financial accounting standard-setters. Do you consider these approaches to be consistent?

2 How useful do you think it is to have a conceptual framework for external reporting based on unspecified users, taking unspecified decisions, at unspecified points in time, with unspecified success?

3 Critically assess the usefulness of historical costs.

4 Users take decisions based on the financial statements, and so the argument is that the objective of the financial statements is to enable users to take decisions. How does this differ from the following situation? There are speed limits on the roads, and motorists might exceed the speed limits. Can one therefore conclude that the objective of a speed limit is to enable a driver to speed?

5 Using the financial statements to predict the future financial performance of an enterprise may have been the twentieth-century equivalent of the medieval alchemist's dream. In the current dynamic and volatile business environment, how useful do you consider the financial statements to be in predicting future financial performance and, in particular, in evaluating an entity's ability to generate cash?

REFERENCES

Accountancy (1993) 'Greater expectations', *Accountancy*, January: 1.

Accountancy (2001) 'Wave goodbye to the p & l', *Accountancy*, January: 7.

Accounting Standards Board (ASB) (1991a) *Responses to the Exposure Draft – 'Statement of Principles, The Objective of Financial Statements and the Qualitative Characteristics of Financial Information'*. London: ASB.

Accounting Standards Board (ASB) (1991b) *The Objective of Financial Statements and the Qualitative Characteristics of Financial Information, Exposure Draft – Statement of Principles*. London: ASB.

Accounting Standards Board (ASB) (1992, revised 1993 and 1999) *Reporting Financial Performance, FRS 3*. London: ASB.

Accounting Standards Board (ASB) (1999) *Statement of Principles*, reproduced in *Accounting Standards and Guidance for Members 2001*. London: ICAEW.

Accounting Standards Board (ASB) (2000) *Revision of FRS 3: Reporting Financial Performance*. FRED 22. Milton Keynes: ASB Publications.

Accounting Standards Committee (ASC) (1986) *Accounting for the Effects of Changing Prices: A Handbook*. London: ASC.

American Accounting Association (AAA) (1936) 'A tentative statement of accounting principles underlying corporate financial statements', *The Accounting Review*, June: 187–91.

American Accounting Association (AAA) (1966) Committee to Prepare a Statement of Basic Accounting Theory, *A Statement of Basic Accounting Theory*. Sarasota, FL: AAA.

American Accounting Association (AAA) (1971) 'Report of the Committee on Foundations of Accounting Measurement', *The Accounting Review*, Supplement: 1–48.

American Accounting Association (AAA) (1990) *Report of the American Accounting Association Committee on Accounting and Auditing Measurement, 1989–90*, reproduced in R. Bloom and P.T. Elgers (eds) (1995), *Foundations of Accounting Theory and Policy: A Reader*. Orlando, FL: Dryden Press.

American Accounting Association (AAA) (2000) Financial Accounting Standards Committee, 'Response to the Special Report of the G4 + 1, "Reporting financial performance: a proposed approach"', *Accounting Horizons*, September: 365–79.

American Institute of Certified Public Accountants (AICPA) (1973) (Trueblood Report) *Objectives of Financial Statements*, Report of the Accounting Objectives Study Group. New York: AICPA.

American Institute of Certified Public Accountants (AICPA) (1978) *Report, Conclusions and Recommendations of the Commission on Auditors' Responsibilities* (Cohen Commission). New York: AICPA.

Armstrong, M.S. (1977) 'The politics of establishing accounting standards', *The Journal of Accountancy*, February: 76–9.

Australian Society of Certified Practising Accountants and the Institute of Chartered Accountants in Australia (ASCPA and ICAA) (1994) *A Research Study on Financial Reporting and Auditing – Bridging the Expectation Gap*. Melbourne and Sydney: ASCPA and ICAA.

Beaver, W.H. and Landsman, W.R. (1983) *Incremental Information Content of Statement 33 Disclosures*. Stamford, CT: FASB.

Boulding, K.E. (1962) 'Economics and accounting: the uncongenial twins', in W.T. Baxter and S. Davidson (eds), *Studies in Accounting Theory* (2nd edn). London: Sweet & Maxwell.

Boyd, D.T., Boyd, S.C. and Boyd, W.L. (2001) 'The audit report: a "misunderstanding gap" between users and preparers', *National Public Accountant*, Dec. 2000/Jan. 2001, 45 (10): 56–60.

Cadbury Report (1992) *The Financial Aspects of Corporate Governance*. London: Gee.

Canadian Institute of Chartered Accountants (CICA) (1988) *Report of the Commission To Study the Public's Expectations of Audits* (MacDonald Commission). Toronto: CICA.

Canning, J.B. (1929) *The Economics of Accountancy*. New York: Ronald Press Company.

Carsberg, B., Hope, A. and Scapens R.W. (1974) 'The objectives of published accounting reports', *Accounting and Business Research*, Summer, 4 (15): 162–73.

Chambers, R.J. (1966a) *Accounting, Evaluation and Economic Behavior* (reprinted 1974). Houston, TX: Scholars Book Co.

Chambers, R.J. (1966b) 'A matter of principle', *The Accounting Review*, July: 443–57.

Chambers, R.J. (1998) 'Wanted: foundations of accounting measurement', *Abacus*, 34 (1): 36–47.

Chandler, R. and Edwards, J.R. (1996) 'Recurring issues in auditing: back to the future?', *Accounting, Auditing and Accountability Journal*, 9 (2): 4–29.

Chitty, D. (2001) 'New words for old', *Accountancy*, July: 120–2.

Clark, J.M. (1923) *Studies in the Economics of Overhead Costs*. Chicago: University of Chicago Press.

Company Law Review Steering Committee (2001) *Modern Company Law for a Competitive Economy: Final Report*. London: DTI.

Damant, D. (1996) 'Sticking to one's principles in the line of fire', *Financial Times*, 18 April: 30.

Davies, M., Paterson, R. and Wilson, A. (1999) *UK GAAP*. London: Butterworths Tolley.

Deegan, C. and Rankin, M. (1999) 'The environmental reporting expectations gap: Australian evidence', *The British Accounting Review*, 31 (3): 313–46.

Demski, J.S. and Feltham, G.A. (1976) *Cost Determination: A Conceptual Approach*. Ames, IA: Iowa State University Press.

Drury, C. (2000) *Management and Cost Accounting* (5th edn). London: Thomson Learning.

Edey, H. (1971) 'The true and fair view', *Accountancy*, August: 440–1.

Elliott, R.K. (2002) 'Twenty-first century assurance', *Auditing: A Journal of Practice & Theory*, 21 (1): 139–46.

Ernst & Young (1993) *The Future Direction of UK Financial Reporting*. London: Ernst & Young Thought Leadership Series.

Ernst & Young (1996) *The ASB's Framework – Time to Decide*. London: Ernst & Young Thought Leadership Series.

Financial Accounting Standards Board (FASB) (1990) *Present Value-Measurements in Accounting*. Norwalk, CT: FASB.

Financial Accounting Standards Board (FASB) (2000) *Using Cash Flow Information and Present Value in Accounting Measurement* (SFAC No. 7). Stamford, CT: FASB.

Financial Executive (1986) 'How do CFOs evaluate the annual report?', *Financial Executive*, December: 26–30.

Financial Reporting Commission (1992) *Report of the Commission of Inquiry into the Expectations of Users of Published Financial Statements*. Dublin: Institute of Chartered Accountants in Ireland.

G4 + 1 (1999) *Reporting Financial Performance: Proposals for Change*. G4 + 1 position paper. London: ASB.

Humphrey, C. (1997) 'Debating audit expectations', in M. Sherer and S. Turley (eds), *Current Issues in Auditing* (3rd edn). London: Paul Chapman.

Humphrey, C., Moizer, P. and Turley, S. (1992) *The Audit Expectations Gap in the United Kingdom*. London: ICAEW Research Board.

Humphrey, C., Moizer, P. and Turley, S. (1993) 'The audit expectations gap in Britain: an empirical investigation', *Accounting and Business Research*, 23 (91a): 395–411.

Ijiri, Y. (1975) *Theory of Accounting Measurement*. Studies in Accounting Research No. 10. Sarasota, FL: AAA.

International Accounting Standards Committee (IASC) (1989) *Framework for the Preparation and Presentation of Financial Statements*. London: IASC.

Lapsley, I. (1996) 'Reflections on performance measurement in the public sector', in I. Lapsley and M. Falconer (eds), *Accounting and Performance Measurement: Issues in the Private and Public Sectors*. London: Paul Chapman.

Laughlin, R.C. and Puxty, A.G. (1981) 'The decision-usefulness criterion: wrong cart, wrong horse?', *AUTA Review*, 13: 43–87.

Laughlin, R.C. and Puxty, A.G. (1983) 'Accounting regulation: an alternative per-spective', *Journal of Business Finance and Accounting*, Autumn: 451–79.

Lee, T.A. and Tweedie, D.P. (1977) *The Private Shareholder and the Corporate Report*. London: ICAEW.

Lee, T.A. and Tweedie, D.P. (1981) *The Institutional Investor and Financial Information*. London: ICAEW.

Liggio, C.D. (1974) 'The expectation gap: the accountant's legal Waterloo', *Journal of Contemporary Business*, 3 (3): 27–44.

Mattessich, R. (1995) *Critique of Accounting: Examination of the Foundations and Normative Structure of an Applied Discipline*. Westport, CT: Quorum Books.

Moonitz, M. (1961) *The Basic Postulates of Accounting*, Accounting Research Study No. 1. New York: AICPA.

National Audit Office (NAO) (1988) *A Framework for Value for Money Audits*. London: NAO.

Panel on Audit Effectiveness (2000) *Report and Recommendations*. Stamford, CT: Public Oversight Board.

Pannell, R.L. (1978) 'An inquiry into the meaning of stewardship in financial account-ing', unpublished PhD thesis, New York University, Graduate School of Business Administration, reproduced 1988 by University Microfilms International.

Parker, L.D. (1986) *Communicating Financial Information Through the Annual Report*. London: ICAEW.

Paterson, R. (1995) 'The statement of principles: full steam astern?', *Accountancy*, August: 81.

Porter, B.A. (1993) 'An empirical study of the audit expectation-performance gap', *Accounting and Business Research*, 24 (93): 49–68.

Porter, B.A. (1996) 'Review' [of *A Research Study on Financial Reporting and Auditing – Bridging the Expectation Gap*], *Accounting Horizons*, 10 (1): 130–5.

Power, M. (1994) 'The audit society', in A.G. Hopwood and P. Miller (eds), *Accounting as Social and Institutional Practice*. Cambridge: Cambridge University Press.

Puxty, A.G. and Laughlin, R.C. (1983) 'A rational reconstruction of the usefulness criterion', *Journal of Business Finance and Accounting*, 10 (4): 543–60.

Sikka, P., Puxty, A., Willmott, H. and Cooper, C. (1998) 'The impossibility of elimi-nating the expectations gap: some theory and evidence', *Critical Perspectives on Accounting*, 9: 299–330.

Small, J. (1996) 'Effectiveness – the Holy Grail of accounting measures of performance', in I. Lapsley and M. Falconer (eds), *Accounting and Performance Measurement: Issues in the Private and Public Sectors*. London: Paul Chapman.

Solomons, D. (1989) *Guidelines for Financial Reporting Standards*. London: ICAEW.

Stacy, G. (1987) 'The external auditor's viewpoint', in *Fraud '87* (Proceedings of the Conference given by the Institute of Chartered Accountants in England and Wales and the Law Society, 28/1/87). London: ICAEW.

Sterling, R.R. (1970) 'On theory construction and verification', *The Accounting Review*, July: 444–57.

Sterling, R.R. (1979) *Toward a Science of Accounting*. Houston, TX: Scholars Book Co.

Tweedie, D. and Whittington, G. (1990) 'Financial reporting: current problems and their implications for systematic reform', *Accounting and Business Research*, 21 (81): 87–102.

Vatter, W.J. (1947) *The Fund Theory of Accounting and its Implications for Financial Reports*. Chicago: University of Chicago Press.

Whittington, G. (1991) 'Good stewardship and the ASB's objectives', *Accountancy*, November: 33.

Zeff, S.A. (1999) 'The evolution of the conceptual framework for business enterprises in the United States', *Accounting Historians Journal*, 26 (2): 89–131.

Nothing is more conducive to peace of mind than not having
any opinion at all.

                                        – G.C. Lichtenberg

I n view of the problems already identified, this chapter presents a
  personal view of a potential alterative conceptual framework for external
  reporting that will encompass financial reporting. This chapter argues
that the financial statements should be viewed in the context of corporate
governance as part of the process of communicating corporate performance
and risk to the world outside of the reporting entity's management (Table
9.1). The financial statements can then be recognized for what they are – the
allocation of profit (through the matching of revenue and expenses) to an
accounting period, and an attempt to disclose the financial position at the end
of such a period.

   A conceptual framework for external corporate reporting should relate to
ideas about why, what, and how things are to be reported – these may
radically change over time and thus may require innovative approaches and
new components. This chapter will argue that the focus should be on the
reporting entity rather than the myriad of potential users. The level of detail
required may differ depending on the size of the reporting entity. The
framework advocated here will be underpinned by communication theory as
opposed to decision theory. Thus, the focus will be on the communication of
the directors' message regarding the performance of, and the risks relating to,
the reporting entity. This framework could be seen as a meta-framework –
part of which would encompass financial reporting. The attempt here is to
move away from the current situation where everything seems to revolve
around the financial statements. Then, by clearly defining what the financial
statements are capable of achieving and thus recognizing their limitations, it
should be possible to evaluate critically their usefulness in relation to assisting
with the conceptual problem of the corporate communication of performance
and risk. One can then ask: 'How useful are the financial statements in
communicating corporate performance and risk?' The financial statements are

TABLE 9.1   The changing nature of corporate reporting

	Emphasis	Focus	Orientation
Stewardship	Accountability	Managers of the business	Past financial performance
Decision making	User needs	The users of the financial statements	Predictive ability of the data
Corporate communication	Corporate governance	The message the directors are trying to communicate about the reporting entity	Past activities (financial and non-financial) and qualitative assessment of the future direction of an enterprise

useful as a basis for calculating profit so that dividends and taxation can be computed – these are still important requirements even though they may not be the top priorities of some very vocal users of the financial statements. The balance sheet was never an attempt to value the business, yet the preoccupation of the standard-setters with current values could lead people to think that it has come to represent the current value of the business. If it does not mean this, what does the total current value of the assets mean? When users realize the fact that it is the current value of the bits and pieces of the business that are recognized under accounting rules, this is unlikely to enhance the status of the accountancy profession.

THE SPECIFICATION OF THE PROBLEM

As has been established, the clear specification of a problem is required at the outset. It has already been seen that different problems and/or objectives have resulted in a plethora of accounting 'theories' and thus appear to have clouded the conceptual framework debate. Rather than starting with the financial statements (and then basing most of the subsequent discussion around them and their ability to satisfy user needs), it would seem logical for a framework for external reporting to start with, and be based on, corporate governance (Figure 9.1). Chambers (1996: 126) criticized the FASB definition of a conceptual framework because '[n]ot a word is said here about the affairs of the commercial world in which and for which accounting is done'. Therefore, to develop a framework based on corporate governance would provide a foundation and presumably contribute to the financial statement's being 'useful'. This would also be in line with Whittington's view: 'Financial reporting is an important element of the system of corporate governance. . . . Thus, any consideration of how financial reporting might be improved has to

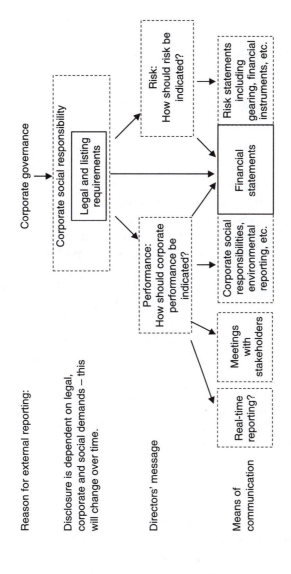

FIGURE 9.1   Corporate communication of performance and risk

have regard to the system of corporate governance within which it operates' (1993: 311):

> *Corporate governance in its broadest sense takes in the whole framework within which companies operate. That framework is partly set by the law, partly by the participants themselves, and more widely by society. While the legal requirements on companies are relatively predictable, the boundaries to corporate behaviour set by the participants and by society are continually shifting. (Cadbury, 1993: 46)*

The usefulness of communication theory to underpin a conceptual framework for external reporting would seem to be relevant: 'Effective communication with a company's shareholders and other stakeholders is a vital constituent of good governance and it is essential that interested parties be given a clear and balanced view of a company's performance' (Sir Brian Jenkins, cited in Carey, 1999: 1). As was seen in Chapter 2, the starting point in terms of communication theory is the identification of the message to be transmitted – which may be hypothesized to be 'the communication by the directors of the performance and risk relating to the reporting entity'. Although communication theory would seem to be a natural basis to underpin the communication process (see Figure 2.1, Chapter 2), it will not per se assist in the determination of what should be reported. In this situation, there is still the need to identify what is meant by 'corporate performance' and 'risk'. However, focusing on the reporting entity, rather than the multitude of users, should help to clarify at least part of the reporting problem. The Hampel Report makes the point:

> *As the CBI put it in their evidence to us, the directors as a board are responsible for relations with stakeholders; but they are accountable to the shareholders. This is not simply a technical point. From a practical point of view, to redefine the directors' responsibilities in terms of the stakeholders would mean identifying all the various stakeholder groups; and deciding the nature and extent of the directors' responsibility to each. The result would be that the directors were not effectively accountable to anyone since there would be no clear yardstick for judging their performance. This is a recipe neither for good governance nor for corporate success. (1998: 12)*

This contrasts with the view of the accounting standard-setters, who have focused on the needs of the myriad of users because of the vogue for the decision-usefulness of the financial statements. If the objective is to satisfy user needs, the users and their needs must be clearly identified. Can all these potential users really have all their needs satisfied? If this is not possible, which users should be satisfied? Another danger arising from focusing the financial statements on user needs is that the debate about what should or should not be contained in them becomes blinkered. At the moment, the argument appears to be that if the users want something the financial state-ments should try to incorporate it – rather than considering potential alternative disclosure mechanisms.

The emphasis on satisfying the needs of the users of the financial state-ments has been challenged, but because accounting has increasingly been seen as a 'service activity', these views have tended to be ignored. The argu-ment advocated in this chapter is that a change in focus is required – away from the users and on to the reporting entity itself. This would be in line with Chambers (1966), who wanted 'to shift the focus of attention from the parties of interest (creditors, investors, managers) to the entity under consideration; to regard the entity as the subject of inquiry; and to regard all participants in its activity as so many interrelated forces bearing on one another as they change position and direction voluntarily or under the influence of forces beyond the entity' (p. 375). Laughlin and Puxty (1981: 74), who were critical of the decision-making emphasis, reported: 'We know of no literature concerned with the provision of external information which takes as fundamentally relevant the well-being of the reporting enterprise.' Anthony (1983: 15) advo-cated that 'financial accounting should focus on the entity as such, rather than on the interest of equity investors in the entity, as is the present focus'. Thus, instead of emphasizing 'the users of the financial statements', and then having everything revolve around the users and the financial statements' ability to meet their needs, it would seem preferable to take a step back and view the overall problem from the perspective of the communication of performance and risk. Indeed, it may be more appropriate to change the discussion from 'users' to 'outsiders' (that is, people outside the inner ring of management). These 'outsiders' (shareholders, employees, analysts, prospective investors, banks, suppliers, customers, governments, etc.) will have a whole range of needs and desires, but whether it is feasible for these to be satisfied by the financial statements (or anything else) is another matter.

It could be argued that the focus on users has resulted in a movement from a 'bottom up' approach to financial reporting (that is, working up from the accounting records to the financial statements) to a supposedly 'top down' approach (based on user needs and the emphasis on trying to meet them). However, are the deliberations of the standard-setters really starting at the 'top'? As depicted in Figure 9.1, it seems likely that the discussions of the standard-setters start some way down this communication hierarchy; thus, they appear to have tried to ensure that the financial statements could be all things to all people – helping to exacerbate the financial statements' expectations gap.

This raises the question of what should be reported and how/when it should be communicated. The identification of these matters is not per se an accounting problem – corporate governance encompasses much more than simply financial reporting. *The Corporate Report* stated:

> We consider the responsibility to report publicly . . . [that is, public accountability] is separate from and broader than the legal obligation to report and arises from the custodial role played in the community by economic entities. Just as directors of limited companies are recognised as having a stewardship relationship with shareholders who have invested their funds, so many other relationships exist both of a financial and non-financial nature. For example, economic entities compete for resources of manpower, management and organisational skills, material and energy, and they utilise community owned assets and facilities. They have a responsibility for the present and future livelihoods of employees, and because of the interdependence of all social groups, they are involved in the maintenance of standards of life and the creation of wealth for and on behalf of the community. (ASSC, 1975: para. 1.3)

Therefore, corporate responsibility extends beyond just reporting on the financial aspects of the business. Since the 1960s, corporate social responsibility and the reporting thereof has received greater recognition (e.g., Adams et al., 1998; Gray et al., 1987; Gray et al. 1996; Jacoby, 1973; Johnson, 1979; Mathews, 1993; Ross, 1971). 'Social reporting (or corporate social reporting – CSR) is the process of providing information designed to discharge social accountability' (Gray et al., 1987: 4). It involves 'communicating the social and environmental effects of organizations' actions to particular groups within society and to society at large' (p. 76). Environmental reporting can be seen as a specific aspect of corporate social responsibility, and environmental accounting (or 'green' accounting) has also been increasingly discussed (e.g., Gray et al., 1993, 1996; Owen, 1992). Consequently, 'there is a growing need to measure environmental impacts in terms of new metrics, including: the number of public complaints; the life-cycle impacts of products; energy, materials and water usage at production sites; potentially polluting emissions; environmental hazards, and risks; waste generation; consumption of critical natural capital; and performance against best-practice standards set by leading customers and by green and ethical investment funds' (Elkington,

1997: 80). Gray et al. (1987: 16) point out that 'much of the likely information to be contained in such a report (e.g. pollution data, health and safety at work) involves concepts beyond our competence qua accountants'. If the problem is bigger than accounting, it cannot be solved by accounting alone. The context of corporate governance provides a basis for the examination of corporate social responsibility (including environmental reporting). Legal requirements, stock exchange listings and accounting regulation determine the minimum amount of data that a company must disclose, but at the moment the cost of further disclosures may have to be justified in terms of the resultant benefit to a business.

Adams et al. (1998: 2) concluded: 'Corporate social accountability is likely to be an increasingly important element of the Western European psyche . . . evidenced not only by corporate, professional and academic developments, but also by the increasing legislative developments of the European Union and the European Economic Area requiring greater corporate social respon- sibility and accountability (see Gray et al., 1996).' While some companies may be genuinely concerned about their greater responsibilities, others may view social and environmental reporting as public relations exercises (e.g., Greer and Bruno, 1996). Cowe (2001: 10) reported that 'research reveals high levels of scepticism . . . about companies' claims to be improving their environ- mental performance and benefiting communities'. He considered that 'the Government will be under pressure to legislate for clearer responsibilities to society, and environmental impacts'.

Therefore, it is suggested that the overall problem which the accountant is trying to help tackle is that of the communication of corporate performance and risk to various interested parties. The financial statements may be seen as a surrogate for corporate performance, although the previous chapter did question whether they really represent performance. What should be clear is that the financial statements can present only a partial picture of the achieve- ments of an enterprise (Figure 9.2).

HOW CAN 'CORPORATE PERFORMANCE' BE INDICATED?

Presumably performance is about whether a business is achieving its objec- tives; however, objectives are often viewed narrowly in terms of financial performance. This section starts by exploring some contemporary notions of financial 'performance' and then proceeds to examine some broader notions of 'performance'.

The ICAEW's publication *Financial Performance: Alternative Views of the Bottom Line* (1999) sought to explore the meaning of the term 'financial per- formance', but much of the discussion appeared to be about assessing financial *potential* rather than financial performance in the traditional sense.

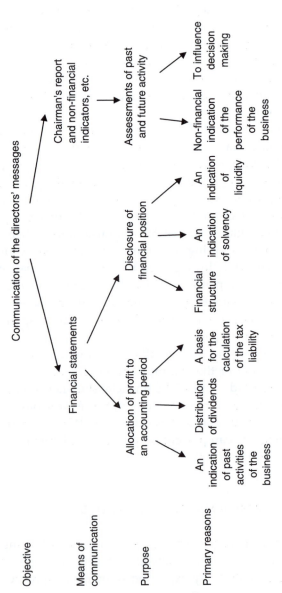

FIGURE 9.2 The directors' communication through the annual report

The report stated: 'The real underlying financial performance of a business during a period is represented by the change in its economic value, i.e. the discounted present value of its future cash flows' (ICAEW, 1999: para. 1.4). Such a statement could lead to questioning of what this has to do with traditional forms of accounting and financial reporting. The report acknowledged that 'because the future is unknown, it is difficult to report this underlying financial performance of a business' (para. 1.4). Consequently, '[o]ne approach to reporting is to provide investors with all the pieces of information that can reasonably be provided so that they can arrive at their own estimates of underlying financial performance' (para. 1.4). This was termed the 'raw materials approach' to reporting. An alternative is the 'ready-made approach' that would contain 'management's own view of underlying financial performance' (para. 1.4).

The 'raw materials' approach to financial reporting would seem to make it even harder to identify the directors' message (as per communication theory) – indeed, with this approach one could almost argue that there is not an intended message and it is simply up to the users to interpret the figures. However, given the complexity of modern businesses and the remoteness of these users from the running of these businesses, there is a real danger that these users do not have a clue as to what is really happening within an organization. In the collapse of Barings Bank, it was alleged that not even the directors knew what was happening in their own organization. Therefore, there must be a danger that the 'raw materials' approach may exacerbate the financial statements expectations gap.

The ICAEW report asserts: 'As a matter of arithmetic, reported financial performance can essentially be equated to changes in financial position other than changes arising from transactions with owners' (ICAEW, 1999: para. 1.5). This may be problematic unless one believes simply that a large profit is 'good' and a small profit is 'bad'. Short-termism means that actions may be taken today to improve today's profit but at the possible expense of future profits. Therefore, a large profit may not necessarily be good and a low profit may not necessarily be bad, but it is very unlikely that users of the financial statements will be able to detect this. Therefore, the arithmetic changes may not really reflect the performance of the reporting entity.

The following six views of the bottom line were set out in the report (ICAEW, 1999).

Cash

'The simplest way in which investors assess financial performance is in terms of changes in cash balances' (para. 4.1), but 'it is clearly inadequate in isolation' (para. 4.6).

Historical cost

With historical costs, 'performance reporting is characterized as a process of allocating income and expenditure transactions to appropriate periods in order to match them in the relevant period's profit and loss account' (para. 4.7). The report pointed out that 'the process of preparing historical cost accounts generates difficult issues of accounting policy and judgement' (para. 4.7):

> The historical cost view of financial performance is relatively simple and cheap to apply because it is derived from the accounting records that businesses need to record their transactions, maintain control over physical assets and keep track of their debts and liabilities. This explains why it is used almost universally for regular internal management reporting. (para. 4.10)

Whether this allocation process represents 'performance' is problematic, as has already been seen. There is the danger that short-term actions by management may distort the picture of 'performance', and 'there is widespread agreement that investors are unlikely to consider historical cost profits on their own to be relevant in assessing financial performance' (para. 4.11).

Modified historical cost

This method may incorporate a mixture of historical costs and current values. Most listed UK companies seem to utilize this combination (para. 4.12). It would seem that this is a result of items of value not being fully reflected in the historical cost accounts and so adjustments were made. However, it should be remembered that the balance sheet was never intended to be a statement of valuation. The development of modified historical cost may have confused the issue of the purpose of the balance sheet. Originally, it was simply a listing of the assets and liabilities in the nominal ledger at a point in time (hence its name). Whether such a revised configuration really represents 'performance' may again be problematic, as short-termism will still persist.

Net assets at current value

'[R]egularly revaluing all assets and liabilities at current value would go beyond present practice and would give users a more complete view of financial performance' (para. 4.17):

> *However, there are two major criticisms of the usefulness of 'net assets at current value' as a means of helping investors to understand underlying financial performance. First . . . the changes in current values do not in themselves affect the cash flows arising from staying in the present line of business. The only direct effect on underlying financial performance comes through an alteration to the rate that should be used to discount the future cash flows. Therefore it can be argued that performance as reported under 'net assets at current value' might be misleading.*
>
> *In addition, 'net assets at current value' only reflects changes in the values of those assets and liabilities that are recognized in a historical cost balance sheet. It would exclude many softer assets arising, for example, from the knowledge of the workforce, research, training, public image, brands and advertising, as well as internally generated goodwill. These are all central to the real financial performance of a business. (paras 4.20–4.21)*

Thus, there is a danger that this approach appears to be turning the balance sheet into a statement of valuation, but this approach can value only part of the business, namely, those bits that appeared in the financial statements. What proportion of the business was being valued will be unknown and therefore the usefulness of 'net assets at current values' may be questionable. This approach could create artificial precision and thus contribute to the financial statements expectations gap.

Businesses at current value

This 'would involve a company reporting financial performance by reporting changes in the value of business units as valued by management' (para. 4.23):

> *In effect, a company would report the price that management would pay to acquire its businesses based on the net present value of future cash flows. This would inevitably involve a considerable degree of estimation and, to be meaningful, would require underlying assumptions about cash flows to be spelled out along with the discount rate that had been used. Doubts about the reliability of current values increase when income streams are valued, rather than individual assets that have net realisable values and replacement costs. Management intentions and uncertainties about the future become more important. (para. 4.23)*

This view may be impossible to implement, but at least its discussion should force people to think beyond the current format of the financial statement. Rather than just making relatively simple adjustments to the asset and liability values in the financial statements, a radical rethink would be required. There are various ways of valuing businesses, but they are all extremely difficult and subjective. It may be that there is not a demand to know management's assessment of the current value of the whole business, in which case one may ask why there would be a demand for the current value of just bits and pieces of the business.

Market capitalization

This data is readily available for listed companies, though it could be argued that it is not really financial reporting by management (para. 4.26). This data may force management to explain changes in the share price; however, in terms of responsibility, accounting people should be held accountable only for things over which they have control. As management does not really have control over the performance of the share price, it may seem unfair to appear to hold management accountable for movements of that price.

This ICAEW report (1999) was an attempt to stimulate a debate as to what constituted financial performance; however, this debate did not seem to happen. The G4 + 1 (1999) also issued a position paper on the reporting of financial performance, but it 'does not attempt to provide a definitive answer to the question of what constitutes financial performance'; instead, 'it seeks a framework within which financial reporting can develop to satisfy the increasing demands being made upon it' (para. 1.3). Fleming (2000), in discussing the responses to the G4 + 1 position paper, reported that most of the respondents stressed the importance of being clear about what financial performance represents.

One problem with using the financial statements as an assessment of 'performance' is that they say nothing about economy, efficiency and effectiveness. Kaplan and Norton (1996: 22) considered that 'an overemphasis on achieving and maintaining short-term financial results can cause companies to overinvest in short-term fixes and to underinvest in long-term value creation, particularly in the intangible and intellectual assets that generate future growth'. Small (1996: 130) expressed this concern: 'The profit measure – while perhaps necessary for judging effectiveness in the private sector – is certainly not sufficient by itself. It can be argued that to rely solely on the profit measure will be at best misleading and at worst totally unreliable.'

In order to allow users of the financial statements to develop a greater understanding of the activities of a reporting entity, more narrative interpretations by the directors have been encouraged, resulting in the development of the Operating and Financial Review (OFR).

THE OPERATING AND FINANCIAL REVIEW (OFR)

'In considering the responsibility of boards with respect to financial reports, the Cadbury Committee concluded that what shareholders need from the report and accounts is a coherent narrative, supported by figures, of the company's performance and prospects' (Davies et al., 1999: 250–1). Many companies already included such statements in their accounts and so the OFR was aimed at building on best practice; however, it 'is voluntary and not an accounting standard' (ASB, 1993, 2.304: Introduction).

The OFR 'is a report on the year under review, not a forecast of future results, it should nevertheless draw out those aspects of the year under review that are relevant to an assessment of future prospects. It would therefore give users of the annual report a more consistent foundation on which to make investment decisions regarding the company' (ASB, 1993, 2.304: Introduction). 'The OFR should discuss the significant features of operating performance for the period covered by the financial statements, covering all aspects of the profit and loss account to the level of profit on ordinary activities before taxation, and focusing on the overall business and on those segments or other divisions that are relevant to an understanding of the performance as a whole' (ASB, 1993: para. 9). Examples of the changes in the industry or the environment that should be discussed in the operating review include market conditions; new products; market share; turnover/margins; exchange rates and inflation; and acquisitions, disposals and significant changes in activities. The operating review should also include 'a discussion identifying the principal risks and uncertainties in the main lines of business, together with a commentary on the approach to managing these risks and, in qualitative terms, the nature of the potential impact on the results' (para. 12). Other aspects include future investment, profit and total recognized gains and losses, dividend policy, and accounting policies.

The aim of the financial review section 'is to explain to the user of the annual report the capital structure of the business, its treasury policy and the dynamics of its financial position' (para. 23):

> *The OFR could also give a commentary on the strengths and resources of the business whose value is not reflected in the balance sheet (or only partially shown in the balance sheet). Such items could include brands and similar intangible items. Where considered appropriate, the value of such items, and increases or decreases in their value, could be*

> *discussed. It is not intended that an overall valuation of the business*
> *be given, nor, in the case of listed companies, for net assets value to be*
> *reconciled to market capitalization. (para. 37)*

As, at the moment, the OFR is voluntary, the Company Law Review Steering Committee (2001: para. 3.34) has recommended that 'all companies of significant economic size should be required to produce, as part of their annual report and accounts, an OFR'. It continued:

> *In terms of the content of the OFR, we propose that all companies*
> *preparing an OFR should be required to report on three mandatory*
> *items: the company's business, strategy and principal drivers of*
> *performance; a review of the development of the company's business*
> *over the year; and the dynamics of the business, including events,*
> *trends and other factors which may substantially affect future per-*
> *formance. These issues are so universally relevant to an understanding*
> *of company performance that there is no reason why all companies*
> *within the scope of the requirement should not report on them. The*
> *OFR will also contain much other important information; for example,*
> *on corporate governance, relationships with employees, customers,*
> *suppliers and others on whom company success depends, and on*
> *environmental, community, social, ethical and reputational issues*
> *[footnote omitted]. (Company Law Review Steering Committee, 2001:*
> *para. 3.39)*

The Company Law Review Steering Committee's 'proposals are designed to put the onus on the directors themselves to give their own account, based on their own judgement, of the matters which are important in assessing the performance and prospects of the business'; consequently, '[t]his is calculated to ensure that boilerplate formulae will be treated by the market with the distrust which they deserve' (2001: para. 3.40). Therefore, it can be seen from this that the Company Law Review Steering Committee have focused on management's assessment of the performance of the reporting entity, and that they viewed 'performance' in terms more broad than just financial performance.

CORPORATE MEETINGS

Rather than relying simply on printed or electronic communication, company directors are being increasingly proactive in keeping institutional investors and analysts informed by means of private meetings: 'Within the bounds of insider trading laws and Stock Exchange guidance on the dissemination of price sensitive information, there remains scope for legitimate exchange of private information' (Holland, 1997: v). Traditionally, the directors have reported verbally at a company's annual general meeting (or at an extra-ordinary general meeting); however, such encounters have tended to be ritualistic. Therefore, larger companies are increasingly conducting private meetings. Marston (1999: 18) reports that it was not uncommon for some large companies to hold over 50 one-to-one meetings (this was during 1996/97). 'The basic message was revealed in the OFR section of the annual report, to be expanded in private meetings' (Holland, 1997: vi):

> The main aims of the investor relations programme are to inform the major stakeholding institutions and broader market of group strategy and objectives, to avoid misapprehensions and misunderstandings about group strategy, and to support the treasury and the financial director with the financial markets in matters such as raising capital. We also use investor relations to feed back market sentiment to top management. Investor relations is therefore a two way communication channel. (Case X) (Holland, 1997: 10)

Other advantages to the company are that '[i]mage, reputation and impressions are important attributes which can be enhanced through the meetings' (Marston, 1999: 44). However, Marston suggests that the analysts did not gain a competitive advantage by merely attending a meeting (p. 77) and that 'all participants were at pains to point out that price sensitive information was not discussed' (p. 103). This may take some believing, especially as 'close periods [that is, those periods immediately before the announcement of corporate results] were not maintained strictly by some companies' (p. 56), and given that stock market efficiency was used to justify 'an incentive for managers to disclose inside information about what the forthcoming results are going to be' (p. 45). The suggestion that '[m]inutes [of the meetings] would have to be edited in certain cases to preserve con-fidentiality' (p. ix) again seems to imply that the institutional investors/analysts at these meetings may have an advantage over those who are excluded. Even the *ex post* release of the minutes (including via the Internet) would leave non-participants at a disadvantage – after all, timing is crucial in terms of potentially price-sensitive information.

The OFR with its narrative discussion of an enterprise's activities and private meetings with institutional investors and analysts, has increased in importance as a channel of communication during the 1990s; however, most of the focus was still on explaining the contents of the financial statements. As the financial statements can present only a partial picture of an organization's achievements, it is perhaps time to start looking for complementary or alternative indicators of corporate performance.

WIDENING THE RANGE OF PERFORMANCE INDICATORS

In the view of Kaplan and Norton (1996), two major factors could be seen to have contributed to the debate as to what constitutes corporate performance. Firstly, short-termism:

> *Inevitably, as managers are pressured to deliver consistent and excellent short-term financial performance, trade-offs are made that limit the search for investments in growth opportunities. Even worse, the pressure for short-term financial performance can cause companies to reduce spending on new product development, process improvements, human resource development, information technology, databases, and systems as well as customer and market development. In the short run, the financial accounting model reports these spending cutbacks as increases in reported income, even when the reductions have cannibalized a company's stock of assets and its capabilities for creating future economic value. Alternatively, a company could maximize short-term financial results by exploiting customers through high prices or lower service. In the short run, these actions enhance reported profitability, but the lack of customer loyalty and satisfaction will leave the company highly vulnerable to competitive inroads. (Kaplan and Norton, 1996: 23)*

The second factor which seems to have contributed to the debate about corporate performance is the change in the nature of business activities:

> *The emergence of the information era . . . in the last decades of the twentieth century, made obsolete many of the fundamental assumptions of industrial age competition. No longer could companies gain sustainable competitive advantage by merely deploying new technology into physical assets rapidly, and by excellent management of financial assets and liabilities. (Kaplan and Norton, 1996: 3)*

Thus, there is concern about the financial statements with their focus on tangible assets:

> In traditional economic theory, capital as a factor of production can come in two main forms: physical capital (including machinery and plant) and financial capital. But as we move into the knowledge economy, the concept is gradually being extended to include such concepts as human capital – a measure of the experience, skills, and other knowledge-based assets of the individuals who make up an organization. (Elkington, 1997: 74)

'In this new world, the notions of what information should be included on performance will . . . be subject to substantial change with more sought on non-financial performance indicators and on, for example, the value of a company's intangible assets, including its human resources and customer satisfaction ratings, the key drivers of wealth in many companies' (Sir Brian Jenkins cited in Carey, 1999: 1). The importance of intangible assets in the new economy is that they enable an organization to:

> • develop customer relationships that retain the loyalty of existing customers and enable new customers segments and market areas to be served effectively and efficiently;
> • introduce innovative products and services desired by targeted customers segments;
> • produce customized high-quality products and services at low cost and with short lead times;
> • mobilize employee skills and motivation for continuous improvement in process capabilities, quality, and response times; and
> • deploy information technology, databases and systems. (Kaplan and Norton, 1996: 3)

Fay reported (in Carey, 1999: 7) that during the 1990s there were changing expectations regarding corporate reporting:

• Companies were no longer being judged solely on economic performance and wealth creation.
• They were seen as having wider responsibilities – to the environment, local communities, and society in general.

- The public were demanding higher standards of ethical and environmental responsibility.
- Company reporting needed to recognize these changes.

The meaning of corporate performance and the usefulness of the financial statements as an indicator of corporate performance has been much debated (e.g., Harvard Business Review, 1998; ICAEW, 1995; Lapsley and Mitchell, 1996; Nickell, 1995). It is increasingly being recognized that to understand an organization the notion of performance needs to be broader than just financial performance (Burns et al., 1997; Kaplan and Norton, 1992, 1993, 1996). However:

> Many firms' performance measurement systems have not been sufficiently redesigned to meet the needs of today's environment. Many systems primarily focus on measuring historical performance of internal operations, expressed in financial terms, using as a basis of measurement a set of budgeted figures against which actual results are compared. . . . These traditional measurement systems must be expanded to deal with the future as well as the past, with external relationships and events as well as external activities, and with non-financial as well as financial measures. (ICAEW, 1995: 2)

Adams et al. (1998: 2) considered that 'most companies have singularly failed to embrace any but the traditional model of accounting . . . the disclosure of social and environmental information tends to be on a fragmentary and ad hoc basis, most disclosures are partial and are not integrated into a composite whole (see, for example, Adams et al., 1995)'. Elkington (1997; 1999) has advocated the 'triple bottom line' approach to external reporting – this integrates financial, environmental and social factors:

> Worldwide, business people are waking up to the fact that key markets are on the verge of rapid change driven by new environmental standards and related customer requirements. As a result, new bottom lines are being drawn alongside the old profit and loss statements. Once rated a low priority corporate citizenship issue, the sustainable development agenda is in the process of becoming a competitive and strategic issue for major tracts of industry and commerce. (Elkington, 1997: 44)

The types of alternative performance indicators that have been advocated (e.g., ICAEW, 1995: 9–11) include environmental indicators, market/customer indicators, competitor indicators, internal business indicators, human resource indicators and financial indicators. One attempt to operationalize a wider set of performance indicators was that by Kaplan and Norton (1992; 1993; 1996), who advocated the balanced scorecard. This retained the tradition financial indicators but then 'complements financial measures of past performance with measures of the drivers of future performance' (Kaplan and Norton, 1996: 8). The balanced scorecard views organizational performance from four perspectives, namely:

- a financial perspective
- a customer perspective
- an internal business process perspective
- a learning and growth perspective.

Thus, they advocate a widening of the discussion of performance:

> The Balance Scorecard should translate a business unit's mission and strategy into tangible objectives and measures. The measures represent a balance between external measures for shareholders and customers, and internal measures of critical business processes, innovation, and learning and growth. The measures are balanced between the outcome measures – the results from past efforts – and the measures that drive future performance. (Kaplan and Norton, 1996: 10)

The balanced scorecard is often discussed in a 'management accounting' context (e.g., Drury, 2000: 928–39); however, the ideas behind it and the indicators it generates could potentially be complementary to the external reporting process. Indeed, there have been very few attempts to devise an operational framework for the disclosure of corporate performance – this may be a sign of the dominance of the financial perspective, and thus a tangible by-product of the financial statements expectations gap.

The broadening of the notion of performance could mean that the financial statements will be recognized for what they are – an attempt to allocate profit (through the matching of revenues and expenses) to the appropriate accounting period and to indicate the financial position at a point in time – the need for which has been brought about by the development of permanently invested capital. The explicit recognition of this would mean that the accounting standard setters could concentrate on producing a subsidiary conceptual framework specifically for financial reporting – to ensure consistency and coherence in the way that profit is allocated to the appropriate accounting period and in the way that the financial position is disclosed.

REPORTING RISK

To understand corporate performance, one also needs to appreciate the risks that have been taken – performance and risk are inextricably linked. Businesses need to take risks as an everyday part of their activities; indeed, a business that does not take risks is unlikely to impress its shareholders. In the financial reporting context, risk was traditionally viewed in terms of corporate gearing (the relationship between the owners' equity and long-term debt), contingencies (FRS 12 [ASB, 1998a]), solvency (the ability to pay long-term debts as they mature) and liquidity (ability to meet current payments as they fall due). The growth in the use of financial instruments has created another type of risk (FRS 13 [ASB, 1998b]):

> A wide range of risks can affect an enterprise's future cash flows. Although, at a given time, it might only be possible to quantify the potential cash impact of a small number of those risks, this should not necessarily restrict what is reported. (ICAEW, 1997: 4)

The greater recognition of risk could result in 'a statement of business risk' (ICAEW, 1997: 10) incorporating:

- the identification and prioritization of key risks
- descriptions of action taken to manage each risk
- the identification of how the risks are 'measured'.

The disadvantages would be that such a statement would include only what was 'not too commercially sensitive to disclose' (p. 10):

> If it is considered that reporting on a risk, an action or a residual exposure would be commercially sensitive to an unacceptable degree, then the sensitive details should not be reported. Withholding information because it is commercially sensitive implies that public disclosure would be seriously detrimental to an enterprise. However, it is not easy to define what is commercially sensitive. (ICAEW, 1997: 14)

The report considered that '[t]he most widely used form of regular risk reporting might be expected to be in the OFR' (ICAEW, 1997: 19). As has been seen, the ASB recommended that the OFR should include a discussion of the principal risks faced by an enterprise and a commentary on how these risks were being managed. However, a survey in 1996 by Coopers & Lybrand found that while 64% of the sample had explicitly referred to risk, it was often very briefly mentioned and that few companies had disclosed key risks. Reporting on risk is clearly a developing area.

AUDITORS AND ADDITIONAL ASSURANCE SERVICES

In Chapter 5, it was seen that the Elliott Committee (1997) considered that the developments in external reporting had provided opportunities for auditors to provide assurance services in relation to the following factors:

Risk assessments

This service would provide assurance that 'an entity's profile of business risks is comprehensive and that the entity has appropriate systems in place to effectively manage those risks' (Elliott Committee, 1997: 3). The types of business risk envisaged include strategic environment risks (such as changes in customer preferences, competing products and availability of capital funds), operating environment risks (for example, inefficient or ineffective business processes, and damaged reputation), and information risks (arising 'from the use of poor quality information for operational, financial, or strategic decision making' [p. 3]).

Business performance indicators

This service would provide assurance that 'an entity's performance measurement system contains relevant and reliable measures for assessing the extent to which entity goals and objectives are achieved and/or performance has met or exceeded industry norms' (p. 3). The Elliott Committee stressed that '[i]n order to evaluate the performance of a business enterprise, decision makers need a comprehensive set of performance measures (both financial and non-financial) that encompass all major activities within the entity's value chain' (p. 3).

Information systems reliability

This service would provide assurance that the enterprise's internal information systems (this would include the financial and any non-financial systems) were designed and operated in accordance with specified criteria.

Therefore, it can be seen that the widening of the notion of corporate performance and risk is being viewed by the auditors as an opportunity to provide additional assurance services.

CONCLUSION

The hypothesis set out in this chapter is that central to external reporting is 'the communication by the directors of the performance and risk relating to the reporting entity'. Rather than trying to satisfy the needs of the users of the financial statements in order to assist them in predicting the future and taking decisions, this chapter has argued that financial reporting should be viewed as part of the corporate governance system and the directors' assessment of the entity's performance and risk. It is then possible to ask: 'How well do the financial statements show performance and risk?' Because of the limitations of the financial statements and their susceptibility to short-termism, it is necessary to consider widening the range of performance indicators (and recognize things such as corporate social responsibility and environmental reporting). To underpin all this, this chapter has advocated the use of communication theory rather than decision theory.

We need to be very careful about future developments. In the theatrical sense, the word 'performance', could be defined as 'an act of make-believe aimed at enchanting an audience'! The existence of the financial statements expectations gap may mean that this fate has already befallen the phrase 'financial performance'; it is important that this does not happen to 'corporate performance'.

DISCUSSION QUESTIONS

1   Outline the relative merits of focusing the emphasis of financial reporting on a) the reporting entity, and b) the users of the financial statements. Where do you think the emphasis should be?

2   How can financial performance be reported? Critically assess the alternative ways of reporting financial performance.

3   How can one assess corporate performance?

4　Company directors have started to have private meetings with institutional investors and analysts. What are the advantages and disadvantages of such meetings?

5　It has been suggested that excess concentration on the financial figures has resulted in short-termism. Suggest the ways in which the expansion of the concept of corporate performance might counter this.

REFERENCES

Accounting Standards Board (ASB) (1993) *Operating and Financial Review*. London: ASB.
Accounting Standards Board (ASB) (1998a) *Provisions, Contingent Liabilities and Contingent Assets*, FRS 12. London: ASB.
Accounting Standards Board (ASB) (1998b) *Derivatives and Other Financial Instruments: Disclosures*, FRS 13. London: ASB.
Accounting Standards Steering Committee (ASSC) (1975) *The Corporate Report – a Discussion Paper*. London: ASSC.
Adams, C.A., Hill, W.-Y. and Roberts, C.B. (1995) *Environmental, Employee and Ethical Reporting in Europe*, ACCA Research Report No. 41. London: ACCA.
Adams, C.A., Hill, W.-Y. and Roberts, C.B. (1998) 'Corporate social reporting practices in Western Europe: legitimating corporate behaviour?', *British Accounting Review*, 30 (1): 1–21.
Anthony, R.N. (1983) *Tell It Like It Was*. Homewood, IL: Richard D. Irwin.
Burns, J., Scapens, R. and Turley, S. (1997) 'The crunch for numbers', *Accountancy*, May: 112–13.
Cadbury, A. (1993) 'Highlights of the proposals of the Committee on Financial Aspects of Corporate Governance', in D.D. Prentice and P.R.J. Holland (eds), *Contemporary Issues in Corporate Governance*. Oxford: Clarendon Press.
Carey, A. (ed.) (1999) *The 21st Century Annual Report*. London: ICAEW (Research Board).
Chambers, R.J. (1966) *Accounting, Evaluation and Economic Behavior*. Englewood Cliffs, NJ: Prentice Hall.
Chambers, R.J. (1996) 'Ends, ways, means and conceptual frameworks', *Abacus*, 32 (2): 119–32.
Company Law Review Steering Committee (2001) *Modern Company Law for a Competitive Economy: Final Report*. London: DTI.
Coopers & Lybrand (1996) *Cadbury Compliance: A Survey of Published Accounts*. London: Coopers & Lybrand.
Cowe, R. (2001) 'Firms "need forcing" to do the right thing', *Observer* (Business Section), 14 October: 10.
Davies, M., Paterson, R. and Wilson, A. (1999) *UK GAAP*. London: Butterworths Tolley.
Drury, C. (2000) *Management and Cost Accounting* (5th edn). London: Thomson Learning.
Elkington, J. (1997) *Cannibals with Forks: The Triple Bottom Line of 21st Century Business*. Oxford: Capstone.
Elkington, J. (1999) 'Triple bottom-line reporting: looking for balance', *Australian CPA*, March: 18–21.

Elliott Committee (1997) AICPA Special Committee on Assurance Services: *Report of the Special Committee on Assurance Services*. New York: AICPA. Found on website: http://aicpa.org/assurance/about/opportun.htm (viewed on 11/09/01).

Fleming, C. (2000) 'Reporting financial performance', *IASC Insight*, March: 15–16.

G4 + 1 (1999) *Reporting Financial Performance: Proposals for Change*. G4 + 1 position paper. London: ASB.

Gray, R.H., Bebbington, J. and Walters, D. (1993) *Accounting for the Environment*. London: ACCA/Paul Chapman.

Gray, R.H., Owen, D. and Maunders, K. (1987) *Corporate Social Reporting: Accounting and Accountability*. London: Prentice Hall International.

Gray, R.H., Owen, D. and Adams, C.A. (1996) *Accounting and Accountability: Changes and Challenges in Corporate Social and Environmental Reporting*. Hemel Hempstead: Prentice Hall.

Greer, J. and Bruno, K. (1996) *Greenwash: The Reality Behind Corporate Environmentalism*. Penang and New York: Third World Network and Apex Press.

Hampel Report (The) (1998) *Committee on Corporate Governance: Final Report*. London: Gee Publishing Ltd.

Harvard Business Review (1998) *Measuring Corporate Performance*. Boston, MA: Harvard Business School Press.

Holland, J. (1997) *Corporate Communications with Institutional Shareholders: Private Disclosure and Financial Reporting*. Edinburgh: Institute of Chartered Accountants of Scotland.

Institute of Chartered Accountants in England and Wales (ICAEW) (1995) Faculty of Finance and Management Good Practice Guideline Issue 9. *Developing Comprehensive Performance Indicators*. London: ICAEW.

Institute of Chartered Accountants in England and Wales (ICAEW) (1997) *Financial Reporting of Risk: Proposals for a Statement of Business Risk*. London: ICAEW.

Institute of Chartered Accountants in England and Wales (ICAEW) (1999) ICAEW Financial Reporting Committee Discussion Paper. *Financial Performance: Alternative Views of the Bottom Line*. London: ICAEW.

Jacoby, N.H. (1973) *Corporate Power and Social Responsibility: A Blueprint for the Future*. New York: Macmillan.

Johnson, H.L. (1979) *Disclosure of Corporate Social Performance: Survey, Evaluation, and Prospects*. New York: Praeger.

Kaplan, R.S. and Norton, D.P. (1992) 'The balanced scorecard-measures that drive performance', *Harvard Business Review*, January–February: 71–9.

Kaplan, R.S. and Norton, D.P. (1993) 'Putting the balanced scorecard to work', *Harvard Business Review*, September–October: 134–47.

Kaplan, R.S. and Norton, D.P. (1996) *The Balanced Scorecard: Translating Strategy into Action*. Boston, MA: Harvard Business School.

Lapsley, I. and Mitchell, F. (eds) (1996) *Accounting and Performance Measurement: Issues in the Private and Public Sectors*. London: Paul Chapman.

Laughlin, R.C. and Puxty, A.G. (1981) 'The decision-usefulness criterion: wrong cart, wrong horse?', *AUTA Review*, 13: 43–87.

Marston, C. (1999) *Investor Relations Meetings: Views of Companies, Institutional Investors and Analysts*. Glasgow: Institute of Chartered Accountants of Scotland.

Mathews, M.R. (1993) *Socially Responsible Accounting*. London: Chapman and Hall.

Nickell, S. (1995) *The Performance of Companies: The Relationship Between the External Environment, Management Strategies and Corporate Performance*. Oxford (UK) and Cambridge (USA): Blackwell.

Owen, D. (ed.) (1992) *Green Reporting*. London: Chapman and Hall.

Ross, G.H.B. (1971) 'Social accounting: measuring the unmeasurables?', *Canadian Chartered Accountant*, July: 46–9, 52–4.

Small, J. (1996) 'Effectiveness – the Holy Grail of accounting measures of performance', in I. Lapsley and M. Falconer (eds), *Accounting and Performance Measurement: Issues in the Private and Public Sectors*. London: Paul Chapman.

Whittington, G. (1993) 'Corporate governance and the regulation of financial reporting', *Accounting and Business Research*, 23 (91a): 311–19.

10 The Elusive Holy Grail

Accounting is probably not the only field of human endeavor in which people are very busy without knowing just what they are doing.

– A.M. Cannon

A generally agreed conceptual framework for financial reporting could be viewed as the Holy Grail of the accounting world. The futility of the search for it can probably be explained by the misspecification of the problem it was supposed to solve, and a misunderstanding about what the financial statements were trying to achieve. Extravagant claims have been made about the objective of the financial statements, and instead of viewing the financial statements as part of the external reporting process, it now appears that there is very little limit to what they can portray. Thus, the conceptual frameworks have been developed on the premise of satisfying user needs and enabling users to take economic decisions. This book has sought to examine current developments in financial reporting in order to see how this has come about. It has been argued that at the heart of these problems is the financial reporting expectations gap – and in particular the financial statements expectations gap. The vague specification of the objective of the financial statements by the standard-setters appears to imply that the financial statements are fit for just about any purpose that their users may want. In terms of setting financial reporting standards, it is doubtful whether such a wide specification of the objective of the financial statements would really help the standard-setters produce consistent and coherent standards. It is also not helpful in terms of educating users for them to be told that the financial statements are there to enable them to do just about anything they want with them. Accounting may even be taught from a user perspective; however, to specify the objective of the financial statements in terms of satisfying user needs would appear to be an example of circular reasoning. Central to all this would appear to be the vagueness of the nature, scope and purpose of accounting 'theory'. One would have expected developments in financial reporting to have been built on theory and thus be conceptually robust. Given the problematic nature of the underlying theory, there is a danger that the standard setters have been building on shifting sands rather than firm foundations.

Stewardship (in the sense of checking on the honesty and integrity of one person who works for another) predated the earliest forms of accounting. The early forms of accounting could be viewed in a 'management accounting' context but were again to do with honesty and integrity – indeed, early accounting could be seen as an early form of internal control. The development of double-entry bookkeeping could be seen as an extension of this need for internal control. The arrival of permanently invested capital gave rise to the need to divide the life of the business into artificial accounting periods. This was so that people who owned shares for part of a company's life could be given some form of return (in the form of a dividend) commensurate with the length of the period of their investment (rather than having to wait until the enterprise was wound up). This periodic division of the life of the company gave rise to what was termed 'profit', and this in turn became a surrogate for the performance of the business and an indication of management's stewardship (thus widening the meaning attributed to 'stewardship').

From the 1960s, the emphasis of financial reporting focused on user needs and the provision of financial data to enable users to take economic decisions. This change of emphasis has consistently been challenged:

- a number of academics do not support it
- auditors do not seem to support it
- the courts do not seem to support it (as in the Caparo ruling)
- the Company Law Review Steering Committee did not seem to support it.

These criticisms appear to have little impact on the standard-setters, who have claimed that an assessment of stewardship will result in some sort of a decision (such as hold or sell shares, or remove or reappoint the directors), and that therefore there is not much difference between stewardship and decision making. Instead of accounting theory being used to buttress one's preconceived notions, 'theory' now seems to have been almost forgotten and mental gymnastics appear to be the order of the day (in order to justify the financial statements appearing to be all things to all people).

In management accounting, the phrase 'different costs and benefits for different purposes' is key, and the point is that costs and benefits which are produced for one purpose may be totally misleading if used in another context. The origins of financial statements may be found in the need to divide the life of an enterprise into artificial accounting periods because of the development of permanently invested capital. Whether this division represents 'performance' or is really suitable for predicting the future has been challenged in the preceding chapters. The fact that the financial statements are used to assess 'performance' and predict the future cannot be denied;

however, just because this occurs does not mean that these are the primary objectives of the financial statements – they may be contributing to the financial statements expectations gap. While there has been much discussion of an audit expectations gap, this other gap appears to have received scant recognition.

The chameleon nature of accounting may have done much to enable it to adapt to the changing business environment, but how far can it change? The danger of trying to satisfy user needs is that these users may not understand the scope and limitation of accounting and thus may make unreasonable requests. Without a strong theoretical basis or a robust conceptual framework, the danger is that the standard-setters will merely end up pandering to the perceived needs of the supposed users of the financial statements.

The nature and pace of business were revolutionized during the final decade of the twentieth century; therefore, it is natural that there have been calls for a revolution in corporate reporting. In responding to these calls, the accountancy profession needs to be cautious about the claims made on behalf of the financial statements, and innovative in assisting in the provision of complementary data. The danger of making excessive claims about the usefulness of the financial statements is that one may not look beyond them for alternative forms of data and disclosure. Viewing financial reporting in the wider context of corporate governance, rather than considering it to be a stand-alone subject, should enable the debate about what constitutes corporate performance and risk to take place. It has been argued that external reporting should focus on the directors' assessment of the performance of, and the risks relating to, the reporting entity, and that financial reporting could provide only part of this assessment. Concentrating on the performance of the entity should obviate the need for different reports for different user groups (and, in particular, the idea that the financial statements should contain multiple columns, each with figures produced following different bases). If there is one reporting entity, it should not be unreasonable to have one set of figures – even though the myriad of potential users may have a multitude of needs.

The calculation of profit for a particular accounting period is subjective and can be only an approximation. By definition, the division of the life of an enterprise (which in total could amount to fifty years, one hundred years, or even longer) into an accounting period (of one year, six months, three months or much less time) involves much judgement and is rarely clear-cut. Management's motivations make the process even more problematic, and it has been seen that the auditors admit that it is virtually impossible to eliminate management bias. While the accounting standard-setters have attempted to limit management's choice of accounting alternatives, variations and differences among companies will always exist because of the nature of the subject matter and the judgements made by management.

IS 'HISTORY' HISTORY?

The focus on enabling users to predict the future and thus aid decision making seems to have resulted in a move away from trying to understand what has happened during an accounting period. Consequently, accountants appear to be very defensive about the 'historical' nature of current financial statements. However, it should be remembered that the 'historical' figures are in fact part of a continuum – the division of which is fairly artificial but inextricably linked to the rest of an enterprise's life. Although the financial statements may represent only a partial picture, they do give an insight into what has been happening and thus should assist the reader in *understanding* developments in an organization. *If* people understand the reporting entity (including its strengths and weaknesses), this in itself may enable them to make assessments about its future direction. These users may want to predict its future cash flows, but predicting the future is not easy, although as an intellectual exercise it is probably easier to predict the future than it is to understand the past. Instead of viewing the latest financial statements as 'historical' documents (and thus 'irrelevant' to decision making), they should be viewed as the most recent part of a continuum (which they assist the reader in understanding):

> Although facilitating the prediction of future cash flows is certainly an important use for accounts, it is not their primary use. A faithful account of the results of an expired period is the first thing that many users want, and it is unlikely to be provided by an approach that concentrates on the unknown future to the neglect of the relatively verifiable past. (Paterson, 2001: 101)

Focusing on the future could be seen as an attempt to build on the economics literature that was 'borrowed' during the development of accounting theory. While this may be an interesting theoretical approach, it would appear to have overlooked basic differences between accounting and economics.

> Imagine that all future cash flows could be foreseen with certainty, and that they could all be linked to existing assets and liabilities. Would this facilitate an ideal form of reporting? It would certainly convert the balance sheet into a true statement of the company's economic net worth, which some accountants would regard as the Holy Grail. But it would be less obvious how to present the movements

between one balance sheet and the next in an informative way. With perfect foresight, every year's balance sheet would be founded upon the same future cash flows. As a result, apart from changes in the discount rate, the reported performance for each year would be confined to the effects of rolling the forecast one year on, so that the current year's cash flows would fall out while the remaining ones were brought a year closer. That may be fine for a valuation model, but it doesn't provide much insight into the year's activity. (Paterson, 2001: 101)

It would appear that there are a number of Holy Grails in accounting, but this is probably because of the fragmented nature of the underlying 'theory' and a lack of overall vision relating to the specification of the central problem relating to corporate external reporting.

AN AGENDA FOR DEVELOPMENTS IN CORPORATE REPORTING

Given the issues raised, the following are potential developments that could help tackle the problems identified here:

- A reassessment of accounting 'theory' and its interrelationship with conceptual framework developments (as presumably a conceptual framework attempts to operationalize the theory).

- Consideration should be given to a tighter and arguably more realistic specification of the objective of the financial statements.

- Increased user education about the scope and limitations of the financial statements and the external audit, and the recognition of bias in the financial statements arising from management's motivations.

- Standard-setters should use principles to derive standards consistent with statutory requirements.

- In recognition of the political nature of standard-setting, consideration should be given to the accountability of the accounting standard-setters for their actions. If standards are produced on the basis of a compromise between contending views, it should be remembered that advances in knowledge seldom come about on the basis of democracy.

- There should be a greater recognition of the implications of corporate governance on external reporting.

- A proper debate about the communication of corporate performance, and in particular what indicators should constitute overall performance is required (that is, both financial and non-financial indicators). Given that performance is traditionally viewed as the achievement of objectives, maybe companies have to be more explicit about their objectives – rather than just issuing general mission statements. This could be perceived as a threat to their confidentiality, but it may be counterbalanced by the recognition that corporations have responsibilities to the societies in which they operate.

- Consideration should be given to the establishment of standards for the disclosure of non-financial data. This would then raise the question of who would be responsible for this.

- Consideration should be given to the auditors' assessment of economy, efficiency and effectiveness being extended from the public sector to the private sector.

- A reflection on the usefulness of outsiders gaining real-time access to accounting databases – what would be gained and would the data be meaningful?

- A clarification of the amount of assurance that can be given by continuous auditing would be useful, as well as a clear delineation of the respective responsibilities of the external and internal auditors.

- There should be a greater recognition of the ever-present threat of fraud.

The challenges of the twenty-first century can be met only once there is *understanding* of the nature, scope and limitations of the financial statements. It is also important to recognize the role of the financial statements within the context of corporate governance, and consider their usefulness in terms of communicating corporate performance and risk. The preoccupation with 'user needs' appears to have resulted in an abdication of the need to educate these people about the role of the financial statements. The adoption of such a pedagogic approach has probably merely exacerbated the financial statements expectations gap, and thus it has prevented a proper consideration of corporate performance and risk.

DISCUSSION QUESTIONS

1   Corporate governance recognizes the importance of directors establishing and maintaining a system of internal controls. Indeed, because of the complexity of business, it could be argued that recording and control are more important now than at any time in the past. Why, therefore, do you think that accountants appear to be so defensive about their traditional role, preferring instead to emphasize the decision-usefulness of their data?

2   In public sector accounting, an assessment of the economy, efficiency and effectiveness of an organization has long been part of the auditors' work. What would you see as the advantages and disadvantages of applying this requirement to the audit of major companies?

3   The orientation of financial reporting appears to be moving from understanding the past to predicting the potential of the reporting entity. Is it important to understand what has happened in an organization? Justify your stance.

4   What is your view regarding the possibility of a financial statements expectations gap?

5   What do you foresee as the major developments in financial reporting?

REFERENCE

Paterson, R. (2001) 'History is not bunk', *Accountancy*, August: 101.

Name index

Subject index